My Kids Can

Making Math Accessible to All Learners, K–5

Edited by Judy Storeygard

TERC

HEINEMANN
Portsmouth, NH

Heinemann
361 Hanover Street
Portsmouth, NH 03801–3912
www.heinemann.com

Offices and agents throughout the world

The authors and publisher wish to thank those who have generously given permission to reprint borrowed material:

Figures 18–1, 18–2, and excerpts from *Investigations in Number, Data, and Space* by S. J. Russell, K. Economopoulos, and L. Wittenberg. Copyright © 2008 by Pearson Education, Inc. or its affiliate(s). Used by permission. All rights reserved.

 This material is based upon a work supported by the National Science Foundation under Grant No. HRD-0435017. Any opinions, findings, and conclusions or recommendations expressed in this material are those of the authors and do not necessarily reflect the views of the National Science Foundation or other funders.

Library of Congress Cataloging-in-Publication Data
My kids can : making math accessible to all learners, K–5 / edited by Judy Storeygard.
    p. cm.
  Includes bibliographical references.
  ISBN-13: 978-0-325-01724-2
  ISBN-10: 0-325-01724-7
1. Mathematics—Study and teaching (Elementary). 2. Effective teaching.
3. Mathematics teachers—Anecdotes. I. Storeygard, Judy.
  QA135.6.M95 2009
  372.7—dc22   2009000232

Editor: Victoria Merecki
Production: Sonja S. Chapman
Cover design: Susan Paradise
Cover photograph: Christina Myren
DVD production: Sherry Day
Typesetter: Aptara Inc.
Manufacturing: Steve Bernier

Printed in the United States of America on acid-free paper
13 12 11 10 09   VP   2 3 4 5

To Jacob Matthew, with love.

May you have teachers as dedicated and knowledgeable
as those who contributed to these resources.

Contents

Acknowledgments

This collection is the culmination of a long strand of work. I have been very fortunate to work with a group of dedicated teachers and colleagues. I could never have edited these resources without their intellect and commitment to the work.

My colleague, Cornelia Tierney, and I began thinking about students who struggle with mathematics ten years ago. Her vision and passion about equity shaped the projects that we initiated. Our project officer at the National Science Foundation (NSF), Dr. Larry Scadden, understood and championed our efforts. The teachers from our Accessible Mathematics project began this work with us. I am grateful to all of them: Candace Chick, Heather Straughter, Eileen Backus, Lisa Nierenberg, Karin Olson-Shannon, MaryKay Resnick, Lisa Davis, Andrea Cerda, Susan Fitzgerald, Leslie Kramer, Karen Ravin, Somchay Edwards, Lauretta Medley, Michelle Anderson, and Lauren Grace.

More recently, the Educational Research Collaborative at the Technical Education Research Center (TERC) provided me with funding to pursue publication. My colleagues, Andee Rubin and Myriam Steinback, have provided unlimited support and wisdom. I am grateful for and humbled by their generosity. Arusha Hollister made major contributions to these resources, in writing the workshops and video context pieces and by imparting her knowledge about primary-grade mathematics.

Keith Cochran, Beth Perry-Brown, and Karen Mutch-Jones have given me thoughtful ideas and comments about several of the essays. Amy Brodesky, Nancy Horowitz, and Heather Straughter were very astute reviewers. The insights of Nicole Feret were incredibly valuable in shaping the writing. David Smith lent his creativity and patience in producing the DVD.

I was also privileged to have a wise group of colleagues from the Professional Development Study Group. Deborah Schifter generously offered to write the Foreword, and members of the group read several entries and provided excellent feedback and encouragement.

Victoria Merecki at Heinemann has provided me with gentle, intelligent guidance and encouragement throughout.

Foreword

All teachers of mathematics face the challenge of reaching the range of students in their classroom. Many teachers feel especially daunted by the task of helping students who are struggling as learners. Faced with a student who lacks confidence, doesn't know how to interpret a task, and loses focus, what is a teacher to do? My *Kids Can* is an important resource for teachers who are ready to tackle this challenge.

The most important message in this book is that *all* children, given appropriate supports, can learn mathematics for *understanding*. This may come as a surprise to those who were taught that the best way to work with struggling students is to break mathematical tasks into small chunks to be memorized. Instead, the key is to find where a student is on solid ground and provide tasks that will help him or her move forward. The examples presented here demonstrate the progress students can make.

My *Kids Can* devotes each chapter to a broad principle: assessing students' understanding as a way of making decisions about how to proceed, making the mathematics explicit, helping students become independent learners. Within each chapter, through written narratives and video cases, individual teachers convey their own stories, illustrating how they worked with their students. That is, readers can see the broad principles enacted within the constraints of day-to-day classroom life: how teachers found time to conduct one-on-one interviews and to keep records of students' progress, which assessments were particularly useful, and what kinds of accommodations were made to make the tasks accessible to students while keeping the important mathematics intact. Readers learn about the kinds of supports that made students who struggle feel confident enough to work with classmates and to speak up in whole-group discussions. We are shown the variety of representations students used to make sense of the mathematics and the connections that students were able to make. And we witness the collaborations forged between classroom teachers and special educators.

Although not explicitly stated, the knowledge these teachers bring to their practice shines through each narrative and video case. They understand deeply the mathematics content they are responsible for teaching and how students learn it. They identify the central mathematical concepts, recognize how concepts are related to each other, and understand how these concepts build from content covered in earlier grades. They situate these concepts in a variety of representations and contexts familiar to students from their daily lives. They assess the correctness of students' reasoning as students explain their solutions to a problem; furthermore, if a solution is incorrect, the teachers analyze that reasoning to determine what is correct about the students' process and where the thinking has gone awry. All of this knowledge—together with a deep sense of care and respect for their students—is applied to the goal of having each student make sense of the mathematics.

A reader might ask, "How can I put so much effort into one or two or a handful of students when I am responsible for so many?" The answer: The knowledge exhibited by the teachers in this volume and many of the techniques they specify and elucidate enhance the learning of *all* of their students. When a teacher is explicit about the mathematics of a lesson, provides additional representations, and helps students figure out how to participate in whole-group discussion, it serves *every* student in the classroom.

Indeed, the challenge of reaching the range of learners in a classroom *is* great. There is much to learn and much to do. But, as illustrated by *My Kids Can*, the rewards are even greater.

Deborah Schifter
Education Development Center, Inc.

Introduction

NCTM Standards-based instruction might be fine for most students, but students who are struggling with mathematics must to be told what to do.

When my colleague, Cornelia Tierney, and I were working on Bridges to Classroom Mathematics, a NSF funded professional development project focused on the implementation of NCTM Standards-based curricula, we heard statements like the one above from administrators across the country. We, however, strongly believe that all children can learn to make sense of mathematics and deserve the opportunity to do so. With funding from the National Science Foundation, we developed the Accessible Mathematics project. This project brought together special educators and classroom teachers to develop principles and strategies to improve the mathematical learning of students who struggle with mathematics. Our work was based on the premise that if these students engage in a variety of NCTM Standards-based activities that *support their strengths*, they can learn to think mathematically. The operating assumptions of the project were adapted from the work of James Hiebert and his colleagues (1997):

- Each student can and has the right to learn mathematics with understanding.
- As the teacher comes to know each child, he/she can select tasks that enable the student to engage in mathematics tasks that pose authentic problems.
- Active student participation in the mathematical community of the classroom increases learning opportunities for all students.
- In a mathematical community, acknowledging and accepting differences in how students learn helps students work together and feel safe to take risks.

Classroom teachers today are expected to have more responsibility for teaching the range of learners than in the past. In regard to students who struggle, there are two major developments that have led to the increased focus on the classroom teacher.

Because of federal legislation, between 1995 and 2005, the percentage of students with disabilities spending 80 percent or more of the school day in a general classroom showed an overall increase from 45 to 52 percent (NCES 2007). The 1997 amendments to the Individuals with Disabilities Act (IDEA) require schools to account for student progress toward higher educational standards and to increase participation of students with disabilities in the general education curriculum (Thurlow 2001). The 2001 No Child Left Behind Act (NCLB) also requires educators to provide children with disabilities access to the general curriculum.

Another recent development that places additional demands on the classroom teacher is response to intervention (RTI), a model that is designed to match high-quality instruction and intervention to student needs and to bring the efforts of general and special education together in working with students who are struggling. The orientation of RTI is to move away from thinking about students in categories and to work toward addressing the learning challenges of individual students through appropriate teaching strategies. The tiers of RTI range from having the classroom teacher plan and implement high-quality instruction for the entire class with ongoing formative assessment that monitors students' progress, to offering targeted differentiated instruction within the classroom for students who are not showing progress, to providing intensive intervention that includes special education teachers for those students who still need more support. (National Joint Committee on Learning Disabilities 2005).

To address the challenges of teaching students who are struggling with mathematics, either already in special education or identified as needing more support through RTI, the Accessible Mathematics project developed strategies to support students to actively engage and make sense of mathematics along with their classmates. For two years, TERC researchers met regularly in an action research group with sixteen teachers, both special educators and classroom teachers working together to present and discuss episodes from their classrooms, plan next steps in their investigations of students' learning, and document what worked. The audience for this work is primarily teachers, either those who are already working with young students or those who are preparing to teach mathematics in the elementary grades.

All of the Accessible Mathematics teachers made sure that their students knew that they expected them to support one another as learners and that they expected their students who struggled to learn along with their peers. They created a culture based on respect and acceptance of differences in which students felt safe to take risks and to admit confusions. The teachers listened carefully to students' thinking, analyzed how students made sense of the mathematics and why they might be confused, and chose representations that could help the children solve the problem. During our seminar meetings, they talked about what students knew as well as what they didn't know.

As our researchers and teachers collaborated, they came to identify five actions that are critical to teaching mathematics to students who struggle:

- make mathematics explicit
- link assessment and teaching
- build understanding through talk
- expect and support students to work independently and take responsibility for their own learning
- work collaboratively

These five principles provide the organizational structure for this collection. A section of the book is devoted to each principle and consists of an introduction with questions to consider, followed by chapters that describe teachers' practices through both written and video episodes that relate to the particular theme of the section. The goal is to give teachers examples of strategies that they can implement in their mathematics to improve the learning of their students who are struggling.

It will become quite evident as you read the essays that these principles overlap. An essay has been included in a particular section because of its primary theme, but you will notice similarities among all of the essays. Any given essay may have elements of several principles because all five characterize good teaching.

Making Mathematics Explicit

The teachers whose essays and videos appear in this section take an active role in helping students who struggle to access mathematical concepts. They analyze activities ahead of time to identify which concepts might be difficult for their students who struggle, preteach necessary skills such as vocabulary, and refer to prior work that the class has completed, such as posting students' strategies in the room. They are purposeful in every teaching move they make, for example, calling on students to share whose strategies are mathematically sound and can help others understand the underlying concepts, and asking that extra question that might seem obvious, but that they know is necessary to build understanding. Providing and referring to specific resources, such as 100 charts and manipulatives, is another strategy these teachers use, and to build flexibility they highlight the connections among different representations. When they find that they have students who need support with particular skills, they plan an intervention, pulling students who are struggling into a guided math group.

These teachers also understand that expectations for doing mathematical work must be clear. Too often expectations for successfully completing a task are indirect. For example, when teachers ask students to explain their answer, unless the expectations have been established that an explanation includes elements such as a sequence of steps and an accurate use of a representation, students, especially those without a solid mathematical foundation, cannot fulfill the request. Being clear about expectations and goals helps all students, but explicit teaching is particularly important for fragile learners.

Linking Assessment and Teaching

The essays in this section illustrate that assessment must be ongoing and must inform planning, as opposed to being used only to measure learning at the end of a unit of study. Assessing students who struggle involves finding out about their strengths as well as their weaknesses, and planning accommodations accordingly. Throughout this section, you will see evidence of teachers' deep knowledge of elementary school mathematics content and how mathematical ideas develop. This knowledge forms the basis for their teaching and assessment decisions. Although finding time for ongoing assessment is difficult, because these teachers had specific goals in mind, they were able to do assessment in a manageable period of time: taking notes as they observe children working in small groups, remembering children's comments during whole-group discussions, or meeting with students for targeted one-on-one interviews.

Building Understanding Through Talk

In recent years, there has been an acknowledgment of the importance of talk in elementary mathematics classrooms. According to the NCTM standards, mathematics instruction should allow students to:

- organize and consolidate their mathematical thinking through communication
- communicate their mathematical thinking coherently and clearly to peers, teachers, and others
- analyze and evaluate the mathematical thinking and strategies of others
- use the language of mathematics to express mathematical ideas precisely (NCTM 2000)

Yet teachers find that including all their students in discussion is challenging. We were often asked, "I want to include all students in class discussions, but some of my students who struggle tune out during meetings. What can I do to make them feel included?"

In this section, teachers describe how they establish community norms so that each student feels valued and safe to participate. During whole-group discussions, these teachers actively involve their students in doing mathematics, making connections to prior work, and targeting powerful strategies that are accessible. Critical work also takes place well before the discussion. Teachers figure out ahead of time where their students might have difficulty following the conversation and plan accommodations accordingly, such as including examples of students' work from prior sessions or providing concrete materials or representations as an entry point. Sometimes the accommodations include pulling together a small group to preview the day's activity so they can follow and participate during the whole-group time or rehearsing one of their strategies so they might later share in the whole group. This extra practice is often key to supporting these students in building their mathematical understanding through talk.

Taking Responsibility for Learning

The teachers who wrote the essays in this section found that their students who struggle often do not see themselves as capable learners. These students tended to not ask for help, participate in groups, or begin or complete work independently. This "learned helplessness" frequently results from experiences of failure and low expectations. The authors of these essays believe that their students who struggle can learn and they find strategies to help them do so. They developed routines to help students feel comfortable and get them started, beginning with making sure the students know what they are being asked to solve. Sometimes this involved retelling a story problem or making accommodations so that the students were able to make sense of the mathematics. The teachers also engaged the students in evaluating their own learning, asking them to answer questions such as "Did I actively participate in learning? Did I use *everything* I know to help myself with the problem?"

This section is closely tied with the Linking Assessment and Teaching section, because when teachers assessed their students of concern, they often found out that the students' lack of confidence stemmed from gaps in their learning. They used assessment to find students' strengths to help build both their confidence and their mathematical understanding.

Working Collaboratively

During the course of our project, we were fortunate to collaborate with Karen Mutch-Jones, a researcher studying collaboration between classroom and special education teachers. Ms. Mutch-Jones' data (Mutch-Jones 2004) revealed that collaboration can have a powerful impact on the classroom community:

- All students form a relationship with and seek help from both teachers instead of seeing the special education teacher as the teacher for *those* kids.
- Expectations for learning behavior (e.g., paying attention, participating in the group) during math class are the same for all students.
- Teachers help each other to establish fair, yet high expectations for learning mathematics for all students.
- All students have access to a standards-based curriculum, to learn mathematics concepts with understanding, and to develop strong problem-solving strategies.

Mutch-Jones' findings showed that collaboration also led to the following benefits:

- Teachers gained a broader or deeper understanding of mathematics content and curriculum.
- Teachers learned to ask each other and their students better questions about mathematical thinking and math curriculum.
- Teachers expanded their ways of thinking about student abilities and needs.

The essays in this section illustrate both the benefits and the challenges of collaboration. Many of the barriers are structural. The schedules of special education teachers and classroom teachers may not overlap and their responsibilities may differ, particularly in regard to administrative responsibilities. Opportunities for professional development, and the amount of mathematics instruction teachers received as part of their preparation are often not the same, with the special educator being offered far fewer courses and inservice programs in mathematics. However, the teachers who wrote these essays were able to meet regularly to plan for and reflect on the students they taught in common. They analyzed student work and conversations to decide on next steps, determined which teacher would take responsibility for what aspect of teaching, and decided how they would assess what the students knew. All parties concerned, whether in a co-teaching or pull-out situation, felt positive about the advantages of the collaborative relationship in terms of what they learned from each other and what students gained as a result of their coordinated effort.

The goal of this resource is to immerse you in the classrooms of skilled practitioners so that you have models and examples of what it means to help *all* students make sense of mathematics. These teachers do not take the "ten steps to success" approach. Instead, their essays are designed to give you a window into their thinking, addressing questions such as:

- How do you get students who are not working independently to find a starting place and learn to explain their thinking?
- When special educators and classroom teachers collaborate, how do they plan? What is it like when they both work with students who struggle?
- How do teachers take the time to engage in ongoing assessment? What happens with the rest of the class?
- How do teachers orchestrate the sharing of strategies—isn't it confusing for students who are struggling?
- When students are far behind, what do you help them focus on in a lesson?

The purpose of analyzing these written and videotaped episodes is not to look at whether what the teacher is doing is right or wrong, but instead to consider the decisions a teacher makes, why he or she might have made those decisions, and what effect those decisions might have on the students' learning. The complexity of the process is always apparent. Many of these teachers have years of experience developing the strategies you will see and read about. Some of the newer teachers write about how they are learning to teach their struggling learners effectively. We hope you will be able to apply or adapt their principles and actions to your own classrooms and teaching situations. We also hope that you will see how the principles and actions described here benefit all students, not just those who struggle. As one of our teachers explained:

> What we've learned from working with our students who are struggling has made us better math teachers for *all* of the kids. Ideas about sequencing, about not being so quick to explain, about really insisting that kids figure some things out for themselves, that models that work for some kids don't work for others . . . Teaching them [students who struggle] effectively *is* teaching the class effectively.

Making Mathematics Explicit

Introduction

For some, making mathematics explicit for struggling students means telling them what to do. The literature is replete with step-by-step directions for algorithms and mnemonic devices designed to foster recall of specific procedures. Although these techniques might be useful in certain circumstances, an exclusive emphasis on memory results in passive learning. When students then encounter unfamiliar situations, they are often at a loss for how to apply the procedures they've memorized (Boaler 2008). A more useful way of being explicit is to make visible the assumptions and processes involved in problem solving that lead to successful solution strategies. Teachers who do this kind of explicit teaching create a "learning environment where students learn about themselves as learners and develop strategies for success" (Asera 2006).

These essays and videos focus on being explicit to help students make sense of mathematics. Students who struggle with a particular mathematical idea or struggle to develop useful strategies to solve mathematical problems often need help seeing the mathematics that underlies an activity, making mathematical connections among different activities, or figuring out what to look for as they solve a problem. The teachers featured here use a series of strategies to reach their struggling students: choosing a mathematically rich problem, carefully sequencing questions that build appropriate skills and orientations, and incorporating prompts to support students who are experiencing difficulty (Sullivan, Mousley, and Zevenbergen 2006).

These teachers do not wait for students to become frustrated or fall behind. They take an active role, analyzing activities ahead of time and preteaching necessary skills such as vocabulary or directions for a game, articulating the goals of the activities and the expectations for completing a mathematical task. When they find students are confused, the teachers work with the students in small groups to review key concepts using authentic contexts and multiple representations. The teachers also model computation strategies that students can make more efficient over time, pose problems to elicit these strategies, and ask students who have used these strategies to share their work. Asking students to make connections among the strategies shared also brings forth mathematical ideas. These teachers do not assume that their struggling students are making these connections on their own—they recognize the need to make the connections explicit through discussion.

In "Are We Multiplying or Dividing?" Ana Vaisenstein writes about the teaching moves she uses to help her students solve multiplication and division problems. She creates a structure for her group of fourth graders in which they think about what they know before solving a new problem, make connections among strategies and representations, work through their misunderstandings, reflect on their learning, elaborate their answers, and explain why their solutions worked.

In "What Comes Next?" kindergarten teacher Laura Marlowe writes about her focus on helping struggling students understand patterns. She helps her students who have difficulty with the concept of patterns by providing repeated opportunities for practice, verbalizing each element of the pattern along with the student, and asking specific questions so that the student knows what to look for, such as, "Where's the part that repeats? Where do you start over?"

In "You Can't Build a Sand Castle on a Classmate's Head," Lisa Seyferth writes about how she carefully goes over the goals and important mathematics of an activity or game both before and after—to preview, and then to assess. She works closely with her students who are struggling to make sure they have an entry point into the mathematics and then, during share time, she names the strategies that students are using, emphasizing the mathematical concepts.

In "Double or Nothing," Michelle Perch notices that a small group of her third graders struggle with the concept of doubling. She writes about how her work with them in a small guided math group to develop their understanding of the concept. She discussed what *doubling* meant, asking them to come up with their own definitions. She used cubes so that the students had the experience of actually seeing objects being doubled and then posed a problem in a familiar context about double scoops of ice cream.

 In "Focused Instruction on Quick Images," Michael Flynn works with a small group of second-grade students on an activity called Quick Images (Russell et al. 2008g). He decided to pull this group of students together because he thought they needed more work with this activity. During the session, he helps students develop strategies that help them visualize the dots in the image so they can accurately record them. For example, he asks them questions about and comments on their own observations. He asks them to explain in detail what they are seeing or doing, and then he repeats what they said and asks them if his restatement was correct.

In "Solving Multiplication Problems," Heather Straughter works with her fifth graders on a set of cluster problems (Kliman et al. 2004). Heather works hard to make explicit the mathematics of the problems her students are solving. She does so through her structuring of the lesson, through the directions she gives, through the questions she asks, and through the decisions she makes about whom to ask to share a strategy.

These essays and episodes about teachers' practice provide insight into what it means to be explicit when teaching mathematics—not to "tell" or "prescribe" but to guide and support with purpose and forethought.

Questions to Think About

What do these essays and videos bring to light about what it means to be explicit with students who struggle?

What strategies do these teachers use to make the mathematics explicit?

What evidence do you see that students understand concepts that the teachers are highlighting in their instruction?

1

Are We Multiplying or Dividing?

Being Explicit in Teaching Mathematics

Ana Vaisenstein

It is common to hear that students with disabilities need explicit teaching. Usually explicit teaching is understood as telling the student what to do, such as explaining what procedure to follow to solve a multiplication problem. The belief underlying this approach is that because of their disability, and in some cases cultural background, students cannot come up with their own strategies for solving problems and/or do not have language to explain their thinking. Therefore, the teacher needs to be the one who talks and explicitly gives these students the necessary information to solve the problem.

Over the last four years, I have worked with students who struggle in math. Some of them have Individualized Education Programs (IEPs), and some of them have not yet been formally identified as students with special needs. I have observed many students who have been taught procedures to solve the four basic operations but who have not been exposed to the concepts underlying these procedures. They are often not able to reason through the procedures or explain the mathematical meaning of what they are doing.

Let me share an example from a student I had last spring. This is how Davel solved 18×12:

$$\begin{array}{r} 18 \\ \times\ 12 \\ \hline 836 \end{array}$$

What procedure do you think Davel used?

This is what he explained to me: "2 times 8 is 16. Write the 6 and carry the 1. 2 times 1 is 2, plus the 1 I carried is 3. 1 times 8 is 8—836." Davel had forgotten or maybe misunderstood the steps of the procedure he was taught, yet he completely trusted the procedure and did not even wonder whether his answer made sense. When his peers commented that the answer could not be in the 800s, he couldn't figure out why. Davel did not reason, he proceeded mechanically and did not understand the meaning of the steps he took.

How can we help students link procedural and conceptual knowledge? What explicit teaching supports students' understanding of key mathematical ideas and gives them tools to reason through problems? I have grappled with these questions for many years and have come to realize that for me, explicit teaching involves particular teaching moves designed to help students become active learners: learners who engage in the process of thinking and reasoning through problems. These teaching moves include asking students to:

- elaborate their answers and explain why their solutions worked
- think about what they know before solving a new problem
- make connections among problem-solving strategies
- make connections among representations: drawings, numbers, contexts, and concrete materials
- work through their errors and misunderstandings with teacher support
- reflect on their learning

In this essay, I discuss a selection of lessons in which I used these teaching moves with a group of six fourth-grade students who struggled in math. These students joined me every day for an hour during their math period. Their teacher and I agreed that learning in a small group would help them move forward. Some were English language learners and some were on IEPs or were referred for special education services. Part of my work with them focused on multiplication and division, topics they specifically identified as being difficult.

Setting Goals for My Students

During my observations of the students, I noticed that, for the most part, they used repeated addition or skip counting to solve multiplication problems. They were not very comfortable working with arrays[1] and had a difficult time memorizing the multiplication facts. My intent was to help them understand the relationship between skip counting, repeated addition, and multiplication. I also wanted them to become very familiar with the array model as a tool to help them think through multiplication, and the distributive property in particular. My goal was to help students develop these understandings, so that they would be able to find the product of factor pairs they couldn't remember and they would develop reliable strategies to solve multiplication problems. Finally, I wanted them to be able to make sense of division story problems.

---

[1]An array is an area model for multiplication that consists of arrangement of objects, pictures, or numbers in rows and columns. See Figure 1–1, page 8, for an example.

From the beginning, I tried to help them take control of their own learning by developing productive work habits. I made it clear that they would be required to explain their ideas to the best of their ability, listen to other students' ideas, and ask questions if they didn't understand what their classmates said. I also wanted them to become aware of what they already knew and how that knowledge could help them solve what they did not know.

We also had a conversation in which we agreed that we were all going to work hard and not give up, even if the ideas seemed difficult. We talked about situations in our everyday lives when we didn't know something and how we dealt with them. The students offered examples from sports and explained how they learned to play by making mistakes and watching others. They also talked about practicing a skill repeatedly before they could do it well. We made the connection between these experiences outside of school and our math class. Although students' motivation to learn math or skateboarding may be different, I tried to highlight the commonalities. Trying hard and not giving up rang true for these children. In school, they had not always been expected to persist to learn, and this was an obstacle at first. However, by putting the students' thinking front and center, over time they got the message that their thoughts and words mattered, and they slowly began to get a sense of satisfaction from their work. Although these conversations helped the students become more focused and engaged, I knew that I needed to implement specific teaching strategies to increase their mathematical content knowledge.

Teaching Moves

Elaborating Their Answers

After students gave me an answer, I often questioned them further. I tried to find out what knowledge they were using to choose their strategies. I asked them where each number came from as they went through the steps of their solution. Sometimes I asked them how they knew their answer was reasonable.

The distributive property was one key idea I wanted these students to grapple with. I decided to introduce this concept through a familiar context for the students: cookies on cookie sheets. I adapted a picture from the book *Amanda Bean's Amazing Dream* by Cindy Neuschwander (1998) in which I drew a rack with 2 cookie trays. The cookies were organized in a 3 × 8 array and a 4 × 8 array (see Figure 1–1).

Modeling multiplication using an array of objects allows children to visualize and make sense of multiplicative contexts. The context was designed to highlight the distributive property, that is, that the problem could be solved by

Figure 1–1.

calculating 7×8 or $(3 \times 8) + (4 \times 8)$. I introduced the picture by explaining that I saw the trays that morning at a bakery around the corner from school. I asked students if they could tell me how many cookies the baker made. Students were very excited to find out. The responses of all six students were the same:

$$3 \times 8 = 24$$
$$4 \times 8 = 32$$
$$24 + 32 = 56$$

I had expected that at least one of the students would offer 7×8 as an answer, but since that was not the case, I shared how I solved the situation using 7×8: "Interesting, I solved the problem by doing 7×8 and I got the same answer as you. How come? Could you show with the snap cubes what I did and what you did and why both ways work? You can work in pairs if you want." I wanted the students to use the manipulatives for two reasons: (1) to represent their ideas in a concrete model, and (2) to ground the discussion about the distributive property with objects they could move around as they were explaining their ideas. Julio and Davel worked together. Alejandro worked with Lucía, and Fleurette worked with Vanessa.

> JULIO: [*after building the arrays*] See we have a 3 × 8 array and a 4 × 8 array and when we put them together it makes a 7 × 8 array.
> ALEJANDRO: The same with us. It is the same.
> TEACHER: Yes, now we see it is the same. I wonder why it is the same to do 3 × 8, then 4 × 8, and add both products or just do 7 × 8?
> LUCÍA: 3 and 4 make 7 but the 8 stays the same. [*Lucía points to the arrays as she moves the smaller arrays closer to each other to make a 7 × 8 array.*]
> TEACHER: Who understood what Lucía explained to us? [*It was very clear to me what Lucía said; however, I wasn't sure everyone followed her and this was a key idea I wanted more students to think about.*]
> FLEURETTE: I don't understand what she said. Can you say it again?
> TEACHER: Who understood that idea? . . . Go ahead, Alejandro.
> ALEJANDRO: When you put together the 3 and the 4 [*pointing to the dimensions of the smaller arrays*] you make 7 rows of 8 cookies.
> FLEURETTE: Ah! Yes, I understand. It is the same! That is what we did.

I could have stopped the exploration there. However, I wanted the children to understand why they could either find the product of both trays at the same time or calculate 1 tray at a time and add both products. I wanted them to have both a conceptual as well as a procedural understanding. They had to articulate that the number of groups (7 or 3 + 4) and the number of items in each group (8) had not changed: "You make 7 rows of 8 cookies." They had to explain the distributive property of multiplication over addition, even though they didn't name it. I did not teach students a procedure but asked them to reason about an important property of multiplication.

In addition to contributing to the class discussion, the conversation also served as a reference for future class discussions, especially when students had to solve problems involving multiplication facts that were hard for them to remember.

Thinking About What They Know Before Solving a New Problem

I once assumed that if I worked on an idea in one class, students would generalize the ideas right away and use them in other situations to solve a variety of problems. However, I have learned that students who struggle often have difficulty applying knowledge from one situation to another. I try to support these students in thinking about how what they already know or learned can help them solve a new problem.

I knew that the students in my small group had a difficult time remembering some of the multiplication facts. Because they had just explored the distributive property of multiplication, they should have been able to use that knowledge to find the products for facts they did not know. I was aware that they might not be able to make that connection by themselves, so I planned to bring it up for consideration.

I explained that we were going to work on facts that were hard for them to remember. I wanted the students to be invested in the activity, so I asked them to choose the facts we would focus on. They suggested 9×8 and 9×7. Before they tried to find the products, I reminded them of the conversation we had the week before about why $(3 \times 8) + (4 \times 8) = 7 \times 8$. They shared their ideas about the equivalency of those expressions, making reference to the cookie trays and how we had the same amount of cookies if we counted the cookies on 1 tray at a time or on both trays together. Then I asked, "Could that idea help you solve problems involving multiplication facts you don't know? Could you use facts you know as a starting point?"

To solve 9×8, Fleurette used multiplying by 5s, a relatively easy times table to remember, and then continued with the additional groups:

$$9 \times 5 = 45$$
$$9 \times 3 = 27$$
$$45 + 27 = 72$$
$$9 \times 8 = 72$$

Julio solved the problem very differently. He used the idea of doubling: if $8 \times 3 = 24$, 8×6 has to be the double of 8×3 because 8×6 is 2 groups of 8×3:

$$8 \times 3 = 24$$
$$8 \times 6 = 48$$
$$24 + 48 = 72$$

Both students identified prior knowledge that helped them solve this number problem. I had not told them in advance which ideas would be helpful. In previous lessons, they had to explain why the distributive property of multiplication worked (even though they did not name it), so they knew that their procedures made sense. I was pleased to see that they did not turn to their usual procedure of skip counting or even counting by ones until they got to the answer, but rather they accessed their knowledge of factor pairs.

Reasoning to solve problems by using what they knew continued very spontaneously when they worked on the second problem: 9×7.

DAVEL: We have just solved 9×8, which is 72. So 9×7 is . . . 1 group less.
LUCÍA: Yes! Yes! $72 - 7$?
JULIO: No wait! First we had 8 plates with 9 cookies, now we have 7 plates with 9 cookies, so we have to take away 1 plate of 9 cookies.
ALL: Yeah!
ALEJANDRO: $72 - 9 = 63$. $9 \times 7 = 63$.

In this conversation, Davel brought to the other students' attention what was already familiar to them and how they could use it to solve a nonfamiliar fact. This time, he didn't need my prompting. Then Julio transformed the problem into a familiar context, one that could help them reason whether they had to subtract 7 or 9.

The process of using prior knowledge in new situations is automatic for mathematicians and successful students but needs to be taught to students who struggle in mathematics. In this lesson, I explicitly helped the students link prior knowledge to the new situation. Our previous discussion about the cookie trays served to anchor the conversation. If I hadn't done so before sending them off to work, they would have treated 9×8 and 9×7 as problems isolated both from each other and from any previous knowledge they had.

Making Connections Among Strategies

As mentioned previously, one goal was to help these students understand the relationship between skip counting and multiplication. To do this, I gave them the following problem: I will pack 23 party favor bags for my son's birthday. Each bag will have 4 toys. How many toys do I have to buy? Some students used multiplication and some used skip counting. I wanted to focus on the connection between those two strategies, so I purposefully chose to share the work of three students who used skip counting and multiplication.

Lucía
$23 \times 4 = 92$
4, 8, 12, 16, 20, 24, 28, 32, 36, 40, 44, 48, 52, 56, 60, 64, 68, 72, 76, 80, 84, 88, 92

Fleurette
$23 \times 4 = 92$
$10 \times 4 = 40$
$10 \times 4 = 40$
$3 \times 4 = 12$
$40 + 40 + 12 = 92$

Davel

$23 \times 4 = 92$

$9 \times 4 = 36$

$9 \times 4 = 36$

$5 \times 4 = 20$

$36 + 36 + 20 = 92$

After the work of these three students was on the board, I asked, "Are there any similarities among these ways of solving the problem?" The room was quiet for a short while. Most of the students seemed to be thinking.

JULIO: Two used multiplication. The number 4 appears in the work of Fleurette and Davel. [*another long silence*]

ALEJANDRO: You can see the work of Fleurette's equations in Lucía's skip counting method.

TEACHER: What do you mean?

ALEJANDRO: You can see the 10×4. [*Goes to the board and points*] 4, 8, 12, 16, 20, 24, 28, 32, 36, 40. When she skip counts by 4s and gets to 40, she skip counted 10 times.

TEACHER: Can you mark that with a marker?

ALEJANDRO: This is 10×4. [*He circles the numbers from 4 to 40.*] Then she does another 10×4. [*He circles 44, 48, 52, 56, 60, 64, 68, 72, 76, 80 with another color.*] 40 and 40 makes 80. Then these 3 are the 3×4: 84, 88, 92. [*He circles these 3 numbers with another color*]. Lucía counted by 4s 23 times. But if you want to do it faster, you multiply.

Alejandro made a very strong connection between both strategies, but I wasn't sure everyone understood his explanation. I continued the conversation by asking Lucía to rephrase what Alejandro had said. Lucía did not completely trust multiplication. She was not using it consistently in her work, or she skip counted first and then wrote a multiplication equation to match it. I purposefully asked Lucía to rephrase Alejandro's idea to help her articulate the connection between both strategies. Had she understood what Alejandro said? Although Lucía explained Alejandro's idea in her own words, it was clear that she was still working through it. Yet, to hear other students say out loud what she was considering silently validated her ideas and at the same time clarified her thinking.

Students don't always say what I would like to hear the first time I raise a question, but I keep asking the question. It is not necessarily that students don't have the language to answer these questions. Their initial silence might mean that they had never thought about finding similarities among strategies, and that takes practice. Although I consider the previous conversation very successful, the initial conversation consisted of the students' descriptions of their own methods, the numbers and operations they used. Yet describing their own strategies was important in helping the students notice similarities. Using their descriptions, I asked targeted questions to draw out their thinking about their strategies and the similarities among them.

Again, these discussions are important not only for what they contribute to one particular moment but for the references they establish for future discussions. I knew that after this class, some students would continue to use skip counting, yet I could refer to the connection between skip counting and multiplication they had begun to make to help them further think about it. I posted the chart with the different solutions and Alejandro's notes for future reference.

Making Connections Among Representations

Some students are able to connect the meaning of words in a multiplication story problem with an array and a multiplication equation. For others, the multiplication story, the array, and the equation are not necessarily connected. Because many students can make sense of multiplication through a real-life context, or through a mathematical model like an array, it is important for them to see how these different ways are related.

When I reintroduced arrays in a subsequent lesson, I began with the familiar context of cookies on a cookie sheet. The students immediately described the trays with cookies as follows: "In one tray, there are 3 rows of cookies and there are 8 cookies in each row. In the other tray, there are 4 rows of cookies and 8 cookies in each row."

They were able to use words to describe the number of groups (rows of cookies) and the number of items in each group (cookies in each row). I then asked them to use numbers to represent what they had just articulated in words. After they wrote 3×8, I asked what the 3 and the 8 meant in the context of the cookies. I wanted them to connect the multiplication expression to the context. I also wanted them to connect the array model to the context and the multiplication expression, so I asked them to build an array with snap cubes. Because the students had already talked about what they had seen in the picture, they made the connection between the cubes and the cookies easily: each snap cube stood for a cookie and each row of cubes was a row of cookies. I purposefully asked students to move from one representation to the other and to explain how they connected to each other. This practice continued throughout the lessons, and became especially helpful in solving story problems.

As you may recall, my students referred to contexts as a way to think through an idea in previous lessons as well.

1. During the initial cookie tray problem, Alejandro used a context to make Lucía's idea clearer for the rest of the students:

TEACHER: I wonder why it is the same to do 3 × 8, then 4 × 8, and add both products or just do 7 × 8?

LUCÍA: 3 and 4 make 7 but the 8 stays the same [*pointing to the arrays as she moves the smaller arrays closer to each other to make a 7 × 8 array*].

ALEJANDRO: When you put together the 3 and the 4 [*pointing to the dimensions of the smaller arrays*], you make 7 rows of 8 cookies.

2. When students wanted to figure out if they had to subtract 7 or 9 from 9 × 8 to solve 9 × 7, Julio clarified the situation by creating a context:

DAVEL: We have just solved 9 × 8, which is 72. So 9 × 7 is . . . 1 group less.

LUCÍA: Yes! Yes! 72 – 7?

JULIO: No wait! First we had 8 plates with 9 cookies, now we have 7 plates with 9 cookies, so we have to take away 1 plate of 9 cookies.

Accessing contexts or models to think ideas through is a very important skill in solving mathematical problems. Alejandro brought up a context to prove why an idea worked. Julio recreated a context to solve a problem. Understanding how different representations relate to each other helped these students pick the representation that worked for them and that related to the initial numerical expression they had to think about. This is the kind of flexibility I want students to develop: to identify the tools that help them make sense of mathematical problems. Once again, the initial work we did with the cookie trays worked as a springboard to understand multiple representations.

Working Through Errors and Misunderstandings

As students began to solve division problems using multiplication, I noticed that when the problems involved larger numbers, students lost track of the meaning of the numbers. They could no longer keep straight which were the groups, the elements in each group, and the total number of things. Their mistakes revealed what they were struggling with and I wanted them to consider their mistakes.

I presented the following problem:

Ms. Melissa was selling popsicles as part of a school fundraiser. There were 168 popsicles in the freezer. Ms. Melissa took out 24 popsicles at a time so they would not melt before they were sold. She sold all the popsicles that day. How many groups of 24 popsicles did she take out of the freezer?

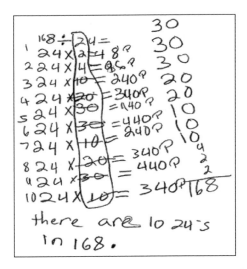

Figure 1–2.

Lucía was able to identify what type of problem it was and which equation repre-sented the problem. (See Figure 1–2.) She wrote 168 ÷ 24. Then she decided to solve it using multiplication.

When I asked Lucía to walk me through her work she said: "I want to get to 168." I asked her to go over her work out loud and think about what each num-ber meant:

> LUCÍA: [*pointing to 24 × 2*] 24 are how many popsicles Ms. Melissa takes out each time. And 2 [*times 2*] . . . , because . . . she took out 2 trays. That is 48 popsicles. And then 4 trays . . . Oops! I messed up!
> TEACHER: What makes you say so?
> LUCÍA: Because these [*pointing to the circled numbers*] are the trays. I did more popsicles than 168.

After reviewing her first attempt and reflecting on her error, she wrote:

$$24 \times 5 = 120 \text{ popsicles}$$
$$\underline{24 \times 2 = 48 \text{ popsicles}} \qquad 120 + 48 = 168$$
$$7 \text{ groups}$$
There are 7 groups.

Lucía knew she could use multiplication to solve a division problem, but she often did it mechanically, without thinking about the meaning of the numbers. Here, she did connect the meaning of the numbers to the procedure and was able to identify her mistake. Lucía was connecting procedural knowledge to concep-tual knowledge.

It is important to consider children's mistakes as learning opportunities. In the past, I tried to explain students' mistakes to them, hoping that they would understand and correct them. Most of the time all I got were blank stares. I was presenting my own reasoning, which did not make sense to them. I have learned that it is better and more lasting for students to develop the habit of reasoning through their own work in order to identify and clarify their mistakes. I facilitate this reasoning through asking them to restate their process and asking specific questions about their steps, if necessary. Of course, the mistakes will not disappear right away, but the fact that students have already talked about mistakes makes it easier for students to revisit, identify, and correct their work in the future.

Reflecting on Their Learning

At different times during my work with this group of students, I asked them to reflect on what they did and did not understand about multiplication. For me, these reflections served as tools for evaluating their knowledge and overall attitude toward their learning. For my students, it served to articulate their understandings and misunderstandings and in the process helped them to see themselves as learners.

At first, most of the students' reflections focused on what they did not understand. They were aware that they did not know how to solve difficult problems and that they did not know all the multiplication facts. But after we had worked together for awhile, their reflections began to focus more on what they did understand:

> "Multiplication is like skip counting and the number gets bigger." (Vanessa)
> "If you have 13×12, you have to times the number you have that number of times, you put the number again that many times." (Lucía)
> "Multiplying by 4 and counting by 4 is the same thing. If you have 9×4, it is counting by 4 nine times." (Davel and Alejandro)

Vanessa, Davel, and Alejandro paid attention to the relationship of skip counting and multiplication, and Lucía tried to articulate the idea of having many groups of the same size. Her statement refers to the transition she was working on between skip counting and multiplying: "You put the number again that many times."

Toward the end of our work together, I asked the students to reflect on whether or not they felt more comfortable with multiplication and division. Their answers were all positive. This is a very important aspect of learning: to become aware that what was difficult before is no longer so. This is especially important to address with students who struggle, as they have a hard time seeing themselves as learners.

Reflections

Although I worked with these students in a small group, I know from my own experience and through talking with other teachers that the teaching moves I've described are applicable in large-group settings and, in fact, help all students learn mathematics with understanding. For example, when teachers ask students to share strategies, they often target a few that illustrate important features of the mathematical operation and then draw out the connections among them. They refer to prior solutions that students have used and contexts and representations that are familiar to the group. By creating a mathematical culture in their classrooms, teachers can encourage students to take risks and use their errors and misunderstandings as learning opportunities for themselves and the rest of the class.

At the beginning of this essay, I referred to Davel and his inability to reason through a multiplication number problem (see page 5). Although he had made a mistake, he could not analyze it because he had trusted a procedure that he thought he remembered properly. Through the process we developed in our small group, Davel began to see mathematics differently. He began to understand that mathematics is about reasoning and making sense. The emphasis on making connections to prior knowledge, among strategies and representations, explaining and analyzing strategies, working through errors, and reflecting on their learning helped Davel think through the problems that I posed. Despite his slower learning pace and his confusions, he showed he was capable of reasoning.

After students felt more comfortable interpreting and solving multiplication problems, we began to work on division story problems. Students spontaneously used multiplication combinations to solve them. After a few sessions, Davel asked, "I don't understand! Are we dividing or multiplying?" Davel wanted to understand, and his question led us to explore an important mathematical idea: the inverse relationship between multiplication and division.

2

What Comes Next?

Being Explicit About Patterns

Laura Marlowe

I have learned that it is important for me to take an active role in helping my students who struggle with mathematics. Instead of waiting for them to discover concepts on their own, I think about the kind of support each student needs. Are they having difficulty getting started? Do they understand the problem or the task? Do they understand both the directions and the goals of the activity? Can I restate the directions or questions to make the goals and concepts more explicit? Can I provide the right support or scaffold? Can I give them the supports in small enough bits so I don't overwhelm them?

Patterns: A Central Mathematical Idea

A major objective in kindergarten mathematics is constructing, recognizing, describing, and extending repeating patterns. Patterns are an essential part of mathematics. We want students to expect regularities in the mathematics they do and to look for and use patterns when they solve problems, using strategies such as skip counting, for example. Over the years, I have noticed that recognizing and creating patterns can be challenging for some children. Many young children have experienced patterns in their lives but cannot identify the repeating parts. In addition, I have found that students who have difficulty with patterns often have difficulty with making sense of number and operations, perhaps because they do not see patterns in their work with numbers. So it is important to get students comfortable identifying and working with patterns starting in kindergarten.

Much of the support I provide to students who struggle with patterns focuses on helping them:

* understand that a pattern is a regularly repeating unit
* figure out what comes next in a pattern
* begin to discover the structure of a pattern by identifying the unit that repeats

What Is a Pattern? Who Needs Support?

The beginning of our pattern unit asks students to name patterns they see in the classroom and in the neighborhood, and then to draw a picture of a pattern they observed. This informal assessment gives me a quick check on which students already know what a pattern is and which students need my attention. If students are struggling with identifying and constructing patterns from the beginning, it is important that I give them immediate support to help them understand what a pattern is.

To help those who are unable to name or draw patterns, I point out the features of the patterns that other students have drawn. For example I might say, "What do you see in this picture that keeps repeating? What part is the pattern? Why is that a pattern?"

We also do body movement patterns early in the unit so that students who learn best kinesthetically can involve their whole body in noticing patterns. When we do body movement patterns, I might say to the students, "We call this a *pattern* because it repeats over and over again. We could go on forever, without stopping, and it would always be shoulders, head, shoulders, head." Sometimes it is difficult during this activity to tell which students understand the idea of a pattern because motor skill development can inhibit some students from being successful. That is why naming each movement as we do it helps students "hear" what the pattern is. These body movement patterns work well at the beginning of subsequent pattern lessons because using their bodies helps some students who are having difficulty make connections to other pattern contexts. They are able to refer back to the earlier work with body movements to recognize other patterns. For example, we use the body movement words to connect with the snap cubes patterns. If the pattern is, "clap, clap, snap," we snap together a green, green, red cube pattern to match.

I also ask students questions as we go along to help them focus on each element of the pattern and on the repetition.

- How did you know what to do next (for body movement patterns)?
- How did you know what comes next?
- How would you tell someone else what the pattern is?

Identifying What Comes Next in a Pattern

When students began working with partners to make patterns with tiles and connecting cubes, I circulated, focusing on children who had been having difficulty with the concepts during the whole-group sessions. I have found that I need to work with them as soon as possible so they practice naming the parts of the pattern, instead of floundering on their own or depending on a partner to set them straight.

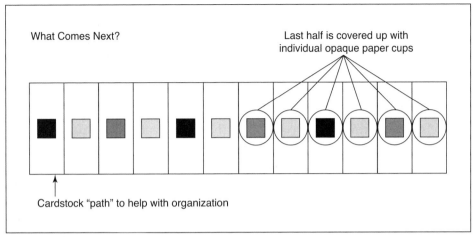

What Comes Next?

Last half is covered up with individual opaque paper cups

Cardstock "path" to help with organization

Figure 2–1.

One day my students played a game called What Comes Next? in which one student builds a linear pattern with twelve color tiles or other manipulatives (Russell et al. 2008n). Then the student covers up the last half of the pattern with cups, and her partner has to tell what comes next (see Figure 2–1).

I knew that one of the pairs, Rashid and Chad, would need my support. This was Rashid's second year in kindergarten. He was born very prematurely and showed developmental delays in language and mathematics. Children tended not to want to be his partner because he struggled *so* much. Rashid needed to develop foundational skills so that he could be successful with patterns. Identifying attributes is a critical skill as students pay attention to which attribute is repeating in a pattern. For example, at the beginning of the year, Rashid could only name color and shapes of blocks as attributes of a set of pattern blocks. Through extended practice, he was able to come up with additional attributes with which to sort a set of objects, such as size, texture, surface features (like holes/no holes on buttons), or thickness (when using attribute blocks).

Rashid was not consistently successful making simple patterns, such as red, green, red, green (AB, AB), but because so many of the other children were moving on to more complex patterns, he really wanted to try and do what his partner was trying. On this particular day, Rashid had made a tile train that started blue, yellow, red, yellow and then did not repeat—it was random. His partner, Chad, became very frustrated because he could not guess what came next. This discussion followed.

TEACHER: Chad, what could you say to Rashid about his pattern?
CHAD: It really isn't a pattern.

TEACHER: How could you explain it to him? Why isn't it a pattern?
CHAD: It doesn't keep going. It doesn't repeat. It should be blue, yellow, red, yellow—blue, yellow, red, yellow, and so on.
TEACHER: Can you show Rashid what the pattern should be?

Chad proceeded to build the blue, yellow, red, yellow. Then all three of us said the pattern and occasionally I asked, "What comes next?" while we were actually looking at the pattern in front of us. Chad then took his turn and built a pattern with the repeating unit: yellow, green, yellow, blue. I suggested that we stop here and name the tiles (yellow, green, yellow, blue). "Let's repeat this much," I said, (pointing to each one: yellow, green, yellow, blue). "We're going to repeat this part again" (yellow, green, yellow, blue). "What would come next?" Rashid still could not identify what came next. So I asked Chad to make a different pattern. Chad made a pattern with yellow, green, red as the unit. "Let's look at how this pattern starts," I said.

This was a simpler pattern than Chad's last pattern—a yellow, green, red (ABC) pattern instead of yellow, green, yellow, blue (ABAC)—so I thought this might be a better place to begin with Rashid to explicitly work on identifying the pattern. I decided it might help Rashid to have him "name" the color and touch each tile as he said the name.

TEACHER: What color is the first tile?
RASHID: Yellow.
TEACHER: Put your finger on it as you say *yellow*. What color is next?
RASHID: Green.
TEACHER: Let's say that much together.
RASHID AND TEACHER: Yellow, green.
TEACHER: Let's keep going. What color is next?
RASHID: Red.
TEACHER: Alright. Let's start at the beginning and go that far. Remember to touch the tiles as you say the colors.
RASHID: Yellow, green, red.
TEACHER: Keep going!
RASHID: Yellow, green, red.
TEACHER: What color do you think comes next? What's under the cup? [*Rashid gives me an unsure look.*] Let's start from the beginning again and see what happens.
RASHID AND TEACHER: Yellow, green, red, yellow, green, red . . . [*I pause.*]
Rashid: Yellow.
TEACHER: Let's see if you're right. Chad, lift up the cup that is hiding the next tile.

21

Rashid's eyes lit up when he saw that he was correct. I asked them to continue doing the activity with the pattern Chad created, but I stayed to support Rashid as he figured out the next parts of the pattern. Each time Chad asked Rashid, "What comes next?" I asked Rashid to start back at the beginning of the pattern and say the color of each tile as he points to it and then say what color he thinks is next. Rashid was able to finish his turn successfully with this extra support. Although he had been successful, I encouraged him to also practice with AB patterns to build his confidence. I asked him to make patterns that would make sense to him.

The next time Rashid worked on identifying what came next in a pattern, he started by repeating the process of saying out loud the part of the pattern that he could see, and I made sure he touched each piece as he said its name. Each time we got ready to name the next missing piece, I asked him to start at the beginning and touch and name each piece up to the next missing piece. Although this process took extra time, it allowed Rashid to experience more success than he had in the past. He was able to name the pattern correctly as he touched each tile. There was something about going back to the beginning each time and the tactile experience along with the voicing of the pattern that made him more confident. Repetitive oral and physical prompts are important with students like Rashid who struggle to retain learning from the previous lessons. Sometimes I also asked him, "Can you lay the units in a row on top or next to each other?" I would often ask students to place each unit on top of each other or lined up flat on the table, one underneath the last one, to see if they match the rest of the units. The consistent restating of directions and cues, what I call "overlearning," or practicing newly acquired skills to integrate them thoroughly, helped him build this critical piece of understanding.

Providing Additional Contexts

Another way I attempt to help students build understanding from one session to the next is to continue the strategies I use with them when we're in the small group at our whole-group meetings. I find these strategies often help make the mathematics explicit for the whole group, so I use the same language when we are having a whole-group discussion to wrap up the lesson. I let the students in my small group know that I will be asking them the same questions in the large group that I already asked them. I prepare them ahead of time so they can contribute to the whole-class discussion. For example, when Rashid was making pattern trains with cubes, I told him I would be asking him to name his pattern in the large group using his written recording to help him articulate his thinking.

To solidify students' ability to make generalizations about patterns, we also play games and do activities that have different contexts and representations. For example, we do an activity called Patterns on the Pocket Chart in which a pocket chart is used to display a 100 chart (Russell et al. 2008n). I make a linear pattern along the first row, and I cover up the last half of the pattern, similar to the What Comes Next? game. Students name the pattern and tell me what comes next. This is a routine that we continue for the entire school year. Students then use what they learned about naming and extending a pattern in the whole group when they do similar activities on their own or with partners. Although Rashid wasn't always successful at the beginning, he was engaged in this activity and often took the risk to volunteer an answer.

Identifying the Repeating Unit

Once Rashid began to have more success identifying what comes next in a pattern, I worked with him on identifying the unit that repeats. When students name patterns, often their voices pause naturally at the end of the unit of a pattern, but some children, such as Rashid, have difficulty identifying where the breaks occur. Sometimes simply asking these students to say the pattern a few times helps them identify the unit. However, I often need to be more explicit. One strategy that sometimes helps is to ask them to say one part of the pattern and ask, "Has any part repeated yet?" For instance, the following is the exchange we had when Rashid was trying to find the unit of a cube pattern train with the unit red, blue, blue.

TEACHER: What's the first cube?
RASHID: Red.
TEACHER: What's the next cube?
RASHID: Blue.
TEACHER: Has the pattern started to repeat?
RASHID: No.
TEACHER: Let's keep going.
RASHID: Red, blue, blue.
TEACHER: Have you started repeating yet?
RASHID: Yes. There are two blues in a row.
TEACHER: But have you repeated the first cube yet? Have you said red yet?
RASHID: No, that's what comes next?
TEACHER: OK. So is it repeating now?
RASHID: Yes.
TEACHER: Then let's break it here and see if it keeps repeating this part.
RASHID: Red, blue, blue—here's another part like the first one we broke off!

By asking Rashid to name each cube in a sequence, first, next, and so on, I reinforced the concept of the repeating unit. Having him physically break the cubes apart and seeing that each unit is the same (or not) brought home the idea that he was looking for the chunk that repeats over and over again. By saying the words out loud while physically breaking off the cubes, he got a feel for the pattern, and his voice almost instinctively said what came next.

Reflections

In thinking about strategies for helping students know what a pattern is, predict what comes next, and identify the repeating unit of a pattern, I realize that especially with my students who struggle, I need to take an active role in making accommodations. Some strategies I use include:

- providing repeated opportunities for practice
- verbalizing each move in a game along with the student, in addition to speaking/using words to describe the pattern
- asking specific questions to help make what they are looking for explicit; for example, to help students identify the repeating unit, I asked, "Where's the part that repeats? Where do you start over?"
- asking the students to say the pattern out loud
- asking the students to touch each object in the pattern as they say the word
- providing a variety of contexts and materials so that these students can flexibly apply their knowledge
- reviewing the concepts we have practiced in the small groups during our large group time and asking the students who struggle to participate with my support

I use these same strategies throughout all of our units of study, particularly for my students who are struggling. I work with these students in small groups to give them extra practice, for example, more opportunities to play games to make sure they understand the underlying mathematical concepts. In our work with counting games, students might lose track of where they started, which spaces to count, and where to stop. So I might repeat students' moves aloud, having the student touch each space as I say the words. "So you were at 3, you rolled a 4, so we move to 4, then 5, then 6, then 7, now you landed on 7." After a few rounds of this modeling, I might ask the students to verbalize their moves as they move the game pieces. To work on the counting sequence, we do a lot of oral counting so they can hear the correct order of numbers, and the students have many opportunities to count all through the day.

For the rest of the year, I purposefully called on Rashid every time we reviewed Patterns on the Pocket Chart. He showed a willingness to take risks and became more confident in explaining his thinking. He literally started to bounce up and down, with his hand in the air, because he felt so sure of himself. His understanding of number also progressed. Understanding the repeating unit in our study of patterns undoubtedly helped him look for and expect to find patterns in the number system. He ended the year being able to rote count to 100, having one-to-one correspondence to about 25, and being one of the first ones picked for a partner for the number games that we played because he was so successful!

3

You Can't Build a Sand Castle on a Classmate's Head

Being Explicit in Kindergarten Math

Lisa Seyferth

Over my years of teaching kindergarten, I have thought a great deal about being explicit with students about my expectations for how they are to behave in class. Each year brings new students and new situations where I have to be very clear about what I want my students to do or not do. This year, for example, was the first time I had to tell them not to climb into the sand table. What is more, I had to tell them not to build a sand castle on top of a classmate's head. The crushed look on their faces when I was not delighted with their innovation (very much like the kids in *Hop on Pop* [Dr. Seuss 1963] when told they must not hop on Pop) was even more surprising to me than the sand castle itself.

I have a tape playing in my head of my former principal saying, "You can teach for the behavior you want." This idea is such a powerful one. I often hear teachers say, "My class always does [this wrong thing]" or "Susie can't [do that desirable social behavior]" as if the thing they are stating is a static, permanent fact. I usually think, and sometimes say, "But you can *teach* them [not to/to]."

In the past few years, my thinking about when to be very explicit about behavioral expectations has extended into when to be very clear about the mathematics of an activity. Again, this is such a powerful, and also simple, idea, but I didn't think about it much before for a couple reasons. One, which is embarrassing to admit, is that it is easy not to be thoughtful. I could present a lesson, teach a game, show a worksheet, and then send the students off to do it. "Here is how you play Racing Bears, here are the materials, this is your partner, now go play." (If I was being explicit about behavioral expectations, I might also talk a bit about how to be a good partner, how to play calmly, and how to clean up.) The lesson might go well from a management point of view, but I was not always successful in making sure that all of the students worked on or thought about the mathematics at the heart of a particular activity or game.

Another reason I have not always been very explicit with my students about the math in an activity is that I believe that young students should be given the opportunity to make their own discoveries. I have always thought that I should not insert my own understanding of the math (or other subject matter), but rather should let the students construct their own understanding. However, as I thought about my struggling students, I decided to take steps to make the mathematics explicit for them.

Grab and Count

In the fall, my class spent a few weeks working on math activities that centered around the idea of comparing. We started our work on comparing with an activity called Grab and Count: Compare (Russell et al. 2008a). In this activity, students grab 2 separate handfuls of Unifix cubes and determine which handful has more cubes. Students color in stacks of cubes on a paper to represent their 2 handfuls and then indicate which stack has more cubes. This activity is a variation of a game we played previously, Grab and Count (Russell et al. 2008a), that requires students to grab handfuls of objects, count how many they got, and represent the quantity on paper.

When I introduced the new version of Grab and Count, I decided to start out with a conversation about the word *compare*. I asked the class if they had heard the word before or if they had any idea what it meant, but none of the students had any inkling. I told them that comparing can happen with a lot of different things and that when we compared numbers or amounts, we were looking to see which was more and which was less. We demonstrated the activity with student volunteers. I reminded them that the point was to compare their 2 towers. I told them, "If you choose this activity, you will be doing lots of counting and lots of thinking about which number is bigger."

Kyle

I knew it was important for me to check in right away with my struggling students to make sure they understood what was required and that they had an entry point. Kyle is a student who is very tentative about academic activities. He often asks for help and reassurance, and he does not like trying new things. He counts objects up to 6 or 8 before losing one-to-one correspondence. I noticed Kyle would play the entire game of Grab and Count without doing any actual counting. He was successful at other steps of the activity; it is in fact possible to determine which of your 2 towers is larger without doing any counting. Kyle would build his stacks and then color his paper stacks by taking 1 cube off, coloring 1 cube, taking another cube off, coloring another cube, and so on, matching one-to-one as he colored. I thought this was a good way for him to solidify his one-to-one correspondence, but I also wanted him to practice counting and to think about how the quantities that went with the numbers compared with each other. So, I told him to be sure to count them because that was part of the important math in this activity. "After all, the game is called Grab and *Count*," I told him. I did notice Kyle counting his cubes on most turns over the following days, and slowly his counting started to be more accurate. He still generally used matching to record the amount in his stacks—taking 1 cube off of the stack, coloring 1 cube on the paper, taking another cube off, coloring another cube, and so on rather than just coloring in the quantity he counted.

Latisha and Briana

Latisha and Briana made their way to Grab and Count: Compare on the third day it was offered as a math choice. In mathematics, Latisha had difficulty counting even small quantities of objects correctly, and Briana could get mixed up after 10 or 11. Over at their table, I noticed that Latisha and Briana were spending much of their time coloring the paper cube strips and arguing over markers. In fact, more than once Latisha colored the whole strips using what she called "girl colors" without interacting with the actual cubes in any way, never mind counting them up and figuring out which stack had more cubes. Briana would grab the 2 handfuls and build the towers, but the task of coloring the paper cubes to match her stacks was challenging for her. She kept switching colors, starting over, and arguing about who was using the pink marker. I reminded Briana and Latisha what good partners do—work, share, take turns, listen to each other, and watch each other count.

I also made the decision that I needed to play a couple rounds with the girls to help them focus on just comparing the amounts without recording. When I grabbed a handful of 7 and a handful of 8 and stacked my cubes, Briana immediately lined the stacks up next to each other and said, "This one has more," indicating the stack of 8. I asked her how many there were in each stack, and she counted accurately. I then said, "So which is more?" She said, "8." On the next round we grabbed 7 and 9. Latisha grabbed the stacks and started coloring before we had counted. She did not compare the stacks nor count the cubes. When I asked her which stack had more she pointed vaguely toward her paper, not the cubes. When I asked her how many cubes were in 1 of the stacks she shrugged and went back to coloring.

Clearly the girls were having difficulty for different reasons, and clearly this was not a good activity for them to work on together. I had Briana work with

Samantha, who was matching her towers directly to the paper cubes and coloring the cubes next to the real cubes. I said to Briana, "I like that you are counting your cubes and comparing your stacks. Samantha has an idea for how to color the paper cubes to show her stacks. It's important that you show how tall your stacks are and which has more cubes." We held class conversations about how to color in the cubes on the paper to show how many cubes were in the towers, and I demonstrated on chart paper some of the strategies students had suggested or had used at their tables. I was glad to see that Samantha was using a good strategy and hoped that Briana might both think about our previous class conversations and take note of what Samantha was doing.

Next, I worked with Latisha for a few minutes one-on-one. I had her grab handfuls of cubes and count them up. She kept reaching for the markers and trying to keep other students from taking her preferred colors until I finally moved the markers and papers off the table. I said, "Latisha, I know you like to color, but the most important thing for you to do right now is count. Counting is an important part of math. I want you to keep grabbing handfuls of cubes and counting them up. Later you can color." I planned the next day to have Latisha compare 2 stacks, and not to work on the recording piece until much later. I felt that the most important math idea for Latisha was counting accurately and thinking about quantity, so my bottom line message to her was "You must count."

Playing Compare

The class chugged along for some days with this and other activities about comparing. Briana was partnered with a couple other students who had different strategies for coloring their cube papers, and she usually ended up aligning her cubes right next to the paper cube strips—the same strategy that Samantha had used. Latisha sometimes fought over markers, but often counted her cube stacks, and could do so accurately up to 7 or 8.

Next, we played the card game Compare (Russell et al. 2008a), which is basically the pacifist version of War, during which players each turn over a number card and the one whose card has a greater number says "Me." We also measured objects by comparing them to a stick of 10 Unifix cubes, and we sorted the objects into groups of "longer than the cube stick" and "shorter than the cube stick." Throughout the lessons and activities, I was sure to use the word *compare* when talking with the students. I wondered if they realized that all of the activities hung together around the idea of comparing. I decided to ask them. At the end of math time one day, I said, "Raise your hand if you did some comparing today." Almost all the students, including Briana and Kyle, raised their hands. Many kindergartners talked about how they compared numbers or lengths during the different math activities. Briana said that she compared numbers when she played the card game. Kyle said he compared cube towers at Grab and Count.

A few days later, Kyle was playing with our phonics puppets. He approached me with two of them and said, "Look, I compared Milo Mouse to Frederica Frog, and Frederica Frog is bigger!" I was so pleased to hear him using the idea and the language spontaneously in a new context. He shared his discovery at meeting and, as a result, comparing the puppets became a choice at math time. Later, Kyle measured some of the puppets with Unifix cubes and counted how many cubes long each was. I was pleased that he was applying the counting piece, particularly because he had avoided it at the start of our investigation.

Briana also showed that she was building an understanding of the math we were working on. The students made stacks of Unifix cubes with 1 cube for each letter in their names and then put letter stickers on the cubes to spell their names. Many of the students spontaneously started talking about whose names were longer and shorter, and they lined up 2 names to compare them. I wasn't planning to introduce any recording until another day, but Briana said, "We can use the papers from Grab and Count [the paper cube strips] and copy the names into the squares and circle the bigger name." I was so pleased that Briana had made sense of the idea of comparing and had connected to the process of recording her math.

More Comparing

Our investigation of comparing ended with an activity called Comparing Inventory Bags, a variation of a previous counting activity called Inventory Bags during which students counted small collections of objects in paper bags and showed on paper what was in the bag and how many (Russell et al. 2008a). When I told the class that each pair of students would be given 2 inventory bags and I asked them to guess what they were going to do, several children called out "Compare them!" They knew what we were studying in math! I asked how they could compare the collections in their 2 bags, because they couldn't stack them up and line them up next to each other like Unifix cubes. They had lots of ideas. Off they went.

Again I kept careful track of my learners who struggle to see if they were able to make connections from the previous work. Briana and her partner had a bag of 6 checkers and a bag of 9 dominoes. Briana drew all the checkers and all the dominoes, making the first one detailed and the rest just a round or square shape. She also wrote 6 next to the checkers and 9 next to the dominoes, and circled the 9. When I asked her how she knew that 9 was more she said, "I drew 6 checkers, and then I drew 6 dominoes, and I had to draw more dominoes then." Not only was she counting and recording, but her method of recording helped her reason about the quantities and compare them.

Kyle had a bag of 8 chess pieces and a bag of 7 dominoes. He wrote an 8 and drew one chess piece, and wrote a 7 and drew one domino. He said he knew that 8 was more because 7 comes before 8 when you are counting. This was a strategy that some children used and shared to figure which number was higher when playing the card game Compare, and Kyle applied the strategy to a different comparing task.

Latisha worked with Taryn. They had 6 Halloween pompoms and 5 crayons. Taryn wrote the numbers and drew one of each object to show what they had, and circled the 6. Latisha counted the pompoms over and over. She was accurate every time. One time, Taryn interrupted her after 4, and Latisha answered her and continued to count correctly, 5, 6. After each count she made marks on her paper. She looked like a very young child playing Mommy or Teacher as she spoke in a grown-up voice and mimicked how an adult writes on her clipboard. Her writing is a collection of protonumbers and suggestions of letters, but she has made significant progress in her willingness and ability to count quantities under 10. I was pleased that she was persistent and understood what the task required.

Reflections

I will continue to think about how and when to be explicit about the mathematics we are working on with this and future classes. There are times when it is really helpful to tell the whole class, "This is the math idea in all these games," or, "If you are doing this activity the way I expect, I will see lots of so-and-so and hear lots of such-and-such." My experience with the Compare activities showed me how important it is for me to direct my struggling learners to focus on an important part of a math activity or an important behavior that will help them become confident, independent learners. My experiences with this class, which needs so much direction from me to have smooth and productive days in school, also show me that being explicit doesn't preclude those important chances for students to make discoveries or think independently. My telling them to think about a certain topic, or to try a certain strategy, actually helped my struggling learners to have good ideas like comparing puppets' sizes or using paper cube strips to record and compare the lengths of classmates' names. They needed me to make the mathematical focus clear for them to play the games successfully. The repeated practice then helped them gain the skills they needed to see connections among the activities and learn the important mathematical concepts. It has been very helpful to extend what I have learned about being very explicit about desired behaviors to being very explicit about what math the students should focus on. And really there is a way in which building a sand castle on someone's head is an interesting idea.

4

Double or Nothing

Guided Math Instruction

Michelle Perch

When teaching the range of learners in my classroom, I find that making the math explicit is a key factor. Very often as teachers, we assume that most, if not all students have understood the concepts taught previously. But in working with students and with groups of teachers, I have realized that what I think everyone understands and what is truly understood are often not the same. I have learned that taking the time during a lesson to make the math explicit increases comprehension and therefore saves time in the long run. To make the mathematics concepts accessible to my students who struggle, I have to consider the way I deliver instruction and facilitate student conversation.

A central feature of my instruction is working with students in small groups. There are times when I allow students to choose their own partners or small group to complete an assignment and times when I preselect the group. Deciding how to group students is extremely important, and I consider many factors, such as ability level, attention span, cooperative learning skills, and learning styles. The nature of the assignment also influences the type of groups I choose— homogeneous or heterogeneous—and whether I need to adjust the assignment for my students who are struggling. Heterogeneous groups (groups of students with mixed ability levels) work well when students are working in teams or doing an activity or game that is already familiar to all. Having students help each other and explain concepts to each other strengthens the learning of all students. Homogenous groups (groups of students at or about the same level) are more appropriate when students need to be challenged or increase their confidence (for those students who struggle).

Being pulled out to work with me in a smaller group is not a stigma in my room because I work with different groups throughout the year. Sometimes I pull students who seem to be understanding the mathematics to work with me to monitor their thinking and to make sure they are on task and being challenged.

Other times, I pull out struggling students to provide practice on a particular concept. The following lesson is an example of this latter type of guided math instruction.

Introducing Doubling

The purpose of this lesson that took place in late October was to have students understand what it means to double a number and what happens to a quantity when you double it. We work on multiplication in third grade, so it is important for students to see the connection between doubling and multiplying by two.

I shared the book *Two of Everything* by Lily Toy Hong (1995) and we talked for a few days about the magic pot (a pot that doubled whatever was put in it). We posed questions based on what went in the pot and what came out. For example: "Joseph put $6 in the magic pot. How much money did he get out the pot?" "Susie received $18 out of the pot. How much money did she put in?"

I gave the class an assignment that included story problems about doubling, based on the book. I had been observing the students who seemed less confident. These students would hesitate when their turn arrived, knowing the pattern, but still slightly unsure about what number they were going to say. When I gave students the opportunity to choose partners to work on various math activities, I observed which students chose someone who they felt would give them the answers and which students actively participated and worked efficiently together. These observations and my assessments of the story problems helped me choose a group of five students that I needed to work with for additional guided instruction. These students had difficulty understanding what was happening in the story problems and what the question was asking. These students also had difficulty applying knowledge from one example to the next example. Each problem was like a new experience. They tended to not want to "think" about math, just get through it.

These five students did not see themselves as learners of mathematics. Although they enjoyed some of our math activities, they have never felt very successful in math and often got easily frustrated and shut down. They had difficulty explaining their thinking. Three out of the five really struggled with writing, but all five were very verbal, so I hoped that by working with them in a small group, I could draw on their verbal strengths and build their confidence. Meeting in a small group allowed me to draw out their thinking through questioning and to encourage them to verbalize their strategies. It also allowed me to use a lot of visuals and hands-on material in a guided way to demonstrate the concept.

I gave the class a sheet of story problems asking about doubling situations and reviewed the directions with the whole group. I told the whole class they could select partners to complete the assignment and that they could use whatever manipulatives and materials they needed. When I was sure the pairs were working productively, I began work with the guided math group.

Working with the Guided Math Group

For the guided math group, I put out interlocking cubes, white boards with markers, containers, and scratch paper and asked the students to come to the table with their math journals and pencils. I first asked them, "If someone told you they were going to double your money how would you feel and why?" The students discussed their answer with a partner. (Because there were five students, one student was my partner.) After sharing briefly as a group, I asked, "What happened to the money?" "Who could show me with their hands?" The students showed me by making the space between their hands grow larger and larger. We talked about what the vocabulary word *doubling* means, and I asked the students to come up with their own definition of the word. Their definitions included "Doubling means that a number gets bigger. It is adding a number to itself." We had discussed all of this as a whole class when we originally started this unit, but these students needed a review, and I needed to make sure that they understood the concept of doubling. I then asked the students to choose something that they would like to have doubled. Students shared answers like video games, recess, and money. We next talked about whether doubling everything was necessarily good and discussed things that students would not want doubled. They came up with examples like vegetables and homework. My goal in asking them to choose these items was to relate the concept to their everyday lives and let them see that the mathematics we work on is not just an abstract concept, but an everyday reality.

We then moved to manipulatives so that students would be able to physically show doubling and see what they had done. I instructed the students to build ten stacks of two interlocking cubes. We then reviewed how many cubes are in one stack, two stacks, three stacks, and so on. It was extremely important for them to see and move the cubes as they said the pattern. I then held up one stack of 2 cubes and asked the students to do the same. I asked, "What number did I double to make this stack?" The students took a minute then said, "One." We then took the stack apart to show that it was two groups of 1. I then asked them to record the addition equation that represents two groups of 1 ($1 + 1 = 2$). Next, I asked them to write what the corresponding multiplication statement would be ($2 \times 1 = 2$). We did the same thing with more of the stacks of cubes. For example, we took three stacks of 2 cubes and pulled them apart to make 2 groups of 3 cubes. The two separate groups of cubes illustrated that 3 doubled is 6. Then we wrote equations to represent the doubling: $3 + 3 = 6$, $2 \times 3 = 6$.

I asked the students how we could use this information to help us double numbers. The students said we could just add the number twice. One student said, "If it is an easy number, we can multiply by 2."

After the students had practiced with the cubes and writing equations, I returned to the context of the magic pot. I asked students to take one of their stacks of 2 cubes, and to put 1 cube in a container. I asked the group how many cubes were not in the container. Everyone responded, "One." I then told students to think of their containers as magic pots and to double what was in them each time. I gave them cubes and containers and they wrote the equations showing what was in the container each time they doubled the number of cubes: $1 + 1 = 2$, $2 + 2 = 4$, $4 + 4 = 8$, and so on. Students found that their containers filled up quite quickly. They were very engaged and were fascinated to see what happened when things kept doubling. "Wow, this is filling fast. The bigger the number, the bigger the double." I felt confident that by taking the time to make this concept more explicit, I helped my students comprehend the mathematics of the lesson.

Making Connections to a New Context

After working on the magic pot problems for a few days, I felt the students were ready to move on to a new problem. I wanted to see if students could apply what they had just been doing, so I made up the following problem for them to solve: There are 22 children in a class. Each student wanted a double-scoop ice cream cone. There were 40 scoops of ice cream. Would that be enough? We read the problem together and discussed what was the important information, what would we need to do to solve the problem, and what the question was asking. It was important that these students understood what the problem was asking as they often struggled with comprehending math story problems. We discussed what the important information in the problem was and what it meant to have a double scoop of ice cream. I asked questions such as: "Is the number going to be bigger or smaller than 22?" "How do you know?" "What do you think the answer will be?"

I asked students to work with a partner to figure out the answer and to use their cubes to demonstrate how they solved the problem. The students worked well with their partners and easily solved the problem. Some used cubes and some used pictures. When I asked for someone to share their answer, one student said, "The answer is 44." We looked at the question again and he corrected himself, saying, "The answer is no, there is not enough ice cream. We need 44 scoops and we only have 40."

When we gathered back together as a whole group, I asked the students from the guided math pullout group to explain to the rest of the class how they figured out their answers. We had already shared in our small group. All of the students shared their answers confidently. Some students showed visual drawings of making 22 cones with 2 scoops and counting by 2. Others showed how they just added 22 and 22 together. None, however, used manipulatives to help explain their thinking. They seemed much more comfortable using the manipulatives within the smaller group. Although the use of manipulatives is always an option for my students, sometimes my struggling students want to do the problems mentally as they see other classmates do. I don't want to mandate that everyone use manipulatives for every problem, because there are always students who can solve problems mentally and record their thinking. However, some students, especially those who struggle, often start with manipulatives but when they try to finish by solving the problems mentally, they get confused recording what they did. I want students to use whatever problem-solving strategies work for them, and I want them to know that manipulatives and drawings are valid approaches. I talk with the students about how they might connect the manipulatives or representations to the mathematical equations and ideas in the problem. The manipulatives may help them see the concept, but students must make sure they understand what is happening and why.

I let my students know that manipulatives are also helpful in explaining mathematical ideas to others. Doubling the cubes in the container is the perfect example. The cubes made the solution more accessible because students used them to show the process of doubling, whether it was by doing 22 stacks of 2, or 22 scoops, then another 22 scoops on top of those. Both of these methods reinforced the action of doubling. Working with this group, I was pleased that they could model the problem with manipulatives and explain their work.

The students in the guided math group were able to work on the rest of the problems from this lesson on their own, so I was free to check in with the other students in the class. The guided math group students were now more confident and stayed on task. I could tell that they felt successful. I checked back in with them and reviewed some of the things they noticed about doubling. Some of their statements included, "The numbers get bigger." "You can add the number to itself to find the answer." "You can multiply the number by 2." I sent everyone back to their seats and, as a whole group, we discussed what the students had noticed about doubling. My guided math students were quick to raise their hands to respond, and I was thrilled that they felt successful.

Reflections

The strength of this lesson was making the math explicit and working with a small group of students who needed my support. I needed to be focused in my goals for the session, in the questions I posed, and in the materials and contexts I offered them. I think the most effective part of the lesson was using the containers as magic pots and doubling the cubes. The students were able to internalize that doubling made the containers fill very quickly and the bigger the number, the bigger the double. It was also important to bring the students from the small group back into the whole-group discussion so they could practice what they had just learned and be exposed to their classmates' ideas. This is a process that I use often and in different subjects. When students are allowed to express their thoughts in smaller groups and they are supported and validated, it makes it easier for them to speak with confidence in larger groups.

Making math explicit means making the math concepts as clear as possible and presenting them in a variety of ways. The more deeply I understand a concept, the more I should be able to teach it and show it in different ways. It becomes a personal challenge to present material to students visually and verbally using a variety of methods and materials. The time spent doing this is invaluable in helping the students comprehend, apply the concept, and gain confidence.

• • •

Our dear friend and colleague, Michelle Perch, passed away on August 25, 2009. We are grateful for her contribution to this book, and for her generous spirit that touched the lives of teachers and students.

5

Focused Instruction on Quick Images

A Guided Math Group

Introduction

This video shows Michael Flynn working with a small group of second-grade students on an activity called Quick Images from the *Investigations in Number, Data, and Space* curriculum (Russell et al. 2008g). He decided to pull this group of students together because he thought they needed more work with this activity. While he worked with this group of students, the rest of the class did individual work.

In the Quick Image activity, students are briefly shown an image of an arrangement of dots (see Figure 5–1). Once they have been shown the image, students draw what they remember of the image and then share what the total quantity is and how they remembered the image. Because the goal of the activity is to help students develop their skills of visualizing a quantity and using the way a quantity is organized or grouped to figure out the total quantity, they are only shown the image briefly and then are asked to wait until after the image is no longer visible to draw what they remember.

In the specific Quick Image activity seen in the video, the teacher shows students images of dots organized in ten frames, a tool used to emphasize quantities in relationship to the numbers 10 and 5. Figure 5–2 includes two of the images that students can be seen working on in the video.

Before watching the video, think about how second graders might figure out how many dots are in each of these images. What might they do beyond counting all the dots? How might they use the structure of the ten frame to help them?

As you watch the video, consider the following questions. You might want to take notes on what you notice.

- How does the teacher try to make the mathematics of the lesson explicit?
- How does he structure this activity?
- What decisions and moves does the teacher make?
- What questions does he ask?
- What statements does he make?

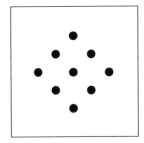

Figure 5–1.

Making the mathematics of a lesson explicit is an essential part of supporting students who struggle with the mathematics of that lesson. Students who struggle with a particular mathematical idea or struggle to develop strategies they can use to solve mathematical problems often need help seeing the mathematics that

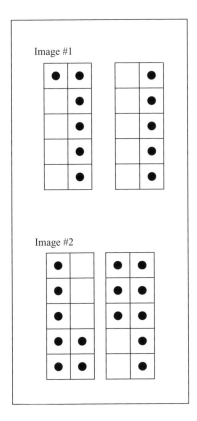

Figure 5–2.

underlies an activity, making mathematical connections between different activities they have done, or figuring out what to look for as they solve a problem.

Examining the Video Footage

Michael Flynn chose to work with this group of students because they seemed to be missing or not understanding important aspects of the mathematics of the activity, and most were trying to count all the dots during the three seconds he was showing the image. It may be that they did not realize that the ways the dots are arranged could help them figure out how many there are particularly in relation to 5 or 10. They also might not have realized they can figure out smaller subsets of the quantity first and then combine the subsets to find the total.

In the second interview, Michael said of the group of students seen in the video, "What they need [are] strategies for doing this activity because it's all about paying attention to the right thing and not trying to count." Throughout the video, you see him helping the students by making the strategies students are using explicit, nudging them a little further in the strategies they are using, and making the mathematics in the activity explicit. He does this not by telling them the strategies to use, but instead by asking them questions and making comments about their strategies and thinking. He asks them to explain in detail what they are seeing or doing, and then he repeats what they say and asks them if his restatement is correct. This helps the students think through their strategies and at the same time makes them clear for others. In asking the students whether they agree with the strategy being presented, Michael gets everyone involved in examining the strategies. His emphasis with the students is on how they got the answer; however, through this discussion, students with an incorrect answer often correct themselves.

The following are some examples of the Michael's questions and comments that helped make explicit for everyone the strategies students were using and helped the students further develop their strategies for doing the Quick Image activity.

> After doing a couple of easier images with the students and asking them to share their strategies, Michael asks, "So when I show you the image, what are you paying attention to? What are you trying to remember in that three seconds I give you?" Asking these questions highlights that there are certain things that are useful to pay attention to in general as students do this activity. It also helps them focus on the strategies they are already using.

> One student shares that she knows there are 10 boxes in 1 frame and that if 1 row is filled, there are 5 dots, and if 2 rows are filled, there are 10 dots. Michael focuses on this strategy and asks, "When you're looking at the rows, how does it help you when I'm showing you something for three seconds and then covering it up?" Through this question and follow-up questions about the

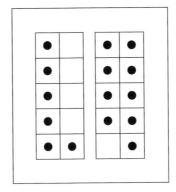

Figure 5–3.

student's strategy, Michael tries to elicit from the student a detailed description of her strategy. This seems to be a strategy that a number of students are already using, so Michael highlights it and then helps students build on this strategy.

Later, after the students work on the second image (see Figure 5–3) and decide there are 15 dots, Michael asks, "When you see this, is there any way that you fit these two together to help you find the total?" By asking this question, he is pointing students toward a way to look at the images that might lead to a strong strategy (i.e., looking at how to fit the dots from one ten frame into another ten frame).

For the third image (see Figure 5–4), Michael says, "Remember the last one we did, we talked about bringing the cards together? When you see those 2 cards, what is a way you can show someone that it would be 15?"

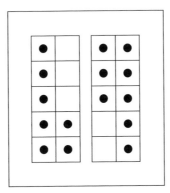

Figure 5–4.

Michael connects a strategy the students used for a previous Quick Image to what they could do for this one. This helps the students see they can use what they already know and that there are strategies that they can apply to many situations. He is also trying to highlight again the idea of using the dots from one of the ten frames to complete rows of 5 or to make 10 in the other ten frame.

By the end of the video, there is evidence that students are using strategies beyond simply counting all the dots to determine the total amount of dots in an image. The students talk about how many groups of 5 and 10 there are and how many groups are left over. Some students use the strategies of thinking about "filling in the blank spaces" by combining one group of dots with another group of dots.

In the last interview Michael talks about how doing the Quick Image activity might help students with their work with numbers. By doing Quick Images, the students might begin to have visual images of certain quantities. It could also help them with counting on by having a visual image of one quantity and then counting on from that quantity. It might help them realize that when they are adding numbers, they can break them up in different ways and combine the parts in easier ways (if you are adding 8 and 7 you can break up the 8 into 3 and 5 and add the 3 to the 7 to make 10 and then add the 5). Working with ten frame Quick Images might also help students with building an understanding of place value (thinking of numbers in terms of the number of 10s and the number of leftovers).

6

Solving Multiplication Problems

Purposeful Sharing of Strategies

Introduction

This video shows Heather Straughter working with her fifth-grade students on a set of multiplication cluster problems from the *Investigations in Number, Data, and Space* curriculum (Kliman et al. 2004).

Cluster problems are a set of related problems. Students are asked to solve the easier problems in the set and then use one or more of the easier problems to help them solve a more difficult problem. Here is the cluster problem you will see the students solving on the video.

$$4 \times 25 \qquad\qquad 10 \times 25$$
$$40 \times 25 \qquad\qquad 50 \times 25$$
$$6 \times 25$$

$$46 \times 25$$

Before watching the video, you might want to solve this cluster problem yourself. Solve the smaller problems and choose one or more of the smaller problems to help you solve the problem in the box.

As you watch the video, consider the following questions. You might want to take notes on what you notice.

- How does the teacher make the mathematics of the lesson explicit?
- How does she structure this activity?
- What decisions and moves does the teacher make?
- What questions does she ask?
- What statements does she make?

Making the mathematics of a lesson explicit is an essential part of supporting students who struggle with the mathematics of that lesson. Students who struggle to grasp a particular mathematical idea or develop strategies they can use to solve mathematical problems efficiently, often need help seeing the mathematics that underlies an activity, making mathematical connections between different activities they have done, or figuring out what to look for as they solve a problem.

In this video, you see the teacher, Heather Straughter, making the mathematics of the problems her students are solving explicit. She does so through her structuring of the lesson, through the directions she gives, through the questions she asks, and through the decisions she makes about whom to ask to share a strategy.

Examining the Video Footage

In the first interview, Heather talks about some of her goals for her students. As she introduces the task, she clearly states her expectations for how students will do the work. For example, she tells the students they can use one of the cluster problems, a few of them, or even a problem that is not on the list. Before they start, Heather asks how many people know where they are going to start. These directions fit with her goals of having them figure out for themselves how to approach a problem and solve a problem efficiently in a way that makes sense to them.

After Heather is sure all of the students have an entry point, the students solve the problem individually. As students solve the problem, she pays close attention to the strategies students are using and decides on the specific strategies (and the order of the strategies) she wants to be shared with the whole group. As students share their solutions, Heather asks them questions designed to make the strategies clear to others and to herself and to highlight the mathematical ideas within their strategies. She records their solutions on chart paper as they share them, carefully writing down each step, including those they just did in their head. By writing their solutions on chart paper for all the students to see, Heather models a way to record a solution and to write a clear and organized explanation. Her recording of the strategies also allows the others to see the steps the students used in the strategy written out fully.

Stephen's Strategy

In the second interview, Heather says she chose to have Stephen share first because "His strategy was one that many other students used and would probably be accessible to most students." As Stephen shares his solution, Heather asks questions and makes comments. For example, she explains that she is going to put 4×25 in parentheses because this was a step Stephen did in his head. She asks him to fully describe each step he took, for example, she asks him to continue his counting by 25s when, initially, he only repeated the beginning of the count. She asks him how he figured out 6×25 so quickly to highlight the understanding he was using to solve the problem. She asks other students if they solved it in the same way: "You broke up the 46 right away." Her questions and comments help clarify the mathematics of how Stephen solved the problem, help Stephen articulate his thinking, and make connections to the strategies other students were using.

Sam's Strategy

Sam's strategy was one Heather thought was mathematically powerful but might be less accessible to many of the students in the class, so she decided to have Sam share his strategy after Stephen. Her questions and recording of Sam's strategy help other students understand his strategy. She has him explain each of his steps and she records each step, even the steps he "just knew" and therefore probably didn't write down for himself. By writing the steps he "just knew" in parentheses, she is trying to make his reasoning apparent for students who might not "just know" those steps. For example, she asks Sam questions such as "How did you do 50×25 so quickly?" which encourages him to think about and explain what he knew that helped him solve that step of the problem.

Stephen's Mistake

When Stephen says that his second strategy was similar to Nashaya's, but that he didn't get the correct answer, Heather uses his mistake as a learning opportunity not only for Stephen, but for the whole class. She uses his mistake to highlight the important mathematical ideas that students need to consider as they solve the problem.

She asks another student to listen carefully as Stephen explains his mistake because she thinks the student had made a similar mistake. This emphasizes that everyone can learn from a mistake and highlights that the students use similar strategies. When the class tries to figure out Stephen's mistake, Heather asks the students to look at the strategies that were successful and compare them to Stephen's strategy. She tries to help them see what components the other strategies include that Stephen's did not. She uses what Nashaya did correctly to help the students figure out what Stephen did incorrectly. She focuses on one step that Nashaya did that connected to Stephen's mistake: "Why did [Nashaya] add 10×25 four times? Because that's key. Why is that so important?" Through this question, she highlights that there is an important idea here to pay attention to when multiplying these numbers. She summarizes the mistake for everyone in the end, "It is very important that when we're breaking the numbers up, we're keeping the value of the numbers right."

Computation Strategies in an Inclusion Classroom

In this video, you see students in an inclusion classroom using a variety of strategies to solve a computation problem. Through her questions, her recording of students' strategies, connections she makes to other strategies, and her summarizing of what they did in their strategies, Heather works to help all the students in her class make sense of the strategies they use and understand the mathematical ideas that underlie them.

During part of an interview not included in the footage, Heather shares the following reflections:

> In the beginning of teaching, I agreed with people when they said, "Special needs students should only be taught one strategy." And then I realized the danger in that is the same as lumping all kids together and saying, "Do this one way." Within [a group of] students with special needs or students on IEPs [Individualized Education Programs], there is such a range of disabilities, and a range of learning abilities, and a range of everything that there is no one approach that meets everyone's needs, whether you're special needs or not.
>
> So, I like to expose students to the different strategies so that they have a way to access [a problem]. I realize that there are certain strategies that are way more sophisticated than some students can access, and we talk about that. We talk about that if someone is sharing a strategy that you cannot understand at all, it's OK to sort of shut that off for a little bit, and not understand it. It's OK to not understand it. It's OK to not try it. But if there is something that really seems to be like, "Oh wait, I know that. I understand that," then there's no hurt in trying it and trying to make meaning of it.
>
> So, I think that students need to be exposed to all different strategies so that they can figure out what actually is easy for them, as opposed to just memorizing something that is meaningless.

In this video, you see how Heather Straughter carefully chooses strategies for students to share during their whole-group discussions. She chooses at least one that all students can understand, and she selects others that present opportunities to highlight important mathematical ideas. By exposing students to a variety of strategies and explicitly comparing the strategies and highlighting the mathematical ideas in the strategies, her goal is that the students increase their computational fluency. Although some students may only be able to solve problems one way, her goal is that they can explain that solution and that they might begin to see connections with other methods.

Linking Assessment and Teaching

Introduction

Assessment in mathematics has traditionally involved giving students an end-of-unit test and then simply moving on to the next lesson. But to include all students in meaningful mathematics, assessment must be continuous and linked with teaching. In this way, teachers can address the learning needs of their struggling students and help them make sense of the mathematics along with the rest of the class. Assessment in the context of these essays and videos refers to an ongoing process of planning accommodations and anticipating where students may have difficulties, observing students in class and posing questions to elicit information about their understanding, analyzing their written and oral work, and planning next steps.

In some cases, these teachers do find that more traditional assessment measures, such as end-of-unit tests or interview protocols, can provide them with additional insights into their students' strengths and weaknesses. On the other hand, the mathematics tests required for an Individualized Educational Program (IEP) are not likely to give a full picture of students' knowledge. These tests are developed in isolation from the general education curriculum and generally focus solely on students' deficits. They do not provide a window into students' thinking or give teachers information on their repertoire of strategies (Nolet and McLaughlin 2005). Often there is a disconnect between the instruments used in the IEP process or required achievement tests, and National Council of Teachers of Mathematics standards-based math instruction. The teachers in these essays do not rely on this kind of test to plan their mathematics instruction. Instead, they trust that all of their students are able to learn, and they

47

focus on how they can help that to happen. "[Instead of asking] 'What are my students' deficits?' classroom teachers who include all learners tend to ask, 'What are their strengths?' Beginning with what students can do changes the tone of the classroom and builds confidence in reluctant learners" (Tomlinson 2003).

These teachers also recognize that understanding mathematics means more than mastering a set of number facts or using a particular manipulative to solve a problem. Students need to understand the mathematics deeply enough to flexibly apply concepts in a variety of situations. A student may do well solving addition problems with linking cubes, for example, but when the same numbers appear in a story problem or a game, that student may be unable to make connections to his prior work. These teachers use assessment to identify where students are not making sense of a concept, then help students see the connections among various representations and contexts and use what they know to integrate new knowledge.

Each of these examples of linking teaching and assessment begins with the teacher's understanding of the mathematical content, how mathematical ideas develop, and what teaching strategies are most likely to be effective in reaching struggling students. The teachers in these episodes bring this vast array of knowledge to each decision that they make. Although the content ranges from counting to fractions, the processes the teachers go through have many similarities. They find ways to manage their classroom routine so that they spend targeted one-on-one or small-group time with students who are struggling and make adjustments as they monitor what and how their students are learning. The information garnered from these ongoing assessments allows the teachers to carefully consider the sequence of activities and the variety of models and representations they offer their students in order to build an understanding of key mathematical concepts.

In "Assessing and Supporting Students to Make Connections," math specialist Ana Vaisenstein writes about her experience supporting a group of students who are not fluent in counting by numbers other than one. She provides a variety of activities, routines, and games designed to strengthen students' conceptual understanding by highlighting the relationships across all of these learning opportunities.

In "The Pieces Get Skinnier and Skinner," Marta Johnson writes about her work with fourth-grade students to compare fractions based on numeric reasoning. She provides them with a variety of activities and models, all the while adjusting her teaching based on what she discovers about what students are learning and where they are confused.

In "After One Number Is the Next!" first-year teacher Maureen McCarty draws on her preservice education, professional articles, and her own insights to develop an assessment interview for a student of concern. She discovers that spending the time and effort to conduct a relatively brief interview can yield valuable information in helping her understand what this child needs to learn.

In "Assessing and Developing Early Number Concepts," second-grade teacher Anne Marie O'Reilly marvels at how much she learned by reviewing the development of counting and beginning number sense ideas from kindergarten to grade 2. She then explains how she uses that information to assess and plan a consistent course of action, as opposed to a series of unrelated accommodations, for one of her struggling students.

In "How Many Children Got off the Bus?" Ana Vaisenstein works with a small group of fourth graders on a subtraction word problem. She asks them to solve the problem independently so she can assess their knowledge of subtraction. Ana's goal is to help the students recognize a subtraction situation and find an entry point (a model, representation, or drawing) to help them solve the problem.

In "Get to 100," Michael Flynn introduces the game Get to 100 (Russell et al. 2008g) to his second-grade class and then works with two students as they play a variation of the game that he adapted to meet their needs. When he observes that they are having difficulty, he poses questions and makes additional accommodations to facilitate their understanding.

One of the clear messages of all of these stories is that there are no easy answers, no shortcuts to understanding and planning for students' growing mathematical understanding. However, knowing the content well enables these teachers to have many strategies at their disposal for listening to children's thinking, analyzing their work, and planning appropriate accommodations.

Questions to Think About

What are some assessment strategies that the teachers use?
What did the teachers learn from their assessments?
What evidence is there that the assessment informed their planning and teaching?
How did the assessment process benefit the student or students in each episode?

7

Assessing and Supporting Students to Make Connections

Developing Flexibility with Counting

Ana Vaisenstein

Since 2003, I have focused my work on better understanding how to teach students who struggle with math. Whether I work with students in general education classrooms or students with special needs, I want all my students to understand math and be efficient problem solvers. For students to understand math, they need to make connections between what they already know and new information. They also need to integrate knowledge they have from different contexts and use it in flexible ways—for example, applying information they learn from playing a game when solving number or story problems and vice versa.

Some children easily make these connections by themselves, and other students need assistance from a teacher. My students challenge me to think deeply about how to support them in making those connections. It is only when I comprehend how they are making sense of an idea through their words, actions, and written work that I can identify how many of those ideas they are connecting from one context to another and what connections they are not yet making. This ongoing assessment guides my teaching. Instead of just following the sequence in the curriculum, I make decisions about what to do based on what I know about my students and the mathematical ideas they need to learn.

Children, like adults, make connections in different ways. Often my mistake has been to think that by providing a specific activity, manipulative, mathematical model, or representation, the student will slowly "get it" by automatically making the connections I expect them to make. What has become clearer to me is that (1) no one activity, manipulative, mathematical model, or representation guarantees understanding, but it is what students do with them over time that facilitates understanding, and (2) students will make connections in ways other than the ones I expect.

So what is my role as a teacher? I need to go beyond just knowing the lessons well. I need to have clear goals for my students and to anticipate difficulties they might experience as they explore mathematical ideas. I also need to listen carefully to what children say and watch what they do to determine what they understand and where they are confused. This ongoing assessment informs the type of questions I need to ask and allows me to plan or adapt the activities in the curriculum.

The Context

In September, I met with the second-grade teachers at my school to identify students who struggled in math. The list of students was primarily based on the teachers' observations. I administered the Early Numeracy Interview to assess the children's knowledge of counting, place value, strategies for addition and subtraction, and multiplication and division (Clarke 2001). Once I gathered this information, I shared it with the teachers and together we picked six students who we felt were at greatest risk of falling further behind grade level in math. These students had a variety of needs: some were English language learners, others had Individualized Education Programs, and some had already repeated a grade. The plan was that I would support them in the classroom daily during the math period. My role was to observe the students closely and provide the necessary accommodations to the activities so that they could participate in the regular curriculum. After a couple of months, it became evident that they needed additional help outside of the classroom. They had a slower learning pace, were not fluent in counting by 1s, and struggled with the meaning of counting by a number other than 1. We began the second-grade math support group in November. Children met with me three additional times a week for forty-five minutes.

Counting by Tens

One big idea I wanted to work on with the students during the support group sessions was that of unitizing: understanding that one group of objects stands both for the group and the objects in it, and that the group constitutes a unit. For example, when students say 2, 4, 6, they should understand that they are counting 3 groups of 2. I often asked the children to count collections of objects in more than one way (i.e., by 2s, 5s, and 10s) and to think about whether they would get the same answer each time. Although the answer may seem obvious, it was not for these students. The activity exposed their confusions about counting by a number other than 1.

One of my students, Michele, preferred to always count the collections by 1s. When her partner suggested counting by 10s or 2s, Michele said that it was too hard and that she would count by 1s. As her partner grouped objects by 2s or 10s, Michele watched or joined in until the skip counting became too difficult. With ongoing practice, Michele felt more confident skip counting but stumbled over how to count the loose items, those that did not make a group. For example, she once counted a collection of 53 buttons by putting them into groups of 10. She had 5 groups of 10 and 3 loose buttons. She said, "10, 20, 30, 40, 50" as she counted the groups of 10, and "60, 70, 80" as she counted the 1s. Despite being able to recite the counting by 10s sequence, her mistake clearly showed that she had difficulties keeping track of the different units she was counting by. Initially she didn't realize her mistake. The other children corrected her. Instead of simply confirming that the other children were right, I asked Michele: "Can you say 60, 70, 80 for the 3 loose buttons?" Her answer was not immediate; she had to think about the meaning of those loose buttons: Were they groups of 10s or groups of 1s? Ultimately, she responded that they were 51, 52, and 53. I asked her how she knew they were not 60, 70, 80, to which she responded that she was counting only 1 more button each time. I hoped that in the process of explaining her mistake, she would become more aware of her difficulties and keep them in her mind the next time she counted groups of objects. In fact, when Michele made similar mistakes later in the year, she smiled as if saying, "Uh! I made this mistake again, but I know what is wrong!" She became more aware of her mistakes and was able to self-correct, an important skill in the learning process.

Counting at Snack Time

One of our weekly support group sessions took place during the last period on Fridays. During these sessions, the students were usually very tired and didn't have much patience for struggling with hard ideas. They suggested that we have a snack on Fridays. I decided to incorporate counting into our snack time. Using this routine gave the children a lot of experience counting and provided me with many informal assessment opportunities. We counted orange slices, candy bags, and chocolate bars. We compared the number of hard candies in different packages. The children loved it! They didn't care if they didn't have the treat until the very end. They really cared about knowing how many there were.

One Friday, Michele brought in 3 bags of popcorn that she wanted to share with us. As we were getting ready for snack time, Michele said, "I have an idea! We can count how many pieces of popcorn there are!" Inés responded, "But that is too hard!" "Not if we count them by 10s!" said Michele. "We will only count the big pieces. You can eat the small ones."

I could not believe Michele spontaneously suggested counting by 10s given all the struggles she had faced when counting different collections by 10s, 5s, and 2s!

This time, Michele had a real purpose for counting, and she could connect what she had been doing in class and in math group to accomplish her goal. She even gave an explanation for why counting all the popcorn would not be so difficult if we counted by 10s. She definitely understood the advantages of counting by 10s. She was very excited and her excitement was so contagious that we were all interested in knowing how many pieces of popcorn we had. Michele gave each of us a few handfuls of popcorn, which we put in groups of 10 and counted. After each of us counted how many we had, Félix began to count all the groups by 10s. We all joined in. There were so many popcorn kernels (609) that children had to think about the number sequence in ways they had not done before. What number do we say after 100? How do we write that number? And after 200? If we have to count by 1s after 600, what do we say? How do we write that number?

In her book *The Having of Wonderful Ideas*, Eleanor Duckworth (2006) writes: "Learning in school need not, and should not, be different from children's natural forms of learning about the world. We need only broaden and deepen their scope by opening up parts of the world that children may not, on their own, have thought of thinking about" (49). Counting collections of objects is something children do: they count how many cards they have, how many pieces of candy, how many coins in their collection, and, as in this example, how many popcorn pieces. I was happy to see that the work we had been doing in class broadened Michele's experience of counting. Counting the popcorn presented a natural opportunity to count by groups other than 1. There were so many popcorn pieces that counting by 1s would have been overwhelming. I had been prepared to ask questions that would help students think about counting by 10s during the popcorn activity, but, thanks to Michele, I didn't have to ask them. What better way of demonstrating a new understanding could I have expected? I was so excited about the results of this informal assessment opportunity!

I continued to provide other experiences to help Michele build on this important understanding and, as a result, she began to integrate counting by 10s much more fluently to solve different problems. Earlier in the year I had introduced the model of "towers of 10"—10 snap cubes joined together to make a tower of 10—in order to model counting by 10s. Michele relied on the use of these towers to keep track of groups and elements in each group as she solved problems. A few Fridays later, I bought 4 chocolate bars to share. I opened 1 bar, which had accidentally broken in half. I asked children how many small squares were in half of the chocolate bar. With no hesitation they said 6, because they were able to subitize—quickly identify a small quantity visually without counting—3 small rectangles on top and 3 on the bottom. They concluded that there were 12 small rectangles in each bar because 6 + 6 = 12. Then the children had to figure out

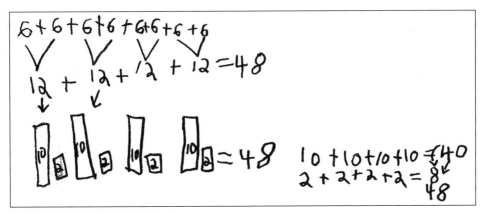

Figure 7–1.

how many small chocolate pieces there were in the 4 bars. Figure 7–1 is a copy of Michele's work. She sat down at her desk and independently worked through it.

The context was real, which helped Michele organize her thinking clearly step-by-step. After writing the number sentence 12 + 12 + 12 + 12, she decomposed 12 into a 10 and a 2, drawing towers of 10 and 2 loose cubes each time. She counted by 10s first, then by 2s, and finally added the subtotals. Michele had begun to make connections between different mathematical experiences: counting a collection of objects by 10s and using towers of 10 to decompose numbers into 10s and 1s to solve story problems. Facilitating these connections was one of my goals during these sessions. What helped this to happen? It was not one particular activity or question. The class had already been working on counting by 10s, and decomposing and recomposing numbers to add and subtract. They played games, counted collections, shared solutions, and reflected on their counting mistakes. They also had conversations about why the total amount was always the same regardless of whether they counted by 1s, 10s, or 5s. On the one hand, listening to other students share their thinking probably broadened Michele's experiences with place value. On the other hand, she also needed time to work these ideas out by herself in order to follow and incorporate her classmates' explanations. In my planning, I had to balance opportunities for students to share and to work independently.

Combinations of 10 Through Games

One of the district's benchmarks for second graders is to use combinations of 10 and knowledge of doubles and place value to solve addition and subtraction problems efficiently. My students had difficulty remembering combinations of

10—for example 7 + 3, 2 + 8—and each time we played a game or added a series of numbers, it was as if they were thinking about combinations of 10 for the first time. I thought that the more children practiced through games, the more fluent they would become with these ideas.

Sometimes I used games from first grade and games children had played earlier in the year. I also included games from Constance Kamii's book, *Young Children Reinvent Arithmetic: Implications of Piaget's Theory*, that are in the spirit of the school's adopted math program (Kamii 2000). I have found that for the students to solidify their number knowledge, my sessions with them must be consistent with the mathematics work they are doing in the classroom.

One of the games the math program offers for practicing the combinations of 10 is Tens Go Fish (Russell et al. 2008b). It is the same idea as the game Go Fish, but instead of asking for the same number, students need to get 2 cards that total 10. For example, if a student has a 2, he or she asks for an 8. This is a game students had played in first grade and early in second grade, so I wasn't sure they would be interested in playing it again. I was very surprised to see how engaged they were. We had been practicing combinations of 10 in many ways in and outside of the classroom, but it was this game that provided the incentive for students to know these combinations. Although they had played the game a few times before in first grade, it was while working in the small group that they really enjoyed it. One reason is that by playing the game over and over again, they began to understand it better. Once again, the game became a meaningful context for the students: they wanted to make as many combinations of 10 as possible, and the better they knew the combinations, the faster they could find the match. Because the children asked to play the game several times, they became more familiar with combinations of 10. I thought that as they became more fluent, they would use this knowledge to solve number and word problems. However, as time passed, I realized that students were not making that connection independently. I became aware that I had to ask questions that would allow students to connect these experiences.

Making Connections from Games to Problem Solving

Sylvia very easily knew 5 + 5 but had difficulties remembering other combinations of 10. However, I noticed that as she played Tens Go Fish over and over again, she began to remember the combinations and relied less and less on her fingers to count on to 10 to figure out what card she needed. One day I was working with Sylvia in the classroom. She had to solve the following number sentence using number combinations. The sentence was:

$$10 + 5 + 7 + 25 + 3 + 8 + 20 + 2 = \underline{\hspace{2cm}}.$$

I remembered how fluent she had become by playing Tens Go Fish. Could she apply that knowledge in solving the number sentence? Sylvia was about to count on 5 from 10 when I said, "Sylvia, pretend these numbers are the cards you have to play Tens Go Fish. Would you be able to make any combinations of 10?" Sylvia replied, "Yes, I can put 7 and 3 together to make 10 and 8 and 2 to make another 10." Then she wrote: 10 + 5 + 10 + 25 + 20 + 10. She continued by grouping all the 10s and rewrote: 30 + 20 + 25 + 5. At this point, Sylvia decided to use the towers of 10 strategy, which she had used since the beginning of the year (see Figure 7–2).

As she worked, Sylvia explained, "I have 3 towers of 10, and 2 more towers of 10; that is 10, 20, 30, 40, 50. Then I have 2 more towers of 10—60, 70. Now I can add 5, 71, 72, 73 . . ." I stepped in, "Sylvia, pretend you are playing Ten Towers of Ten, what would you do next?" "Yes!" she exclaimed. "I can put together the 5 and the other 5 and that makes 10. So now I have [pointing to each tower as she counted by 10s from the beginning] 10, 20, 30, 40, 50, 60, 70, 80. All of that is 80!"

Sylvia had pieces of knowledge that had not yet been integrated. For the most part, she could play the game Ten Towers of Ten (Russell et al. 2008g) and follow the rules, making towers of 10 every time she had loose cubes. She could also solve number sentences using the towers of 10 by grouping the towers of 10 first and counting on the loose cubes next. However, she had not realized that she could combine the loose cubes (in this case, the two 5s) to make a new tower of 10 when solving number sentences. She needed my question to begin to link both experiences and use them to solve the problem.

Some students can easily apply what they learn from playing games to solving number and story problems. They can see the similarities and differences among the

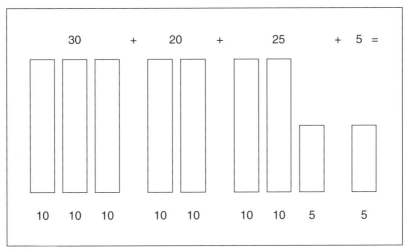

Figure 7–2.

ideas, the contexts, or the representations and establish connections among them. Sylvia, on the other hand, had not thought about how the strategies she learned from repeatedly playing the games could help her solve other number problems. From my ongoing observations of Sylvia, I was able to determine when it was appropriate to push her thinking in that direction. It was not by telling her what numbers to put together or what procedure to use, but by reminding her about a particularly relevant game and asking her if she could apply what she used there to solve the number problem. I knew she first had to be very familiar with the game to draw from those experiences to solve number problems. That is why I want my students to play the same games over and over again. The more familiar they are with the games, the more knowledge they have and can apply to different contexts.

As Sylvia found strategies that worked for her, she found herself doing what many other students in the class had been doing. She grouped all the 10s first, and made a new group of 10 with the loose cubes as she modeled the problem. Then she computed the total. The towers of 10 offered her the possibility to think about the numbers in a more flexible way: as composed of 10s and 1s, which in turn she could decompose and recompose to make the calculation easier. She proceeded slowly, and had a cautious sense of satisfaction, almost as if she couldn't believe her eyes. This sense of accomplishment and of understanding numbers in a new way motivated her to continue solving a difficult problem. She began to see herself as a learner, someone who can have fun doing math. There is a point when math becomes fun, even for students who have been struggling, because they come to understand how numbers work.

Reflections

The work I did with this group of second-grade students made me reflect on important components of how to support students who are struggling. First, I need to be clear about the mathematical ideas underlying the activities. In this case, I wanted children to understand the idea of unitizing and, as a consequence, place value: composing and decomposing numbers by 10s and 1s. Second, I need to develop a picture of the strengths and weaknesses of the students and determine mathematical goals by writing and reflecting on what mathematical ideas children are using and connecting and which ones they are not connecting. Third, I need to give students repeated practice with meaningful games and activities that allow them to engage with the mathematical ideas. I can never assume that providing one kind of manipulative or representation in one class is enough to help the children solidify their understanding. Finally, as students engage in their work, I have to pose questions to students to help them make the connections they need to have a flexible understanding of mathematics *and* solve problems more efficiently. I usually do not have a set of questions ahead of time. I base my questions on what I observe students doing through ongoing assessment. Sometimes my questions are just asking students to explain their thinking. In Michele's case, for example, it was clear to me that she needed to pause and think about whether she could say 50, 60, 70, 80 or 50, 51, 52, 53 when she had 5 groups of 10 and 3 1s. In Sylvia's case, I had to ask her questions that helped her connect her experiences in the games to that of solving story problems. My focus throughout is on understanding how the children are thinking and using this information to provide experiences that help them become independent confident learners who can engage in meaningful mathematics.

8

The Pieces Get Skinnier and Skinnier

Assessing Students' Ideas About Fractions

Marta Garcia Johnson

As a fourth-grade teacher of a self-contained inclusion class,* I use a variety of assessments to monitor my students' progress and drive my instruction. Daily observations of performance tasks, open-ended pencil-and-paper tasks, unit assessments, and anecdotal notes are among the ways I capture how my students articulate their understandings. This picture of individual strengths and weaknesses is especially useful as I plan to engage my students with learning challenges in meaningful mathematics. From my observations and informal assessments, I attempt to pinpoint conceptual "breaks," places where meaning breaks down for students who are struggling. Even if they have attained a benchmark on a unit assessment, their ability to retain and apply the ideas in subsequent work can be tentative. The following vignette is an example of how I implemented this cycle of assessing, planning, teaching, and assessment during our curriculum unit on fractions.

My primary goal for the fractions unit was to help students develop strategies for comparing and ordering fractions using area models, first using physical models and drawings, then without the benefit of making a drawing or using manipulatives. With area models, students divide shapes into the appropriate number of equal sections (the denominator), then color in the number of sections that correspond to the numerator to create a picture of the fraction. I knew that for many of my struggling students, it would be critical that they encounter multiple opportunities to work with these foundational ideas using manipulatives and drawings. As they became more flexible with these, I hoped they could internalize the pictures and relationships to form mental images.

During the first few days of the fractions unit, students worked to name fractional parts of an area model. This helped them develop concrete images of fractions and supported their understanding of fractions as representing equal parts of

---

*Chapter 22 is another essay about this class.

a whole. We first used pattern blocks so that students could easily see that it took 2 equal halves to make a whole or 3 equal thirds. With these models, they could also see that $\frac{1}{2}$ of the area was the same as three $\frac{1}{6}$s of the area.

As I did informal assessments during this part of the unit, I noted that many students were able to compare fractions with numerators of 1 (unit fractions) such as $\frac{1}{2}$, $\frac{1}{3}$, and $\frac{1}{6}$ using numeric reasoning. They recognized that the greater the number of pieces, the smaller each piece is, and they were developing mental images of equal pieces as a strategy for comparing unit fractions. However, there was a group of about five students who needed extra practice with unit fractions at the same time that they were participating in the whole-class work we were doing: comparing nonunit fractions such as $\frac{3}{6}$ and $\frac{5}{6}$ and comparing fractions with different numerators and denominators, such as $\frac{2}{3}$ and $\frac{4}{5}$.

To support the range of learners in my classroom, I often use flexible groups that are formed as a result of the evidence I gather from observations and assessments. These groups provide for temporary homogeneous groupings based on like need. Students can work with other classmates who need practice on the same skills.

Observing these five students in a small group would also be an assessment opportunity. I could note where their understanding broke down or if they applied strategies consistently. I cannot usually get this explicit type of information in a large group. In addition, these students had some language processing challenges; the small-group structure would allow me to make appropriate accommodations so that the mathematics and not the processing of directions became the central focus of their work.

To support my struggling learners, I planned small-group interventions that built foundational skills and allowed me to monitor students' progress. These interventions focused on three areas:

- repeating prior activities to assess understanding
- assessing through talk (rehearsing for class discussions with explicit instruction and practice)
- assessing new learning

Repeating Prior Activities to Assess Understanding

As the class continued their work with comparing fractions, I took these five students aside to evaluate if and how they had incorporated the strategies we had discussed in the whole group for comparing fractions with like numerators and different denominators. I asked them to write a response to the following question: How would you explain to a second grader which fraction is bigger, $\frac{1}{6}$ or $\frac{1}{4}$?

Figure 8–1.

Keisha wrote that $\frac{1}{4}$ is bigger "because the denominator is a lot smaller and you could get bigger pieces."

Tara wrote that $\frac{1}{4}$ is bigger "because 6 is a larger number than 4 but since it is 6th it has smaller pieces and the 4th has bigger pieces."

Ron wrote, "I would say $\frac{1}{4}$ because $\frac{1}{4}$ is bigger than $\frac{1}{6}$." (See Figure 8–1.)

Pete wrote, "You cut the pieces and you cut how many people there are so for one you cut 4 and for the other you cut 6. Four is less but it is more."

Jhali used a picture: She circled $\frac{1}{4}$ and wrote *bigel* (bigger) and then the word *smaller* under $\frac{1}{6}$.

After looking at these responses, I saw that there were some elements of understanding of the numerator and denominator, but I worried that students' understanding might still be fragile. I had several questions that I wanted to explore further based on what I learned: Does Jhali realize that the wholes must be the same size? Would Ron and Pete be able to justify their responses? Would Tara and Keisha be able to apply their reasoning to fractions with like numerators that were not unit fractions?

I decided that this small group of students was ready to compare three fractions at a time, so I asked them to create models for $\frac{1}{4}$, $\frac{1}{2}$, and $\frac{1}{3}$. I chose these particular fractions because I anticipated that the consecutive denominators would provide a scaffold as the students ordered the fractions. It was also important that they begin to view $\frac{1}{2}$ as a landmark fraction and use it as a basis for comparisons. As we progressed through the work, they began to say things such as, "One-half means you have 2 equal pieces. If you make more pieces than 2, you get more pieces, but they are smaller."

All of the students were able to create an area model for each fraction using a rectangle that they knew they needed to divide into equal parts. They were able to explain that the pieces were "equal or fair because everyone is getting the same" and that "the more parts there were in the whole, the smaller the pieces."

Although I was pleased with their work using an area model, I knew that this small group would need additional practice creating a variety of representations, models, and contexts; telling and being aware of their own stories; and holding on to mental images. So, I decided to ask them to compare $\frac{1}{2}$, $\frac{1}{3}$, and $\frac{1}{6}$ without actually drawing a model. I was interested in whether they would be able to use the same reasoning they had applied earlier. The following conversation arose.

KEISHA: $\frac{1}{6}$ is bigger because it has more pieces.

JHALI: Yes, the 6 is bigger.

KEISHA: No! Wait . . . the 6 has more pieces but they aren't bigger.

TARA: Yeah, they are skinny, really little compared to the pieces in this one [*pointing to $\frac{1}{2}$*].

JHALI: But the 6 is bigger.

RON: It is like, remember in class Colton said it is the opposite of the numbers on the number line.' Cause the bigger the numbers, the more, but with fractions when they are more, they are smaller.

TARA: That is confusing.

TEACHER: I agree. It is like our brain has to say: "Stop! Think about what the numbers mean for this fraction." What does the 6 in $\frac{1}{6}$ mean? Remember what we wrote on the anchor chart.[1]

PETE: That is like on the poster (anchor chart) we made that there are people sharing a pizza.

As I spent this extra time revisiting concepts we learned in class, I noted that these students were inconsistent when justifying their thinking. They were not consistent in how they interpreted the denominator. Although they could say "the bigger the numbers, the smaller the fractions," they would sometimes confuse the numerator and denominator. These students were not always aware of how they learned, so they had difficulty applying solution strategies from one problem to another. My concern about what they knew was justified: their understanding broke down when they moved away from the rectangular representation. After considering what I learned about these students, I decided that my next step should be to go back to comparing two fractions and model how I would do the comparison verbally.

---

[1] I used an anchor chart to summarize our mathematical strategies. The anchor charts that we use in both literacy and mathematics provide a structure to recapture our ideas after a discussion and give students a way to see a history of our thinking.

Assessing Through Talk

During our remaining time of this small-group meeting, I wanted the students to consistently connect their representations to a story to explain fractional relationships with unit fractions. Once they could make these connections and talk in class about their ideas, I would feel more confident that their understanding was growing. As the National Council of Teachers of Mathematics (NCTM) Principles and Standards state, "Talk should be focused on making sense of mathematical ideas and using them effectively in modeling and solving problems. The value of mathematical discussions is determined by whether students are learning as they participate in them" (NCTM 2000, 194).

To prepare students for telling stories that would highlight fractional relationships, I told them a story of my own. I explained to them that the story helped me clarify my thinking and helped me better retrieve the strategy the next time I needed to use it. I wanted the story to be a point of reference for them, not just an isolated activity. I returned to the task of comparing fractions, in this case, $\frac{1}{4}$ and $\frac{1}{6}$. I began by saying that I knew that $\frac{1}{4}$ was larger than $\frac{1}{6}$ because the fourths would be larger pieces than the sixths. I explained that for both of the fractions, I would be thinking of the same-size whole.

I then told a story of sharing a pizza to anchor my thinking. I told the students that I wanted to remember how I had just compared those two fractions so I could use my strategy again when I next had to compare unit fractions. So I explicitly stopped and asked myself: "Now what did I say the last time?" I then restated my strategy aloud, for example, "I shared a pizza with 6 people at my birthday party. We cut the pizza into 6 equal pieces. The next day I shared a pizza with 4 people. We cut the pizza into 4 equal pieces. On which day did I get a bigger piece of pizza?"

I modeled similar stories during our subsequent small-group sessions, stopping and explaining how I was returning to my "own story" for explaining how I was comparing two fractions. I explained that as I thought of my strategy for comparing fractions, I was developing mental images. Although the students had used stories when comparing two fractions, I found they were not consistent in their justifications, nor could they apply their reasoning to another situation. I believed that this "oral rehearsing" (similar to the prewriting strategy we use in writer's workshop) would assist these students in developing a story context from which they could make sense of the fraction concepts we were discussing. After each comparison, we stopped to "think about our thinking" and restate the story we had used to compare the fractions. To assess if the stories were building understanding, we spent several more minutes comparing other unit fractions, and I noted that each student seemed to be justifying their choices with a particular strategy or story with more consistency. I asked them to jot down their own story for comparing fractions and let them know that in a few days they would be sharing their stories with the whole class. I wanted to use their sharing as an assessment opportunity. Would they be able to tell these stories appropriately in the whole group without any prompting from me?

During our next whole-class discussion, I invited the students from my small group to remind the whole class how we could use what we knew about comparing unit fractions to assist us in looking at the relationship between the fractions we now were considering. Three of the students confidently read their stories from their journals, and Pete added that he knew that one of the fractions we were considering had larger pieces because the denominator was smaller than the second fraction. Verbalizing their stories helped the students connect the ideas they were expressing to the area models they had drawn previously. I felt more confident that they were beginning to make sense of the ideas we were discussing in class.

Assessing New Learning

When my ongoing assessments in the small-group observations led me to note that students could consistently use a story and representation to explain fractional relationships with unit fractions, I planned to move on to nonunit fractions. Based on what I had learned when the students shared their stories, I wanted to see if the students from the small group could generalize what they learned about unit fractions to nonunit fractions with the same denominator. Would they be able to use the stories they created to explain the order of $\frac{1}{2}$, $\frac{1}{3}$, and $\frac{1}{6}$ to think about the order of $\frac{3}{4}$, $\frac{3}{5}$, and $\frac{3}{6}$? In addition to figuring out that $\frac{3}{6}$ is smaller than $\frac{3}{5}$, would they understand that the fraction of a pizza that 6 people sharing 3 pizzas will get is equivalent to 3 pieces of a 6-piece pizza? I invited them to work with me on a new "game" involving cards that listed fractions with unlike denominators but like numerators that were not equal to 1. My plan was to have the students compare three of these fractions. The first three cards were: $\frac{3}{6}$, $\frac{3}{4}$, and $\frac{3}{5}$. I began the discussion by reminding students of the work they had done comparing unit fractions. We had been using the fraction cards that we made for some of the fraction games.

> TEACHER: So, the other day you all had some very interesting and useful ways to think about comparing fractions like $\frac{1}{2}$, $\frac{1}{3}$, and $\frac{1}{6}$. What do you think about these fractions?
>
> KEISHA: Well, I remember the pizza story! One pizza and then the people come to eat the pizza and now with these fraction cards, there are sometimes lots of people and the pizzas get smaller.

PETE: The pizzas don't get smaller, the pieces do.

TARA: Yeah, remember they get skinnier and skinnier and the more people, the hungrier they get.

TEACHER: Wow! I really love this story about more people coming in and the pieces getting skinnier and the people getting less to eat. I think it is important what Pete said; that the pieces get smaller. All the pizzas are the same size though.

JHALI: But now we have to make a new story because we don't have pizzas with these fractions [*pointing to the new fraction cards*].

TARA: Look, look at $\frac{3}{4}$. We cut 4 pieces and you get bigger pieces. And look at the 5, you get 5 smaller pieces.

TEACHER: Does anyone think they can use the story they wrote in their journal last time with these fractions?

KEISHA: The denominator is the people and now we have more pizzas.

TEACHER: What do you mean we have more pizzas?

KEISHA: Now there are 3 pizzas instead of 1. But the people still have to share them, and it is the same pizzas getting shared.

TEACHER: Well, you are thinking really hard about this idea. And it is really an important idea for understanding fractions. Thinking about what the denominator tells you about the size of the pieces when the numerators are equal.

Using Assessment Information to Inform Next Steps

I was pleased that these students were able to apply the same strategies they had developed in working with unit fractions to thinking about the order of nonunit fractions. But I couldn't tell from the ordering conversation whether they also understood the relationship between the amount of pizza 4 people sharing 3 pizzas would get and $\frac{3}{4}$ of a single pizza. I decided to introduce other ways to visualize fractions to support the connection between these two ways to think about $\frac{3}{4}$. I continued our study of nonunit fractions by using

- fraction cards that included both the drawing and the fraction (see Figure 8–2)
- rectangles on grid paper
- geoboards

The geoboards are related to the rectangle work we had done earlier in the whole-class work, and they gave the students equal-size wholes that they could subdivide into many fractional parts at once, such as $\frac{1}{6}$ and $\frac{3}{6}$. Geoboards eliminated the drawing challenges that some of the students encountered with the rectangle

Figure 8–2.

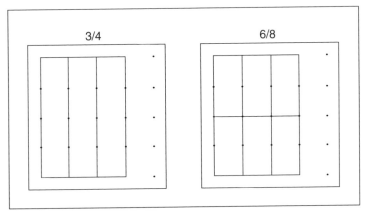

Figure 8–3.

grids so that they could easily maintain equal-size wholes and see the equal pieces. The students worked in pairs to construct two different representations. For example, Jhali made $\frac{3}{4}$ and Tara made $\frac{6}{8}$, and they compared them. (See Figure 8–3.)

The students were becoming more confident in understanding the relationships among unit and nonunit fractions of a whole. I knew that this was a long process and that I must continue to review prior concepts while introducing new concepts, all the while using a variety of representations and contexts. My next goal was to help the students relate what they were doing on the geoboards and rectangular grids to the pizza model they had been using for nonunit fractions.

Reflections

What evidence did I see that these students were beginning to understand fractions? By the end of the fractions unit, most were solid with unit fractions. They could:

- create mental images based on the models and representations we are using
- compare three or more unit fractions

- participate in our small-group discussions and listen to each others' ideas
- contribute ideas to our large-group discussions with the scaffolding of our small-group rehearsal

As I plan for a new unit of study, I will begin again this continuous cycle of reflecting on my students' learning, my instructional strategies, and ways that I can keep assessing to improve both my students' learning and my teaching. I will try to predict what will be difficult for students to grasp during the whole-class discussions while keeping in mind which ideas may have been previously inaccessible or which may need to be kept alive for this particular small group.

9

After One Number Is the Next!

Assessing a Student's Knowledge of Counting

Maureen McCarty

As a first-year teacher, I often felt overwhelmed by all of the decisions I had to make daily. Teaching an inclusive class of first graders, I struggled to determine just what a child needs and then, of course, how to best meet those needs within the given curriculum. How do you support a child with significant needs in a way that addresses a lesson's objective, on a level appropriate for that child? As simple as it might sound, I am learning that to target needs, I must first identify them. Therefore, it is assessment that has supported me in making some of these difficult teaching decisions. Through close work with one particular child, I learned both how to gather useful assessment data and also how this data can guide my teaching. Assessment has helped me target support and provide access for a student struggling with a mathematics curriculum that seems to march unforgivingly forward.

Early in the year, I worked with a small group of students who were all struggling with a majority of the mathematical tasks they encountered. I pulled the five students together during the independent practice part of our math block, which was structured as a workshop format. In the beginning, I presented some of the curriculum's kindergarten-level versions of games and activities that reinforced the goals of that day's lesson. However, I quickly realized that the needs of each of these children were actually quite different depending on the task. I became frustrated. What did they each need? How could I meet all the needs at once? I accepted that I couldn't target their needs until I knew what to target. I decided that focusing more intensely on one child at a time was a more manageable assessment task for me. Perhaps I would form small groups later, but not without identifying a more specific reason for bringing the students together. It was also at this time that I became especially concerned and curious about one particular child in the group—Tamara.

Tamara is an active little girl. She is by far the most kinesthetic individual I have ever met—she devises ways to make almost any task include a physical component.

I observed her countless times standing at her desk rhythmically touching, tapping, or shifting whatever it was she was working on with such force that she managed to move her entire group of tablemates and their desks across the floor. In mathematics, I noticed that she had difficulty focusing during independent practice and often seemed to just write down numbers or spend the time counting aloud on the classroom number line over and over again.

Children were drawn to Tamara, and she was skillful at attracting their attention. The more she struggled, the more she became a distraction to herself and others. Her behavior seemed in large part a result of her not being able to enter into the math. She desperately needed intervention, but first I needed to assess Tamara's understanding to know how make the daily lessons accessible to her.

Finding Out What Tamara Knew

The curriculum's end-of-unit tests and assessment checkpoints seemed like the most obvious place to start. And so, for a few months I dutifully compiled these data. Although the data provided me with some information, they did not give me insight into her thinking. For example, the evaluations seemed to indicate she could accurately compare values 0–10, but how did she do it? What strategies did she use? Essentially, these formal assessments confirmed that Tamara was struggling in math. This I already knew! It made me stop and think: How do I know that? I realized that, through informal observation—working one-on-one with her and watching her in small groups—I had already gathered some important data about her strengths and needs.

Returning to my graduate school training, I reviewed what I already knew by writing down a list of what Tamara understood and how she demonstrated that and what she did not yet understand and how she demonstrated that. What emerged was her ability to count verbally, use one-to-one correspondence with objects, and recognize that the last number word in her count told "how many" were in the set. She did not yet seem to understand that each number is a quantity, not just a label. She treated each number as a separate entity in the sequence of the number line—always counting up from 1 to get to the name of a number. Yet, I also saw evidence of her ability to compare numbers. She could play a number comparison card game (similar to War or Battle) with number cards 0–10 quickly and accurately.

The exercise of writing down Tamara's strengths and needs proved a valuable assessment tool. I was surprised at how much she understood. Plagued by my own frustrations over how to help her, I had been fixating on what she didn't know and it had come to seem this was everything! Using end-of-unit tests as the only form of assessment was dangerous in the same way because I was highlighting only her areas of need and then feeling overwhelmed by the amount.

After I had spent nearly a week mulling over the list of Tamara's strengths and needs, I was still unsure what to do next. On my morning commute, I was leafing through my new issue of *Teaching Children Mathematics* when I came across the article, "Focal Points—Pre-K to Kindergarten" (Clements and Sarama 2008). In this article, Douglas Clements and Julie Sarama explicitly identify and analyze the components of building early number sense. Both the detailed way in which number sense was broken down and the developmental sequence that the authors illuminate allowed me to see not only *where* Tamara fit in, but also *that* Tamara fit in. Knowing where she fit in would help guide my interventions with her because I could be more precise about what areas of her mathematical understanding she most needed support with to move forward. Knowing that she fit in made me feel more confident that the work I was doing with her was worthwhile, valuable, and sensible.

The Interview

I was curious about Tamara's ability to compare values and, yet, her need to count up from 1 each time I asked her how many there were in a set. To understand her thinking, I needed to ask her about it. I returned to my graduate school work of conducting math interviews with students. These interviews are built from one question you have about a child's understanding. Interviews are short sessions that present increasingly challenging tasks aiming to reveal a child's thinking on a topic. The teacher records the exchange (notebook, audio recorder, or video) and analyzes the thinking.

So, my assessment of Tamara's understanding continued with an interview. It took place in the fifteen to twenty minutes of independent practice time for the rest of the class. My question was: How does she compare numbers 0–15? In the frame of reference of a card game, at which she demonstrated success, I asked her to compare different pairs of cards and explain how she knew which number was greater. Although she did not articulate that a certain number comes after another when you count, it was clear that she was thinking about the number line when making comparisons. Discussing which number, 13 or 15, was larger she noted, "This [pointing to 15] is the front and this [pointing to 13] is behind," referring to their placement on the number line. Again, comparing 5 and 8, her explanation was in reference to the number line: "7 separates them. 8 is far away from 5." After comparing 5 and 8, I specifically asked her to compare 6 and 7 because there was no whole number separating them. This time I encouraged her to use interlocking cubes to see if the visual representation would support her in explaining her thinking. Our conversation follows.

TEACHER: What about 6 and 7? Which is bigger?
TAMARA: 7.
TEACHER: How do you know?
TAMARA: 7 is biggest and 6 is smaller.
TEACHER: Can you show me with the cubes?
TAMARA: [*makes sticks of 6 and 7 and holds them up together*] See?
TEACHER: How many bigger is 7 than 6?
TAMARA: 7.
TEACHER: Hold them up together again. How many more is 7 than 6?
TAMARA: Oh! One more.
TEACHER: Yes, 7 is 6 plus 1 more.

Planning an Intervention

Analyzing the interview, I was thrilled to have so much information about Tamara's mathematical thinking. It had taken months to gather the end-of-unit tests, but in just fifteen minutes, I had learned so much more about her strategies. This individual interview provided me with a picture of her strengths as well as her needs. I saw what she understood about comparing numbers and discovered that the number line was an important foundation for this thinking. She did not seem to have internalized the idea that each number is quantitatively one more than the number before it. This information gave me a place to start to plan appropriate instruction for her. To help her further develop her number sense, she needed support in working on the +1 or "one more" pattern. Looking at our interview, I also decided to work from the number line, because it was her strength, and to continue comparing quantities using the concrete model of interlocking cubes. I thought that the cubes would help her connect her understanding of the numbers in a number line to a concrete model that we could use to highlight numbers as quantities.

I was eager to try out my plans, but as a first-year teacher, I was concerned about how to manage the rest of the class during multiple one-on-one intervention sessions. Timing was important. I wanted Tamara to participate in the minilesson and sharing with the whole class, but, during independent practice, I planned to work one-on-one with her. So, like the interview, the intervention also took place while the rest of the class was practicing independently.

I gave Tamara a large piece of construction paper with a 0–10 number line draw across the bottom and asked her to make sticks of cubes to show each number on this number line. She went right to it.

After finishing her stick of 8, she laid it down next to the stick of 7 and independently made an observation.

TAMARA: Almost the same size.

TEACHER: Yes, they are almost the same size, but how much bigger is 8?

TAMARA: 8.

TEACHER: [*reminded of the interview, I try to rephrase*] How many more cubes are in 8 than in 7?

TAMARA: [*slowly touching the top cube on the stick of 8*] Just 1! [*finishes the 10 stick and lays it in place.*]

TEACHER: What about the 9 and 10? How many more is 10 than 9?

TAMARA: [*running her finger horizontally from the top of the 9 to the 10 stick and then up one to the top of the 10*] 1. [*moves all the sticks together on the paper forming a stair*] Look! A stair, Ms. McCarty! Everybody get up out of bed! [*lifts each stick up vertically from 1 to 10*] I'm walking the stairs. [*Using two fingers like legs, she "walks" up the stairs.*]

TEACHER: How many more cubes are there at each stair step?

TAMARA: 1. [*points to each step*] 1, 1, 1, 1 . . .

TEACHER: Why?

TAMARA: Because. [*She pulls out the consecutive pairs of number sticks 6 and 7. Then she twists of the top cube off the 7 stick and gestures to show that they are now the same height.*] You can take 1 away and you can put 1 on. [*She reaffixes the cube to the 7 stick*].

This felt like such a success! She discovered the stair step pattern on her own, and, through my questioning, she was able to explain that each stair step was just 1 more than the next. Obviously, she needed more practice, but the task was well suited to developing this understanding. My next goal was to provide accommodations for upcoming lessons in the curriculum that would both meet her need to explore the +1 pattern in counting and also meet the lesson's objective.

Learning the +1 Pattern

One lesson for which I provided accommodations was called Dice Sums from *Everyday Mathematics* (Bell et al. 2007). The objective was to provide experience with sums generated by rolling a pair of dice. First, I introduced the game to the whole class. Then for independent practice, the children worked in pairs rolling two dice and recording the equations. Additionally, they observed which sums occurred most often. Last, we gathered back together and discussed strategies and findings.

In Dice Sums, I saw an opportunity to give Tamara access to the objective and more experience with the +1 pattern with just a slight modification of the activity. Working with me, she rolled two dice, found the sums, and recorded the number models. Her dice, however, included one with written numerals 1–6 and the other with the number 1 on every side. The probability component of the objective was eliminated. For the recording piece, I asked her to make a stick of interlocking cubes for the sum she rolled on each turn, because I wanted to revisit and build on her success with the stair step pattern and reinforce examining numbers as quantities. Holding the dice in her hands, she quickly noticed the die with a 1 on every side. "Hey, what's this?" she asked suspiciously. I asked her what she thought and she said they were all 1.

"Hmm," I puzzled. "So, what do you think you will get every time you roll this die?" She responded that it would be 1, but before I could ask more about the sum, she starting rolling. After three "rounds" of her counting all on her fingers and then counting out all of the cubes from 1, I stopped the game. This task was not reinforcing the +1 pattern for her, so I decided to try another strategy.

I wrote the following on a piece of graph paper:

$1 + 1 =$
$1 + 2 =$
$1 + 3 =$
$1 + 4 =$
$1 + 5 =$
$1 + 6 =$

Upon seeing this, Tamara immediately abandoned the dice and started counting all on her fingers. She was solving the equations and recording the sums.

TAMARA: [*finishing 1 + 1 = 2 and 1 + 2 = 3 quickly*] This is easy!

TEACHER: Do you notice a pattern? [*Tamara keeps working without responding to my question. It is clearly satisfying work, but again it is not achieving the objective.*]

TEACHER: [*covering the left side of the equations or the 1+ column with my hand*] What do you notice about these numbers?

TAMARA: [*reads the sums she has just written*] 2, 3. [*Then looking down the vertical column she recognizes the pattern and fills in the last four sums quickly saying them aloud.*] 4, 5, 6, 7.

TEACHER: [*wanting her to extend the pattern further, I prompt her.*] So if $1 + 6 = 7$, what will $1 + 7$ be?

TAMARA: [*grabs her pencil and writes out the next equation: 1 + 7 = 8*]

TEACHER: So—

TAMARA: [*interrupts without looking up from her paper*] I want to keep going.

As I watched, she repeated each equation aloud to herself and then wrote it down. She worked diligently, carefully looking at the number above in each column to assure she was continuing the pattern. Although I was thrilled she noticed a pattern and was eager to extend it, I still didn't think she recognized that any number plus 1 is the next counting number. When she came to the end of the paper, at $1 + 11 = 12$, she looked up at her large 0–10 number line (where we were earlier placing the sticks of cubes).

TAMARA: We should do longer. [*I jump up to get her another large piece of paper and quickly tape it to her other number line. She draws the line and marks and writes up to 23.*]

TEACHER: So if you move from 9 to 10 how many do you move?

TAMARA: [*looks at number line*] 1.

TEACHER: What about 6 to 7?

TAMARA: 1.

TEACHER: Any number plus 1 is the next number. After 6 is 7.

TAMARA: [*taking ownership of the language, she follows along the number line chanting.*] After 7 is 8 . . . After 8 is 9 . . . After 9 is 10 . . . [*Hoping she will transfer this to the dice, I ask her to roll the dice again. She takes the dice and rolls a 4 and a 1. Before she can count all, I ask her what comes after 4. She responds 5.*]

TEACHER: How do you know?

TAMARA: Because you can see the number line. [*She begins to roll the dice and rapidly call out in a rhythmic tone.*]

TAMARA: After 6 is 7 . . . after 3 is 4 . . . after 5 is 6 . . . [*I am delightedly cheering her on. In response, she quickens her pace, equally excited by her discovery. I stop her one last time to ask how she knows each sum so fast without counting the numbers up.*]

TAMARA: After one [number] is the next.

I felt that Tamara was recognizing that what she already knew from counting and the number line (i.e., after 7 is 8), the same thing as adding 1 or plus 1. Even though she already knew that "after _____ is _____," she was still counting all when asked to add 1 to any number. I wanted her to realize that she knew what came next and that was what "adding 1 more" meant.

Reflections

Since that day, Tamara has frequently requested that we "play that game with 1" and we have. Empowered by her understanding, she even proudly demonstrated and explained +1 to her classmates in a share or wrap-up one day. Returning to the language "after _____ is_____" triggers her to the +1 pattern and supports her with the concept when visited beyond the context of our dice game. She is now recognizing, with some teacher support, and solving the +1 addition problems in our math facts games. Although she is still working to transfer her new understanding to other mathematical tasks, it is clearly building that foundational number sense. And, because I am more clearly aware of her understandings and needs, I can be there to support her through this.

The process of accepting my own informal observations as valid data, drafting a list of Tamara's understandings and needs, interviewing her directly to understand her thinking and strategies, and finding ways to address her needs within the curricular objectives were all critical parts of my assessment process. Has the assessment I have done so far answered all my questions? No, there are still questions and there are still difficult decisions to make. However, what I learned from the assessment did help me make better-informed decisions. It is an ongoing process that continues to show me the progress a child is making, which, although perhaps not evident on the curriculum unit tests, is essential to mathematical understanding.

The process was also decisive for me in knowing where to start. As a first-year teacher, feeling overwhelmed by the fast-paced curriculum, I needed to figure out what to target for my struggling learners. I was relieved and pleased with the way this assessment process allowed me to identify what supports these learners needed. I began to apply what I learned from my work with Tamara to my other young mathematicians. Yet, I was most surprised by how much the process supported me as a teacher. It gave me both the confidence and focus that I could in fact support a child with significant needs, in a way that addresses a lesson's objective, on a level appropriate for that child.

10

Assessing and Developing Early Number Concepts

Working with Kristen

Anne Marie O'Reilly

Although I am an experienced mathematics teacher, I find that every year brings new challenges that help me think and learn about mathematics in different ways. Meeting the needs of a broad range of learners is one of my greatest challenges, particularly with students who are having a difficult time with mathematics. Over the years, I have struggled alongside many of my second graders, trying to understand how best to help them engage in the mathematics of our curriculum. At the root of many of my students' difficulties is the fragility of their number sense. This year, I've been reminded by one of my second graders that a student's ability to work independently and take responsibility for her work depends on the development of her number sense.

Before I can figure out how to help a student, I must first understand as much as I can about what the student knows, how she learns, and what confuses her. I use student work, informal conversations, and interactions with the child in small and large groups as assessment techniques. I use this assessment information to plan appropriate instruction. This year, I have been particularly challenged by how to best support Kristen, one of my struggling students. Her performance in both math and reading on standardized tests is significantly below grade level. My work to assess and teach her has forced me to reexamine how a student's number sense develops.

Initial Assessments and Accommodations

During the first few weeks of school, I kept an informal eye on Kristen, along with the seventeen other students I was getting to know. Kristen often seemed unable to follow directions and was notably reluctant to engage in classroom discussions. She never raised her hand. When asked to contribute, she usually declined the invitation to participate. I was puzzled about why she wasn't participating in our math discussions. However, when the mathematics began to focus more specifically on counting and quantity, Kristen's confusions about number began to surface. I realized that her reluctance to participate in discussions probably stemmed from the gaps she had in understanding the mathematics. As the rest of the class was learning how to make choices from a list of activities and keep track of their work, it was clear that Kristen required frequent check-ins to help her complete tasks. After observing her struggles with numbers for the first month of school, I began changing the size of the numbers for Kristen so that she was only dealing with sums less than 20. She was more successful with smaller numbers. She was able to model the actions in addition problems with these small numbers, usually drawing tally marks, circles, or pictures to explain her thinking. She also successfully completed activities designed to support the learning of addition combinations to 10 + 10.

Although she experienced some success with my accommodations, I noticed that she was inconsistent in her counting. She tended to count quickly, and she sometimes skipped objects or said more than one number per object. I reminded her to slow down and helped her find ways to keep track of what had already been counted and what remained to be counted.

As I collected additional samples of Kristen's work, I saw more evidence of her struggles with counting. For example, for an activity called Counting Strips (Russell et al. 2008b), in which students write the numbers by 1s on a strip of adding machine tape, Kristen consistently skipped over the multiples of 10 after 20 (28, 29, _____, 31, 32 . . . 38, 39, _____, 41, 42).

The Magic Pot

Once we began working on story problems, Kristen continued to struggle, although she did not ask for help. In mid-October, the class spent some time learning about what it means to double a quantity. The context that we used to introduce the idea of doubling was a Chinese folktale about a couple that found a magic pot (Hong 1995). Any set of objects that was dropped into the pot would be doubled, so that twice the amount of objects that went into the pot would be taken out of the pot. For example, if a bag with 5 gold coins fell into the pot, 2 bags with 5 coins each would be taken out of the pot. To reinforce their understanding of the action of doubling, the students wrote and solved their own magic pot riddles.

Toward the end of this series of activities, the children were asked to solve a problem asking what would happen if our class of eighteen students fell into the magic pot (Russell et al. 2008b). When I walked past Kristen, I saw her usual series of tally marks on her paper, along with the equation, $9 + 32 = 36$. She also had a collection of cubes scattered on her desk. I checked in to try to make sense of what she was thinking and soon discovered that there was no apparent connection between the cubes on her desk and the tally marks on her paper.

TEACHER: What was your plan for using the cubes? [*silence*] Can you just go ahead and count and tell me how you counted?

KRISTEN: [*touches and counts each cube*] 1, . . . 37.

TEACHER: Then what did you do, once you knew that you had 37 cubes?

KRISTEN: Then I counted these 1s and it made 36.

TEACHER: Show me how it made 36.

KRISTEN: Count them?

TEACHER: Can you show me what you did? [*Kristen counts the same cubes again and gets 37.*]

TEACHER: Then what?

KRISTEN: [*continues counting some other cubes on her desk*] 38, 39, 30 . . . 40, 41, 42, 43, 44, 45, 46, 47.

TEACHER: [*I still could not see the connection between the cubes and the problem. Perhaps she didn't understand the story context.*] What's happening in this problem? What's it about?

KRISTEN: There were people going in the magic pot and then they all come out and then there's 9.

TEACHER: [*In retrospect, I wish I had asked Kristen where the 9 came from. Instead, I focused on her understanding of what the problem was asking.*] Let's see if you remember how the magic pot works. What happened when Mrs. Haktak put a hairpin in the magic pot?

KRISTEN: One other 1.

TEACHER: Then when they put 2 bags in the magic pot, how many bags came out of the magic pot?

KRISTEN: Two more.

TEACHER: What would happen if we put our class into the magic pot? How many more people would come out? How many people are in our class?

KRISTEN: I forgot.

TEACHER: You wrote it on your paper.

KRISTEN: 18.

TEACHER: So 18 people would come out of the magic pot. Then how many more people would come out?

KRISTEN: 18.

TEACHER: So could you use the cubes to show that? How would you use the cubes to show that? [*Kristen counts 18 cubes.*] Then what would you do after that?

KRISTEN: Count more.

TEACHER: How many more?

KRISTEN: 18?

TEACHER: Go ahead. [*Kristen counts 18 more cubes.*] Then what would you do?

KRISTEN: I would count them all together.

TEACHER: Why would you count them all together?

KRISTEN: To get the number? [*She successfully counts to 36.*]

TEACHER: So what's the answer?

KRISTEN: 36.

Although she ultimately arrived at the correct answer, I felt I was dragging the math out of her. I didn't have confidence that I was offering her a way to build understanding. This problem was clearly too difficult for her, but it wasn't completely clear to me what aspects of the problem were making it inaccessible. Was it the size of the numbers or coming up with a strategy to solve it? Did she not understand the concept of doubling or was it a combination of these?

Early Numeracy Assessment

I wanted to know more about what Kristen understood about numbers in general and counting in particular. I used some of the tasks that I found in the Early Numeracy Research Project assessment materials (Clarke 2001). I found these tasks valuable in helping me develop a sharper picture of what Kristen knew about counting and where her understanding was breaking down. While the rest of the class was working on our daily Today's Number routine,[1] I met with her for three 5- to 10-minute interviews.

I began by asking Kristen to start counting from 1 and to continue until I told her to stop. She counted successfully until I told her to stop at 32. Then I asked her to start counting from 48. She counted 48, 49, then paused before continuing from 50. She counted from 50 to 59, then paused again: 50, 51, 52, 53, 54, 55, 56, 57, 58, 59 . . . 30. She corrected herself; 60, and then continued successfully to 65.

---

[1]Today's Number is a classroom routine during which students generate and discuss different expressions that equal a given number to develop fluency with addition and subtraction (Russell et al. 2008b).

Next, I asked her to count starting at 76. She counted 76, 77, 78, 79, 30, 31, 32, 33, 34, 35. Then I asked her count from 93. She counted from 93 to 100, then paused. I encouraged her to continue. She counted from 100 to 109. She stopped at 109 and said that she forgot what comes next. Kristen's knowledge of the counting sequence started to break down after 40. She was able to count correctly between the multiples of 10s, but she was unsure of what to do when going over a decade, sometimes losing track of the sequence (e.g., 79, 39).

In a related task, I asked Kristen to say the number word that comes after a given number. She was unsure of the number after 19. She said, "91." After 12, she paused for several seconds, then responded in a questioning voice: "13?" After 29, she said: "22?"

Kristen also could not identify some numerals. For the number 13, she said "31." When she wrote numbers backward, I had assumed that this was simply a writing reversal. In fact, she confused the names of the two numbers, and at times needed to count from 1 on the number line to figure out which number is correct. She was also unable to count backward from 15. When asked to say the number that comes before a given number, she found it difficult to say the number words before numbers that have 0 in the 1s place. She also struggled to recall which numbers come before 11, 13, and 14. Although she was able to say the correct numbers, she required extra think time.

I presented her with the following missing addend task: "Here are 4 green counters under this paper. While you look away, I'm going to put some yellow counters under the paper." I added 2 more counters that she could not see. "Now there are 6 counters. How many more counters did I put under the paper?" Kristen responded, "Six?" She had no way into this task so I lowered the numbers. This time I showed her 3 counters. I asked her to turn away while I added some more. I said, "Now there are 5 counters. How many more counters did I just put under the paper?" Once again, Kristen responded, "Six?"

These assessment tasks provided me with valuable information about Kristen's mathematical understanding. I came away from these brief meetings with a better understanding of why Kristen was struggling with the second-grade curriculum. Her knowledge of numbers, beginning with the number sequence, particularly around the multiples of 10, and her numeral recognition were very fragile. The work of the second-grade curriculum seemed beyond her reach. The accommodations I was making, such as simply changing the numbers in word problems, were not enough to address her needs.

It did not appear that Kristen expected math to make sense. She seemed to approach problem solving in a hit-or-miss fashion, unable to consider the reasonableness of her answers. She needed to connect more meaning to numbers before she could consider the reasonableness of her answers. I wanted Kristen to experience some success so she could build her confidence. When a child has so many gaps, like Kristen, it can be challenging to find activities that build success.

Further Accommodations

Knowing that she had been successful with some of the activities I provided her using small numbers, I began to provide Kristen with some first-grade counting activities from *Investigations in Number, Data, and Space*. One activity, called Start With/Get To (Russell et al. 2008f), involves marking the number 1 on a number line as a "Start With" number, then choosing a card with a "Get To" number. The student counts the distance between the two. I also provided opportunities for Kristen to play Compare, in which two players each turn over a card (Russell et al. 2008f). The student with the highest number wins. Kristen was successful with both games, including a variation of Compare in which two cards are turned over and combined.

At the same time, I continued to modify the activities that the rest of my students were working on, and to work to identify places where meaning broke down for Kristen. We had begun a series of activities designed to develop an understanding of place value, and students had been solving the following problem: *Sally has 3 towers of 10 cubes and 7 single cubes. How many cubes does Sally have?* (Russell et al. 2008l). I modified the problem for Kristen by changing 3 towers of 10 cubes to 2 towers of 10 cubes. I asked Kristen to work with a partner to model the revised problem with cubes to solve it. Sometimes I paired Kristen with a student who had similar needs, especially when I wanted to provide both students with individualized practice or support. In this case, Kristen's partner was a student who benefited from talking through her work with someone to solidify her own thinking. When I checked in, Kristen had disconnected from her partner and appeared to be struggling. I asked her to build the towers of 10 and singles so that we could think about the problem together. Once she had the cubes organized, I asked her to count. She pointed to the towers of 10 and counted, "10, 20." Then she continued counting the 7 single cubes, "30, 40, 50, 60, 70, 80, 90." I removed one of the towers and asked her to count again. This time she counted, "10, 11, 12, 13, 14, 15, 16, 17." When I returned the tower of 10, she again counted to 90.

Once again, we had moved away from the problem at hand and I found myself exploring where Kristen's understanding fell apart. The accommodation that I had made with the tower activity was not addressing her needs. Now I wondered what counting meant to Kristen beyond being able to use the counting sequence to count a set of objects up to 20. Is she ready to count by more than 1s? Does she understand that 24 is 2 10s and 4 1s?

Revisiting Counting

My assessments of Kristen's work forced me to revisit what I thought I knew about counting. I began to refine my thinking and worked to identify the specific ideas about counting that form the foundation for numerical thinking and number sense. I wanted her to understand that counting is more than a sequence of numbers, that each number has a quantity attached to it. My most immediate goal, in a nutshell, was that she develop a deep understanding of small numbers, up to about 20, and specifically that she develop fluency in sequencing them forward and backward, attach quantities to each, and compare amounts. Kristen needed to develop counting as a tool that would help her develop an understanding of the important number relationships that will lead to a stronger number sense. Instead of providing her with various supplemental counting activities from the kindergarten and first-grade curriculum, I realized that I needed to develop a deeper understanding of how the activities in those grade levels build the ideas about counting that Kristen needed to understand. I needed to plan a consistent series of activities that would allow her to build this understanding while exposing her to some of the activities in our second-grade curriculum.

On most mornings, when the rest of the class was working on independent morning work, Kristen played games from the first-grade curriculum that allowed her to work on her fluency with numbers to 20. She often played these games with a partner who needed extra practice. I focused on games that could be modified by changing the size of the numbers. In this way, I only needed to teach her a limited number of games and she was able to put more of her thinking into the mathematics of the game, rather than learning and remembering directions. She played Start With/Get To, in which numbers are chosen from a set of number cards. She identified the numbers, found them on a number line, and then counted from one to the other. This game helped her develop fluency with the rote counting sequence, both forward and backward. By varying the size of the numbers, I could easily adjust the game. Compare Dots is a game in which two players compare dot cards and decide which player has more dots on their card (Russell et al. 2008f). Once she was familiar with that version of the game, she played Double Compare Dots, in which both players turn over two cards and determine which player has the most dots. Here again, by changing the cards, I could easily adjust the game.

I also had Kristen work on modified versions of some second-grade games. When the rest of the class was playing Get to 100 (Russell et al. 2008g), Kristen played Get to 20. This game involves rolling two multiples-of-5 number cubes, finding the sum, and moving a game marker that many spaces on a 100 chart. Kristen played with one number cube. Like the rest of the class, she recorded her

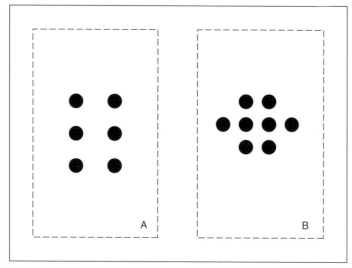

Figure 10–1.

moves on a worksheet and made sure that her numbers added up to 20 at the end of the game. Once she was familiar with the routine, she played Get to 30. She used interlocking cubes in towers of 5 to build the numbers on her worksheet. When the class played Collect $1.00 (Russell et al. 2008g), Kristen played Collect 25¢. She was able to work on some of these games independently, and some with a partner.

I was able to find some time to work with Kristen one-on-one, playing Compare Dots. I asked her to tell me how she decided which card had more dots (see Figure 10–1). I was heartened listening to her thinking. Rather than counting individual dots, she looked for familiar chunks and combinations. She regularly used combinations of 3 + 3, then counted on any additional dots to find the dot totals. I was so pleased that the sequence of first-grade activities I provided had helped her solidify her understanding of some basic number concepts.

Evidence of Kristen's Mathematical Thinking

When the class studied categorical data midway through the year, I was pleased to see that Kristen was more successful with these ideas. She was able to sort objects by their attributes and was noticeably more engaged in these activities. Counting was an integral part of the work. The numbers were relatively small, usually less than 20. She was able to participate without accommodations and worked successfully with a partner to generate survey questions about her classmates' favorite things (Russell et al. 2008j). She created a representation of her

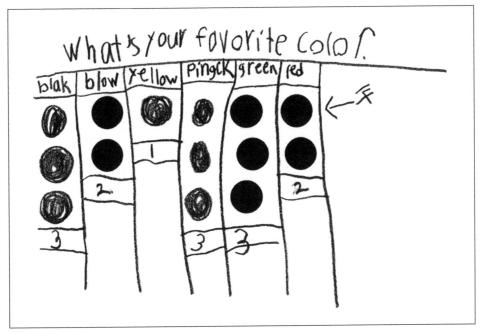

Figure 10–2.

data and was able to share with her classmates what she had learned about their favorite colors (see Figure 10–2). Observing her engagement and her relative strengths in collecting, organizing, and interpreting data reminded me that I cannot assume that students who are weak in one area are necessarily weak in all areas. It is important to be attuned to students' strengths as well as their gaps.

Kristen also experienced success during the patterns and functions unit in March. She was able to complete and extend tables that represented the relationship between the number of floors in a building and the number of rooms (Russell et al. 2008e). Although the activity called for completing the table up to 10 floors, she was consistently successful when working up to a total of 5 floors. The activity required her to make each floor of the building with cubes. The cubes created a model for what was happening in the activity and provided a structure for noticing and counting by equal groups. Throughout these activities, Kristen sat with a partner to solidify her own understanding of how the number relationships were represented in this table. Both students benefited from working with this abbreviated version of the table. To encourage some collaboration, I asked both students to work together to build each floor and keep track of the how the building was growing on their individual worksheets. After some redirection, both students got used to the idea of taking turns adding floors, then

Total Number of Floors	Total Number of Rooms
1	3
2	6
3	9
4	12
5	15

Figure 10–3.

counting the total number. When I asked Kristen to tell me what each row on the table meant, she was able to generate a sentence that related the number of floors to the corresponding number of rooms ("When the building has 2 floors, there are 6 rooms"). (See Figure 10–3.)

Once she was solid with the 5 floors, I worked with her to extend the relationships to 10 floors, something the rest of the class was able to do on their own. Kristen faltered when the total number of rooms grew greater than 20. However, I was pleased that she was able to persist and recognize the relationships that were generated up to 5 floors. Having the cubes to count helped her solve this problem. Without the counters, her understanding was still fragile when working with a number as large as 30 rooms.

Reflections

Working with Kristen has been difficult at times, but it has forced me to think more deeply about the mathematics I teach. It has been an opportunity for me to deepen my understanding of how early counting and number sense lay the foundation for the counting work and development of number sense that we focus on in second grade. I spend so much time with second-grade activities that I don't always have the opportunity to spend time thinking about how number sense develops before second grade. I learned that it is important to have the understanding of how number sense develops at the forefront, instead of planning one accommodation at a time. Once I deepened my own understanding, I was able to begin to integrate the early counting and number sense experiences into my planning for

Kristen. I had a more consistent course of action, planning a sequence of activities over time. I was able to find ways to include her in our classroom mathematics, while continuing to provide her the practice she needed to build her number sense.

Using both formal and informal assessments was critical in helping me learn more about how Kristen thought. Administering individual interviews, analyzing her student work, and listening to her conversations during small-group work all added to my knowledge about her strengths and gaps. I am now using that information to inform my planning. My own deepening knowledge of number and counting is beginning to inform my work with other students as well. I trust that I am developing a body of knowledge and refining my teaching in ways that will be effective beyond this year and this student.

11

How Many Children Got off the Bus?

Assessing Students' Knowledge of Subtraction

Introduction

This video shows Ana Vaisenstein working with a small group of fourth graders on a subtraction word problem. Ana worked with this group of students, who were struggling with math, throughout the year and knew that subtraction was especially difficult for them. In previous years, they had been taught to subtract using the standard algorithm. They had neither mastered this procedure nor understood what subtraction means. Ana's goals were to help them:

- recognize and solve a subtraction situation (removal, comparison, difference between numbers, distance between numbers)
- find an entry point (a model or representation or drawing that was useful for them to solve subtraction)
- build fluency with counting and number relationships (e.g., counting forward and backward by 10, knowing that subtraction is the inverse of addition—if 5 − 2 = 3, then 3 + 2 = 5)
- develop a stronger number sense (be able to break up numbers into parts that are easier to work with; e.g., 62 can become 50 + 12)

In the video, the students share their strategies for solving the following word problem that Ana wrote: There were 62 children on the school bus this morning. 48 children got off at the Sumner School. How many children continued the trip on the bus? She chose this problem because most of the children take the bus so it was a familiar context.

This problem is one that should be easy for most fourth graders to solve. But Ana knew that these students had not yet developed strategies for solving subtraction problems that they could use consistently and with understanding, so she chose to have them work on developing strong, efficient strategies for solving subtraction problems with smaller numbers before moving on to apply these strategies to problems with larger numbers. She also chose this problem because she felt they were still most comfortable with two-digit numbers, but she wanted them to work on problems that involved regrouping. She chose a word problem because she wanted them to be able to make sense of a subtraction situation and connect their strategies to an actual situation. This also gave them a context in which to ground their strategies.

In the video, three students share their strategies for solving the problem. Ana asks them questions about their strategies to make their thinking clearer for herself and the other students and to help one student recognize and correct a mistake she has made. She uses the information she learns about their understanding to plan future lessons.

When students are asked to develop and use strategies that make sense to them, the strategies they use to solve subtraction problems usually fall into four basic categories: subtracting in parts, adding up or subtracting back, changing the numbers to numbers that are easier to subtract, or subtracting by place (Russell et al. 2008h). (You might solve the problem yourself and take note of which category your strategy fits in.) Here are examples of strategies students might use to solve the problem $62 - 48$:

Subtracting in Parts	Adding Up or Subtracting Back
$62 - 48 =$ $62 - 40 = 22$ $22 - 2 = 20$ $20 - 6 = 14$ (the 48 can be broken apart in a variety of ways)	$62 - 48 =$ $48 + 2 = 50$ $50 + 12 = 62$ $2 + 12 = 14$ *or* $62 - 2 = 60$ $60 - 10 = 50$ $50 - 2 = 48$ $2 + 10 + 2 = 14$
Changing the Numbers	**Subtracting by Place**
$62 - 48 =$ $62 - 50 = 12$ $12 + 2$ (took away 2 too many, needed to add back on 2) *or* (add 2 to both numbers) $62 - 48 = 64 - 50$ $64 - 50 = 14$	$^5\cancel{6}^12$ $\underline{-\ 48}$ $\ \ 14$ *or* $60 - 40 = 20$ $2 - 8 = -6$ $20 - 6 = 14$

As you watch the video, consider the following questions. You might want to take notes on what you notice.

- How is the teacher using this as an assessment and teaching opportunity?
- How does she structure this sharing of strategies?
- What questions does she ask?
- What statements does she make?

Using assessment to inform decisions about teaching is an essential part of helping students who are struggling in mathematics. Looking at students' work on formal assessments can be useful, but observing students and asking them questions as they do activities that have not been labeled as assessments can be even more informative. The more specifically a teacher can figure out what aspects of mathematics concepts or skills a student is struggling with, the better the teacher can decide what to focus on with the student and the class, how to support the student's participation in whole-group discussions as well as individual work, and how to perhaps modify an activity to fit a student's needs while still addressing the important mathematics in the activity.

Examining the Video Footage

In the first interview, Ana Vaisenstein explains that in this lesson she "wanted to assess what kinds of strategies the children were going to use independently for a subtraction problem. We had been working on subtraction for a while, then we stopped and did something else. So I wanted to see how much they kept from what they had been doing." She chooses Carlos and Kassandra to share first because they both got correct answers, she thought the other students would understand their strategies, and she "wanted those responses to be there as points of reference for the future discussion."

Carlos uses a "subtracting in parts" strategy. To use his strategy to solve the problem, Carlos needed to know that the problem is a subtraction problem. He knows he could take away the second number in parts and that he could break up 48 into 40 and 8. He also seems to realize that it can be easier to take away a multiple of 10 first.

Kassandra uses the U.S. standard algorithm (a "subtracting by place" strategy) to solve the problem. She also understands that the problem is a subtraction problem. Through Ana's questioning about the value of the numbers, we can see that Kassandra seems to understand that she is using 10 from the 60 to change the 2 to 12 and knows when she does this that she no longer has 60. She is perhaps still working on the place value of numbers as she seems a little unsure that the 1 in 14 is really 10.

Ana next asks Yamilka to share her strategy. Yamilka has made a mistake in her strategy and has come up with the answer of 26. This is what she writes on the board:

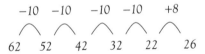

This is actually her second way of doing the problem. She had gotten the incorrect answer of 26 using her first method, and she is trying to make the second strategy equal 26 because she knows that the answer to a problem is supposed to be the same no matter which strategy is used.

Ana asks a series of questions to help her better understand Yamilka's thinking and to help Yamilka identify and work through her mistake. For example:

- Ana asks Yamilka, "Why did you add 8?" to help Yamilka reflect on and voice her reasoning.
- Ana asks, "Are you taking 48 children out of the bus? Did you take these 8 children out of the bus?" Does Yamilka think she has taken away all 48?
- Ana asks, "Where do you think you messed up? Why do you think so?" Does Yamilka recognize her mistake and does she understand why it is a mistake?
- Once Yamilka changes her answer to 14, Ana asks Yamilka if she knows that answer is correct. She asks this perhaps to see if she is choosing that answer because others got to that answer or because she had a strategy to figure it out.
- After Yamilka has identified and corrected her mistake, Ana asks, "Why did you make that mistake? What can help you not make that kind of mistake again?" Does Yamilka understand her mistake? Can she generalize what she now understands to think about how she could prevent a similar mistake?

Ana and the other students help Yamilka work through her mistake. The students ask Yamilka why she added on 8, and a student points out a computation error. Ana asks her to look carefully at what is happening in the problem and whether that matches what she did. Together they look at specific numbers to see if what Yamilka did matches the action of the problem. Finally, Ana asks Yamilka to name her mistake and think about preventing a similar one in the future.

From the questions Ana asks Yamilka, it is possible to gather some information about what Yamilka understands about subtraction and numbers in general. She understands that the problem is a subtraction (removal) problem. She knows that she should get the same answer to a problem no matter what way she solves it. She knows she can take away the quantity in parts and uses 10 as an easy number to take away. She counts backward by 10s and not by 1s. It seems as though Yamilka is still working on how to figure out whether she should add or subtract particular chunks of numbers and making sure what she does with the numbers matches what is actually happening in the problem. She is also still working on figuring out whether her steps and her answer make sense and not just whether her answer matches the answer she got using a different strategy.

In a part of the interview not seen in the video Ana says:

> Yamilka said you never add when you're taking away, I had to think "OK, this is what she's taking out of this situation." But it was very interesting because we had been adding up to solve subtraction problems. But the kids struggle with that because they could do it but they did not know why it was working, and that was something that I wanted to continue exploring.

Ana's assessment of the students' understanding of subtraction indicated to her that she has more work to do to address the range of understandings within the group. Some, like Carlos, had developed some useful strategies and were learning to apply them flexibly. Some, like Kassandra, will need more help in using strategies in which the value of the numbers are clear to them, and most likely all need more practice in understanding the relationship between addition and subtraction. As she continued to work on subtraction with her students, Ana planned to continue to use familiar contexts. For example, Yamilka's family owned a store, so Ana planned to introduce a "store" context so that children could practice giving change. Working with prices and giving change would give them the opportunity to use a variety of strategies, including adding up or counting back, and reflect on the relationship between addition and subtraction. Ana planned to continue to focus on understanding the operation of subtraction and developing efficient strategies for solving subtraction problems in the next series of lessons.

12

Get to 100

Assessing Students' Number Sense

Introduction

This video shows Michael Flynn first introducing the game Get to 100 from the *Investigations in Number, Data, and Space* curriculum to his second-grade class and then working with two students as they play the game (Russell et al. 2008g).

In the game Get to 100, students take turns rolling 2 multiples of 5 dice (the dice have the numbers 5, 10, 15, and 20 on them) and moving their game pieces the amount they rolled on a 100 chart. As they play, they record the amount they move each time in a continuous number string. For example, if a player rolls a 5 and a 10 during one turn and then on the player's next turn she rolls a 15 and a 10, the player's number string would read 5 + 10 + 15 + 10 (see Figure 12–1). The object of the game is to get to 100 on the 100 chart. Once a game piece lands on 100, the player checks that it should have landed on 100, by adding up the number string.

As students play Get to 100, they work on adding numbers, particularly adding on multiples of 5 and 10. The structure of the game encourages students to count by groups rather than by 1s. Students also learn about the structure of the base ten number system and about what happens when you add on multiples of 5 or 10 to a number.

Some students may find playing Get to 100 challenging. They might find it difficult to navigate around the 100 chart or to keep track of where they are and where they are moving to on the chart. Some students may not realize that their number string should show where they are on the 100 chart and that at the end of the game, the number string should add up to 100. Some students may have difficulty adding 2 double-digit numbers or, even if they can add on 5, 10, or 20, they might have trouble adding on 15 to a number. Some students may have trouble adding the entire number string at the end.

As you watch the video, consider the following questions. You might want to take notes on what you notice.

- How is the teacher using his interaction with the two students as an assessment and teaching opportunity?

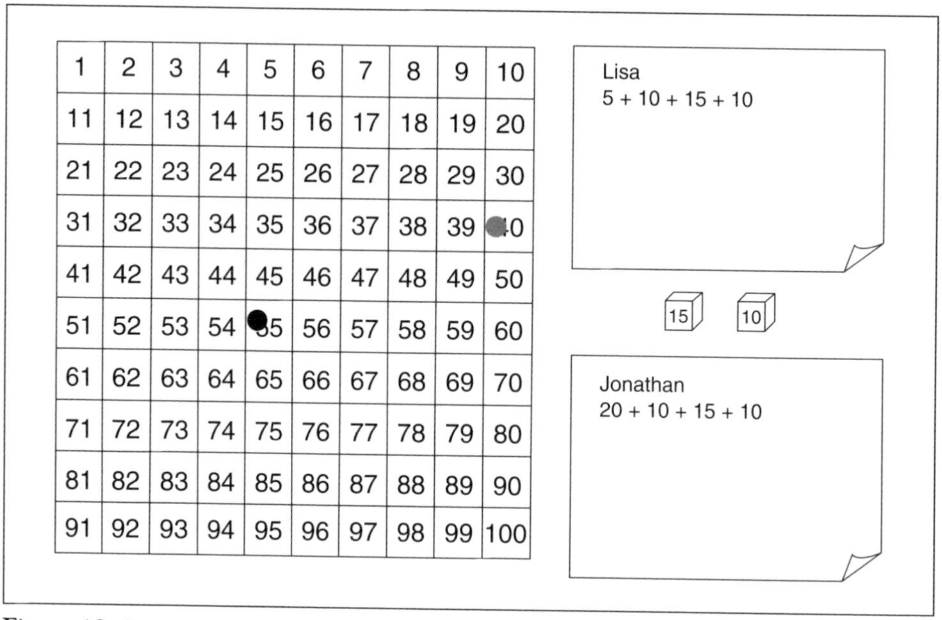

Figure 12–1.

- What questions does he ask?
- What statements does he make?
- What does he ask the students to do?

Using assessment to inform decisions about teaching is an essential part of helping students who are struggling in mathematics. Looking at students' work on formal assessments can be useful, but observing students and asking them questions as they do activities that have not been labeled as assessments can be even more informative. The more specifically a teacher can figure out what aspects of mathematics concepts or skills a student is struggling with, the better the teacher can decide what to focus on with the student and the class, how to support the student's participation in whole-group discussions as well as individual work, and how to perhaps modify an activity to fit a student's needs while still addressing the important mathematics in the activity.

Examining the Video Footage

At the beginning of the video, Michael Flynn plays a demonstration round of the Get to 100 game with the whole class. As they play, some ideas are highlighted that might be useful to students as they begin to play the game in pairs. For example, Michael asks a student how she knows that jumping down 2 rows on the

100 chart would equal adding 20. The student says that it is 2 jumps of 10, which highlights that jumping down 2 rows on the 100 chart is the same as jumping down two 10s, which is the same as adding 20. He also asks a student to count by 1s to check that jumping down 2 rows really is 20. Some students may need to count by 1s to really see that the amount is 20 and to connect the familiar counting by 1s to perhaps an unfamiliar idea of counting by 10s.

Most of the video shows Michael working with two students, Amanda and Michael, while the other students are working independently in pairs. As he works with these two students, Michael asks questions about how they are making their moves and makes decisions about what he asks them to do to assess what they are understanding and not understanding. He uses some of the information he gathers to immediately try to help the students move forward in their understanding. For example, Michael (the teacher) notices that Michael (the student) is counting each space, but is doing it in groups of five. He asks Michael about this and then begins to build on this strategy by asking him to mark off every fifth square. Michael then seems to see the jumps of 5 he can make without counting every space, though he later reverts back to counting each space.

Right after they talk through counting by 5s, the teacher asks Michael to do another move (to start at 20 on the 100 chart and then add 20). By doing this, he may want to find out whether Michael would make the same mistakes or whether he would incorporate anything they just talked about. When Michael gives three different answers for starting at 20 and adding 20, the teacher responds, "Show me" to each of Michael's answers about where he would land when he makes the move. This communicates that he wants Michael to prove his answer no matter whether his answer is correct or not.

Because Michael is unsure of the answer, the teacher urges him to use the strategy of counting groups of 5 that he used before. By doing this, he is encouraging Michael to use and build on a strategy that he already knows. He also repeatedly asks Michael to show his answers by actually moving the game piece. By doing this, he can see how Michael is coming up with his answers and it helps Michael see the answer visually on the chart by actually moving the piece.

He asks Michael explicitly to jump by 5s. He thinks this is a strong strategy that uses what Michael already knows and he wants to see if Michael can use that knowledge to carry out the counting by 5s strategy and move away from counting by 1s. When Michael goes back to counting groups of 5 by 1s, the teacher asks Amanda to jump by 5s, perhaps because he wants Michael to see how another student can use that strategy.

When Amanda jumps backward by 5s instead of forward by 5s, the teacher poses a story about pennies to help Amanda reflect on whether where she landed makes sense. He also asks Michael to help Amanda figure out where she would land, which might help both of them think about jumps of 5.

Throughout his interactions with both students, the teacher asks them questions such as, "Why that number?" and "How do you know?" These questions allow Michael to hear his students' thinking and also force the students to justify their moves. He also asks them to name the amounts they are jumping so they are not just jumping but also thinking about the amount they are jumping and where that brings them on the 100 chart.

The questions the teacher asks are designed to elicit specific information about both Michael and Amanda's understanding. Because he spends the most time working with Michael, there is more information about what Michael understands and doesn't understand. Michael seems to understand that grouping a count by 5 can be useful. He knows how many groups of 5 there are in 20, and he knows that when he has counted 4 groups of 5, he has counted 20. He recognizes patterns of counting by 10 and saw the pattern of 5s going down the 100 chart. Michael still seems to be working on counting by 5s on the 100 chart and navigating around the 100 chart. It seems unclear why Michael knows the number of 5s in 20 but doesn't count by 5s and why exactly Michael is having difficulty with directionality on the 100 chart.

In an essay he wrote about this interaction with Amanda and Michael, Michael Flynn describes what he decided to do when these two students next played Get to 100.

> I decided to have them play Get to 100 with the numbers cubes that didn't have 15. That was just one more thing to worry about. I also had them begin the game by counting off by fives and marking those numbers on their 100 charts. This would serve as a visual reminder. I also had them play with other partners during the next few choice times so they could see different strategies. They both had the hardest time with the game compared to the rest of the class, but with repeated practice on the 100 chart, they both began moving efficiently and accurately on the board.

By eliminating the number 15 on the die for these two students, Michael allowed them to focus on adding on 5, 10, and 20 and not be distracted by trying to add on 15, which can be more challenging. Asking them to mark off multiples of 5 on the 100s chart highlighted the multiples of 5, helped them to count by 5s, and perhaps made it more likely for them to count by 5s. His decision to have them play with other partners was designed to expose them to some other strategies for adding on multiples of 5.

The work Michael did with these two students was both an assessment and a teaching opportunity. He was able to learn about the students' understanding of counting, adding, and the number system, and also help them move forward in their understanding. As Michael himself said in an interview, listening to what students are thinking is an essential ingredient of assessment. Looking at student work, although also critical, is not sufficient.

> When I'm looking at the student work afterward, that's helpful. But a lot of times I miss the critical thing because the student work is the product, kind of what happened at the end. And although they sometimes will explain their thinking, and I can figure out what they've done on paper, I get more information from the process by being there in the moment.

What Michael found out from this careful questioning during this interaction informed what he planned to do next with these two students and most likely with the class as a whole.

Building Understanding
Through Talk

Introduction

My struggling students get confused from hearing so many strategies.

My students with learning disabilities tune out when their classmates are explaining strategies.

I just teach my struggling students one way to do a problem; they need to be told what to do.

My students with special needs can't sit long enough to participate in discussions.

These statements express some concerns teachers have about focusing on talk in their inclusive mathematics classrooms. Including all students in discussions is challenging for teachers and not something that many have been taught to do. Yet communication has become an important part of mathematics instruction.

Communication is an essential part of mathematics and mathematics education. It is a way of sharing ideas and clarifying understanding. Through communication, ideas become objects of reflection, refinement, discussion, and amendment. The communication process also helps build meaning and permanence for ideas and makes them public. When students are challenged to think and reason about mathematics and to communicate the results of their thinking to others orally or in writing, they learn to be clear and convincing. Listening to others' explanations gives students opportunities to develop their own understandings. (National Council of Teachers of Mathematics [NCTM] 2000, 60)

This statement from the NCTM *Principles and Standards for School Mathematics* reveals the emphasis on communication in mathematics instruction, a decided change from when mathematics in the elementary school focused solely on the mastery of arithmetic operations. Not only does talk help students solidify their understanding, it also provides a window into children's thinking. In regard to their students who are struggling, teachers have often been surprised by something their students express that indicates understanding or a question a student asks that indicates confusion. In either case, the information the teachers learn informs instruction. When these students are given the opportunity to justify their answers, discuss similarities and differences among strategies, and ask questions, teachers have found that they are more prepared to solve a variety of problems (Behrend 2003).

The teachers who wrote these essays and appear in these videos share a fundamental belief that their struggling students can learn mathematics along with their peers and that promoting classroom talk aids their mathematical understanding. Including all students in classroom discussion is complex and requires careful planning (Hiebert et al. 1997; Boaler 2008). Students who are struggling in mathematics need support to actively and productively participate in whole-class discussions. These teachers strive to make their classroom a safe place for all of their students, one where clear routines and expectations for behavior are established, taking risks is encouraged, and mistakes are viewed as opportunities for learning.

Meticulous preparation before discussions and documentation of student thinking during and after the discussions characterize these teachers' practice. They anticipate concepts or strategies that might be difficult for their students who struggle, they plan accommodations, and they find ways to take notes afterward to assess what students understood and what confusions might have emerged. These teachers also provide multiple entry points into discussions so that a variety of students can participate. For example, some of the teachers post strategies the class has developed to be used as a reference point for discussions. Others provide a variety of models and representations that allow students to visualize the problem and organize their thinking. When sharing strategies, the teachers begin with one that is accessible for all class members, and the teachers record all students' contributions, using notation that others can follow.

These teachers often structure small-group time with students who find it difficult to participate in the whole-group discussion. This time might be used to review an activity that they introduced in the whole group or to preview a sharing discussion by helping the students rehearse one of their strategies. The practice these students get in talking in the small group helps build their mathematical understanding and prepares them to participate in the whole-group discussion.

In "What's Another Way to Make 9?" math specialist Christina Myren recounts her work in a first-grade classroom. Working in collaboration with the classroom teacher, she structures some experiences and conversations with a small group of students who are struggling with composing and decomposing numbers. She debriefs with the teacher about what the students know, what extra support they need, and how they can best participate in the whole group.

In "Lightbulbs Happen," third-grade teacher Nikki Faria-Mitchell explains that when she introduces and works on an activity she knows will be difficult for some students, she works with pairs or small groups beforehand. This structure enables her to facilitate students' talking through their strategies together so that they can then participate more fully in the whole group.

In "Talking About Square Numbers," fourth-grade teacher Dee Watson describes how she builds her mathematics community to create a safe space for her students to express their mathematical ideas, as well as their confusions or struggles. She then describes specific strategies she uses to help some struggling students express their ideas about multiplication to support their understanding and build their confidence.

In "Kindergarteners Talk About Counting," Lillian Pinet facilitates a discussion with her kindergarten class about an activity called the Counting Jar (Russell et al. 2008o). During this discussion, Lillian highlights students' counting strategies and involves the whole group in helping a student recognize and correct a counting mistake.

In "What Do We Do with the Remainder?" Dee Watson leads a discussion about a division word problem with a class of fourth-grade students in October. The students work through one strategy for solving the problem and, through their discussion of the strategy, figure out what to do about the remainder in the problem.

These episodes describe both the teachers' strong commitment to a focus on talk for all of their young learners and how intentional the teachers are in their planning and their goals for the discussions. They detail various aspects of their practice: how they provide multiple entry points and resources to make the mathematics accessible, how they prepare students who are struggling ahead of time for whole-group discussion, and how they assess what students have learned from the conversations and what next steps might be.

Questions to Think About

What strategies do the teachers use to make the mathematics accessible to all students during whole-class discussions?

What strategies do the teachers use to help the students who are struggling participate in the whole-class discussions?

How do the small-group discussions contribute to the students' learning?

What do the teachers learn about their students' understanding by listening to them talk in small and large groups?

13

What's Another Way to Make 9?

Building Understanding Through Math Talk

Christina Myren

What can we do to encourage young learners to participate more fully during whole-class discussion, especially those who are struggling with mathematical concepts and ideas? Often teachers find that these students are not active participants in these discussions. To solidify their understanding, it is particularly important for these reluctant students to be able to focus on the concepts being presented, make sense of the strategies being discussed, make connections with their own learning, and take risks to ask questions and discuss errors. By participating in the mathematics community, they will be more likely to see themselves as learners and become more invested in learning mathematics. When I work with new teachers, I try to model how to engage a range of students in class discussions and how to use the class discussion to assess student understanding. The whole-group discussion can be particularly difficult for new teachers to manage because it may be unfamiliar for teachers in mathematics class and because comments from a wide range of students can be difficult to sort out "on the fly."

Fostering whole-group discussion as a way to include all learners became the basis of my work with Sarah, a first-grade teacher. This was Sarah's second year of teaching, but her first year with first graders. The previous year, I worked with her second-grade students, so she was comfortable having me in her classroom. I initially worked with her students daily for fifteen or twenty minutes. My goal was to find out what they knew about numbers and to help them record their knowledge in little spiral notebooks we called "number books."

To introduce the number books, we began with the number 1. I wrote the numeral *1* on the board and asked the students, "What other ways can we show 1?" Students' ideas included the word *one*, 1 penny, a domino showing 1, 1 triangle, 1 person. I made a representation of each of their suggestions. Martin held up 1 finger and said, "We could draw a hand with 1 finger. When I go to my sister's soccer game it means that they are the number 1 team." Next, I asked if anyone knew a number sentence or equation for the number 1. When there were no answers, I added, "It could be adding or subtracting." Suddenly Rachel offered, "I know, 1 + 0 = 1." Then Owen added, "5 take away 4 makes 1." I recorded each of these equations on the board. Then I showed the children their individual number books, telling them that their job was to draw or write things that showed 1 (see Figure 13–1).

Figure 13–1.

Each day we talked about the next number in the series. Most children began to come up with more complex ways to express the numbers. For example, with 5, I wrote the equations in sequential order, leaving a space between $1 + 4 = 5$ and $3 + 2 = 5$. I was hoping the children would notice the pattern. Lukas noticed it first and said, "2 plus 3 equals 5 goes in that empty place." When I asked him how he knew, he replied, "The first numbers count up and the second numbers count back," referring to the addends. As we got to greater numbers, some children began to use the number line to come up with subtraction equations. They began seeing patterns and making generalizations about the operations of addition and subtraction.

Although I was pleased that some of the children in the class were building from each other's ideas and were challenged to think about the numbers in a more abstract way, I noticed that others were struggling. For example, when we worked on the number 6, Kelvin volunteered, "6 and 0 makes 6." Kelvin had already become quite predictable. He knew that any number plus zero equaled that number, so he had shared it with all the numbers so far. He also showed some confusion when he shared other combinations and often included the number as part of a different equation. For 6, he had volunteered, "6 plus 2." When Owen said, "That makes 8 and we're doing 6," Kelvin looked puzzled. Even after I asked Kelvin and Owen to use the linking cubes to find combinations for 6, Kelvin seemed confused. When writing in his number book, he most often chose to illustrate sets of quantities rather than write equations.

Mia also struggled. She often chose to draw pictures, and when she wrote a number sentence, it was not always accurate, even if the correct numbers were on the board. Fernando preferred to draw rather than write numbers, and often used $1 + 1 + \cdots + 1$ as his equation for the number of the day. Stacy confused addition and subtraction and frequently gave incorrect answers.

Given their struggles, I wondered what these particular children were learning from the whole-group discussion. I decided that they could benefit from additional opportunities to practice counting and recording combinations in a small group prior to their work with the whole class.

Sarah and I met to identify children who needed more support. We decided that Nicole, Stacy, Fernando, Keith Allen, Connor, Mia, and Kelvin would form the intervention group. After working with the numbers 1 through 12, my plan was to work with the intervention group for ten to fifteen minutes two or three times a week reviewing one of the numbers. Next I would revisit the same number as a review for the entire class. I wanted to see if the extra practice and review in the intervention group would help those children participate more successfully with the entire class.

Working with the Intervention Group

In planning the first intervention lesson, I wanted the students to see the number 9 and its parts by using linking cubes. I knew they needed experience with concrete models and in verbalizing what they were doing before they could begin to see patterns and make conjectures about how addition and subtraction work. My plan was for each student to build a train of 9 with the cubes, and then break that 9 apart into 2 groups. I would record the combinations on a small whiteboard and watch the children carefully as they worked.

Although the plan seemed simple and direct enough to me, I was surprised by the children's responses. I began by telling them that we would be reviewing the number 9 using cubes. I asked them to use the linking cubes to build a train of 9 cubes. As they were working on this task, I noticed that Mia had 10 cubes, so I asked everyone to count their cubes again. Keith Allen was taking a long time looking for specific colors so that he could make a pattern, so I had to tell him not to worry about the colors. When everyone finished their cube train, I asked the children to break the train into 2 parts. The children seemed confused, so I modeled with my own train of 9 cubes. When I saw that each child had broken their train into parts, I said, "Tell me how many you have in each part. I see you broke the 9 into different numbers of cubes."

Mia was the first to volunteer. While we all watched, she said, "Two," as she pointed to 1 group of cubes, and then counted the other group, "1, 2, 3, 4, 5, 6, 7." I wrote $2 + 7 =$ on the whiteboard and asked her, "How many is that?" Mia then started with the group of 2 and counted all the rest of the cubes by 1s to answer 9. Kelvin was the next to share. He had broken his cubes into 3 and 6. When asked the total, he too began counting the cubes from 1.

Connor then shared that $9 - 3 = 9$. I knew that he was confused, so I tried using a context to help him realize that you can't subtract something and end up with the starting number. I asked the group, "If I had 9 pieces of gum and gave 3 pieces to my friends, how many would be left?" Nicole used her train of 9 cubes, took away 3, and yelled out, "6." Even though the task was to make 9, not subtract from it, I felt it was important for the group to visualize this problem in a real-life context. We then continued for a few more minutes using cubes to find combinations of 9—sometimes connecting the numbers to stories.

After giving this small group additional practice, I wanted to bring the ideas we worked on to the whole group, both as a review for the whole class and to assess if and how the intervention group students would be able to contribute to the whole-class discussion. I prepared the intervention group by telling them that after recess we would review the number 9 with the whole class. I ended the session by asking them to put down their cubes and look at all the ways we found to make 9 with 2 numbers. I wanted to prepare them for the discussion that would move us from concrete objects to written symbols, so I asked them to tell their neighbor the number combinations they saw that made 9. After they finished, I said, "Remember the ways you told each other so you can share them when we review 9 with the whole class."

Whole-Class Talk

After recess, I began the whole-class lesson. As we began the review, I paid close attention to the responses of all the children, and especially made an effort to include the students from the intervention group. From my work with them, I knew what questions to ask to elicit their thinking.

"What do you know about 9?" I asked. Colin shared first and offered, "8 + 1." Lukas then added, "5 + 4 and 4 + 5 'cause they're the same." When Stacy shared next, she said, "1 + 6." Owen quickly told her she needed to check that answer so she walked over to the cubes. While she worked with the cubes, I called on Kelvin who predictably said, "9 + 0 = 9." Stacy then came back to the group with her correction and proudly announced that 1 + 8 makes 9. Next I asked Mia, "Do you have a way to make 9?" When she responded, "Tally marks," I added 9 tally marks to the board. Owen shared 10 − 1, and then Keith Allen said 11 − 2. When Owen seemed to be adding to the problem with 12 − 3, I asked him how he knew that fact. He said, "I just add 1 to each side." Other children shared, including Connor, who said 4 + 5, which I added even though it was already there, to encourage his participation. Skylar and Trinity then shared subtraction equations beginning with 100 − 91, then 101 − 92, and continued the pattern. When I asked Skylar how she knew what would come next, she replied, "It's just like Owen's. I added 1 to each side."

I was encouraged that a range of students was able to enter in the whole-class discussion. The various entry points of the children, whether Mia's tally marks or Kelvin's predictable equation, were acknowledged as I wrote each contribution on the board. I was also pleased with Stacy's willingness to listen to Owen and with her choice of using the cubes to proudly correct her answer. Although Stacy needed the cubes to help her think about the number, Keith Allen seemed on the verge of seeing a subtraction pattern. When I chose to ask Owen how he knew the next fact in the pattern, 102 − 93, Keith Allen listened thoughtfully. Later Skylar was able to use Owen's ideas when she and Trinity were using larger numbers. Children were beginning to build on each other's thinking and access the number in a variety of ways.

Small-Group Intervention: Addition Equations

After school, Sarah and I debriefed the small-group lesson. We realized that these children needed much work in seeing the numbers within the larger number—subitizing. Most of the six children, with the exception of Keith Allen, had difficulty even remembering the starting number. After they broke the train of 9 cubes into 2 parts, they counted the cubes in each group separately, and then counted the total over again, not realizing or trusting that the original number they began with was 9. Sarah was also surprised with the amount of time it took the children to make the original train of 9 accurately. We both felt that the distraction of all the colors of linking cubes led this group to think of color patterns rather than focus on the 9 cubes. I decided that next time we worked together, I would only give the children 2 colors of cubes.

For the next small-group lesson, the children only used white and red cubes, which were already separated. I showed them Meredith's page in her number book that depicted 8 and asked them what they noticed about the addition equations. I hoped that the students would be able to model the equations with cubes but also notice the order of the equations and maybe represent the patterns found in Meredith's book (see Figure 13–2).

"I see 4 + 4," Mia offered. My response was, "Can you build 4 + 4 using the cubes?" Connor and Nicole went right to work, while the rest of the children watched. I asked Nicole to share about her train, and she pointed to the colors and said, "Here's 4 red and 4 white. That makes 8." We then went on to build the rest of the addition equations in Meredith's book. As the children were building, I listened for someone to mention something about the way Meredith arranged her equations. Not one child mentioned the patterns. From this conversation, I could see that the children needed more practice with building and naming each combination before they were ready to discover the patterns. At the end of the small-group discussion, I asked the children to place their trains on the chalk tray so that they could share some of them during the whole-class discussion. I again wanted to have their representations available to help them recall the work they did and participate in the group talk.

Whole-Class Talk

After recess, the whole class gathered to review the number 8. Mia explained how we used Meredith's book to make the cube trains for 8. Then I asked the class to look carefully at the cubes to find 4 + 4. Connor volunteered and chose the train that showed 2 white and 6 red. I wanted him to be explicit about his choice and asked, "How many cubes are white? How many are red?" He counted each time, and Keith Allen said, "2 plus 6 makes 8." Then I directed the class back to the original question by asking again, "Can you find the 4 + 4?" Mia picked out the

eight 8 ̶I̶H̶H̶/|||

14 - 6 = 8
13 - 5 = 8
12 - 4 = 8
11 - 3 = 8
10 - 2 = 8
9 - 1 = 8
8 - 0 = 8

4 + 4 = 8
5 + 3 = 8
6 + 2 = 8
7 + 1 = 8
8 + 0 = 8

Figure 13–2.

4 red and 4 white cubes and said, "I know this one because I made it." For the next combination of 3 + 5, Kailey quickly found the cube train of 3 red and 5 white. She said, "I just saw the 3 and I didn't have to count the 5." Nicole chose the train of 3 white and 5 red. She referred to Kailey's comment: "I saw the

3 white, so I didn't even count the reds. I just saw them with my eyes." When I asked for 1 + 7, Stacy picked the correct train and said, "There's 1 white and 7 red." During the discussion, I was pleased that some of the students from the intervention group were beginning to visualize and talk about the number combinations, while building on what other children in the class were sharing. For example, Fernando said, "There's 2 red so there has to be 6 whites to make 8." The practice in the small group, review in the large group, and the experience of hearing their classmates' ideas were helping to build their understanding of number combinations.

Reviewing Student Progress

After these lessons, Sarah and I sat down to review the progress of the intervention group. I particularly wanted to help her analyze their contributions to the large and small groups. The intervention group was, from our notes, participating more confidently in the whole-group discussions. Mia's progress, after just three meetings, was good and she seemed ready to be phased out of this special group. Nicole, Stacy, Fernando, Connor, Keith Allen, and Kelvin were progressing but could continue to benefit from the additional intervention. We needed to capitalize on their gains and solidify their understanding so they could begin to see patterns. Even though I had sequenced the equations to highlight a generalization about addition, the children were not ready to see this. I decided to be patient and not force the issue. It was important that this "aha" moment come from the students themselves, after they had seen the patterns several more times and heard the other children explain what they saw.

Working on Notations

During our discussions about the students, Sarah and I began to focus on how Sarah would soon take over the small-group discussions and whole-group work with the number books. From reviewing students' work on the number books, we decided on some additional themes she would emphasize. For example, we noted that Nicole still had difficulty notating her work symbolically, often confusing the plus and minus sign as well as the horizontal and vertical formats of addition and subtraction. We decided that she needed more explicit instructions in these formats and that perhaps other children in the class might benefit also. Sarah was going to weave how to notate both vertical and horizontal equations into her number discussions, asking children what to write next and talking about the symbols. She planned to have the children respond on individual whiteboards so that she could get a quick overview of what the children understood during the discussion.

Building Understanding of Story Problems

Keith Allen and Fernando also needed help with understanding story problems. With Fernando, the language of the problems was confusing. He would often add the numbers rather than subtract when comparing two things. When solving the problem, "Maria has 6 marbles, and Mark has 10 marbles. Who has more marbles? How many more?" he added 6 + 10.

For the children in this group, conversation had to be accompanied by manipulating objects. The children needed multiple sessions to make and verbalize number combinations. To clarify the language in the problems, Sarah and I decided that acting out story problems first in the small group and then in the large group would be a helpful strategy for Fernando, Keith Allen, and other children as well. She would also adjust the contexts to find ones that made sense to the children.

Next Steps

Through our discussions, Sarah became convinced of the benefits of the small-group intervention to give the students confidence and practice in explaining their ideas. She has chosen to continue to work with the small group of students. She uses the small-group instruction in very particular ways to zero in on what the students need the most. To make the schedule manageable for her as a classroom teacher, she meets with students for ten to fifteen minutes at a time to front-load the number that the whole group will be using. She also reviews smaller numbers with them and the whole class. Sarah is also carrying out some of the ways we worked out for her to document and assess the classroom conversation when I am not there. Taking brief notes as soon afterward as possible and making sure to keep artifacts, such as the equations that came up during the discussions, are important to inform planning the next steps. Sarah also finds it helpful to use her camera to document children at work.

Reflections

In my conversations with Sarah, I have tried to share additional strategies that can engage all of her learners in the classroom discussion. For example, acting out story problems and asking children to share and talk about their representations (e.g., number cube trains) can benefit all children. Sometimes we forget that children who seem to understand beginning number concepts well can benefit from a visual model and representation, whether that is working with models or acting out the story problem. Also, by explaining their thoughts and reasoning, all children learn to value themselves as mathematicians and to challenge themselves to think about and then verbalize their understanding of mathematical concepts and ideas.

As I think about my experience with Sarah's group, I realize how much I learned about the students' understanding through the classroom conversation. The range of understandings was evident. As evidence of students' confusions emerged, I was able to plan the small-group intervention to give these students extra practice. We have found that these opportunities both to preview and review are crucial in helping the intervention group make connections from one day to the next so that they have ways to enter and participate in the whole-class discussion and continue to build their understanding. They are being exposed to their classmates' talk about patterns in these whole-group discussions. This talk will be a reference point for them as they move toward discovering patterns and making generalizations.

14

Lightbulbs Happen

Making Connections Through Math Talk

Nikki Faria-Mitchell

Knowing that my class includes a range of learners with diverse learning styles, I need to make my students aware of the importance of each other's ideas. I need them to understand that our math classroom is a place to learn and a safe place to take a risk. This is particularly true for my struggling students. I want them to know that they are capable of learning mathematics and that they can learn from the ideas of other students.

At the start of each school year, I facilitate a discussion with my third-grade students about how to create a mathematics community. Together, we establish the routines that guide our work throughout the year. We use the workshop model—we meet as a whole group for a minilesson devoted to a particular skill for the day, then the students work independently, with partners, or within a small group, and finally we come back together to share what we have learned. This model allows my students to contribute in a variety of situations and encourages participation in many forms.

Building a positive math community is vital from the beginning because it sets the stage for our work throughout the year. My role as a teacher and facilitator at this stage is crucial. I not only need to establish the routines but also have to teach students how to have a mathematical discussion. I begin this process early in the year by gathering the students together and directly addressing the purpose for whole-class conversations.

Establishing Expectations for Classroom Talk

The following is a piece of a September conversation that was devoted to the importance of our mathematics community. I hold this conversation each year so that all my students understand my goals and expectations for expressing their mathematical ideas and becoming responsible learners who take ownership of their own learning. Our math community is new. No matter how confident the students were in math the previous year, and even if many of the students were together the year before, I am a new facilitator for this group of students. They need to figure out what I expect of them.

I open the conversation by asking students: "Can someone tell me why we meet at the carpet before and after each math lesson?" By asking this question, I'm hoping the students will realize how much I value this piece of our mathematical learning. I also pose this question to get a sense of my new students' experiences: Are they at ease sharing in a whole-group setting? Are they willing to take risks and answer questions that may not be straightforward? Do they feel comfortable within our classroom?

September

TEACHER: Can someone tell me why we meet at the carpet before and after each math lesson?

LISA: We come here to review our work, find out if the answer is right or wrong.

JOHN: I think it's to share.

BETHANY: Yeah, but we also get more ideas.

TEACHER: Do our conversations help you as a math learner?

DARRYL: It helps you understand something.

LISA: Well, we see different ideas.

JOHN: You might see that someone else did the same thing as you.

TEACHER: How do you feel talking about the math we are working on? [A long, uncomfortable minute of silence follows.]

CODY: It's hard, I don't want to say the wrong answer. [Many children nod their heads in agreement.]

During this conversation, I asked the students three different questions and still did not get many responses. The children who were brave enough to give an answer gave very generic responses that felt like what they thought I wanted to hear. *Ideas* were referred to, but what are these ideas? Why do we talk about them? Eventually, these "things" we share will be the strategies the students use to solve problems, the questions we ask to clarify a classmate's thinking, and the connections we make while investigating different mathematical concepts.

Reflecting on this conversation, I could sense the uncomfortable feeling that filled the classroom. At times, the silence was so intense I found myself shifting in my chair, trying to think of different questions that I could ask to fill the quiet "dead air." But even this brief initial discussion helps me to get to know where my students are and allows me to quickly assess how to best reach them all. I think about the range of learners when I analyze this conversation. Which students already feel comfortable enough to share? Who is looking down or away to avoid eye contact with me or with the student who is sharing? Which students seem to be actively listening to each other and trying to build ideas off of one another?

John and Darryl are both learners who are struggling with math. From this brief conversation, I learn that they understand that sharing is considered important and recognize that they benefit when they see how someone else has approached a problem. However, they don't typically share their thinking in the larger group. Cody is quite the opposite. He is a confident math learner, but he understands how other students feel. He too hesitates when he isn't 100 percent sure of himself because he doesn't want others (including me) to know that he doesn't get it. His comment summed up many of the students' feelings.

Facilitating Math Conversations

After our initial conversations in September, we jump right into the math and address concerns as we encounter them. We don't formally generate rules for "math talk," but there is an understanding of what is acceptable math conversation. The students are encouraged to express what they are thinking about the particular activities we are working on as well as to admit when they aren't sure and need some help. I carefully plan my actions and questions so that I am making our discussion process explicit for the students. In the beginning of the year, I will give the students a minute or so to think about their response. Then I may say something such as "Do you need some help?" "Would you like to call on someone to help you?" "Do you need more thinking time? I can come back to you when you are ready, just be sure to raise your hand again." Students can then choose to call on someone to help them out or just pass. This strategy helps build camaraderie, allowing an individual to share as much as she is comfortable with before calling on someone else for help. As the year goes on, I find myself continuing to use these questions, but not as frequently. The students take more ownership of their thinking and learning and will say things such as "I'm not sure, can you come back to me?" or "Can I ask someone to help me?"

When sharing, the students' ability to articulate their responses changes over time. In the beginning of the year, the students may just restate or repeat what a classmate has said. Slowly, with my guidance, we evolve into rephrasing what a classmate has said in a student's own words. I may ask, "Can someone repeat what Darryl just said?" in the fall, but by the winter, I may ask, "Can someone explain Darryl's thinking in their own words?" The students begin to find ways to communicate their thoughts so others will understand their thinking. If an idea is not clear, the students tend to question each other. The students then begin to articulate each other's thinking and move into agreeing or disagreeing with someone's idea.

Providing Multiple Entry Points

When I plan discussions, I am always aware of the needs of my struggling learners, and I try to create multiple entry points so that the ideas we are discussing are accessible to all my students. Finding entry points for all my learners is time consuming, but an essential part of their learning. I need to foresee the challenges: Is there difficult vocabulary or words we have not discussed yet? Is there an accommodation I can make to assist a child in the activity (breaking the directions down into smaller steps, reviewing strategies, meeting with a small group before or after the minilesson)? Do I have manipulatives available? Are the students' ideas posted on the board or on a strategy chart?

I usually begin a discussion by reviewing what we have been focusing on; then I ask for students to volunteer and walk them through their thinking step-by-step. I often will ask the students to explain why they did what they described, what the numbers represent, how they decided on their strategy, and so on. I will also ask the other students *to repeat or explain* what they have heard. By being very deliberate in these teaching moves, I am trying to model mathematical discourse for the students, especially for those students who are struggling and may have difficulty following the ideas we are discussing. I have general questions in mind to direct the conversation, but I first need to hear what the students are thinking before I can be more purposeful with my questioning. With this guidance, the students can eventually carry on a discussion without my leading. Initially, I do not insist that the students do these things on their own. I am there to assist and model what will eventually be expected of them.

I recently created a bulletin board titled "Math Talk" as another way to provide an entry point for my students who are struggling. This is a place for students to look when they are at a loss for the words to describe their learning. Basically, the board lists a series of conversation starters, such as "Can you repeat that?" "I agree/disagree with . . ." "My idea is similar to . . ." "I don't understand . . ." This Math Talk board has given the struggling students, as well as everyone in the class, a place to refer to when they have difficulty expressing their ideas. Many times students choose not to share or leave blank space on their papers because they aren't sure how to say what they are thinking. I've noticed that students who have more difficulty sharing will at least try to ask a question we have posted to show that they are participating, such as, "Can you say that again?" or "I agree with . . ." (They may possibly repeat what someone has already said, but it is a start to get them to participate.)

Before share time, I may ask a reluctant student to share his findings with me, giving him time to mentally prepare for this. I may also just refer to a student's strategy and make the connection as I think aloud: "This idea is very similar to what I noticed Yasmine doing today. Yasmine, is there something you can add about your thinking?" This allows the student to have the opportunity to state what they did, share something I purposely left out, or just pass.

Keeping Track of Student Thinking and Understanding

Strategy Charts

We keep track of student ideas on chart paper for the students to refer to during the current lesson or for future days. Having these strategy charts available allows my struggling learners to take the time to process the discussions. It also gives me a starting point when meeting individually with a student. I can suggest that a student try the "adding by place" strategy, for example, or have her "explain what Tommy did in your own words." For example, if we were solving $54 + 32$, a student might write:

$$50 + 30 = 80$$
$$4 + 2 = 6$$
$$80 + 6 = 86$$

Questions that I may ask include: Can someone tell me where the 50 and 30 came from? Why did you add the 4 and 2? What does that 4 represent? Can you tell me why we had to add the 80 and 6 in your last step? Where did the 80 and 6 come from? Are you finished? How do you know?

Conference Notes

Keeping notes on conversations I have with my students (see Figure 14–1) aids me in recognizing who may or may not need accommodations or who has an idea or strategy that should be shared with the entire class. I find that these conference notes provide me with a structure for keeping track of my students' growth. My notes include my thoughts and/or observations about a student when I meet with her individually. I may note that I need to check in with someone again, who understands an idea, who is confused, and so on. It also helps me keep track of children who are struggling in similar ways. That way I can meet with a group who are weak in the same area.

117

Making Accommodations: Close to 100

Meeting with a small group that needs help with a particular skill or activity gives the students a safe place to process what is expected of them and to express their ideas with my support. One lesson that often requires accommodations is a game called Close to 100 (Russell et al. 2008m). The students choose 6 cards from a set of digit cards (digits 0–9 and wild cards). Out of these 6 cards, they need to choose 4 cards to make 2, 2-digit numbers that when combined will result in a sum as close to 100 as possible. For example, if a student drew a 2, 7, 6, 0, 3, and 9, they would ideally pick 26 and 73 or 37 and 62.

Before we begin the game, the whole class has a conversation about how to get close to 100. Many students jump right in and start putting together the digits, whether or not they get as close to 100 as possible. Many will discuss the importance of paying attention to the 1s, others will focus on making the 10s equal 90 or 100. This initial conversation can be somewhat overwhelming for the students who do not have a strong number sense background or are not computationally fluent. So, I will meet with a small group before they begin the game to preview it. I help them understand what they need to know to play the game and to reinforce the connections with what they already know about 100. We develop a set of "rules" for them to work with. Usually, we tend to focus just on the 10s and find ways to make 90, 100, and 110. The students record these ideas and create their own strategy chart to use as a reference during the game. We talk about what 100 is and then different ways to make 100. (We've already done lots of work using a 100 chart, building 100, working with 10s, moving up and down both the number line and the 100 chart by 10s.) The students usually begin by naming the ways with which they are familiar, such as: 50 + 50, 60 + 40, 70 + 30, and so on. These are then listed on one strategy chart. They may also add 25 + 75 or 99 + 1, 98 + 2, 97 + 3, and so on. Expressions such as these will be placed on an additional chart. Below is an excerpt from a conversation I had with three students who were struggling when moving around on the 100 chart.

TEACHER: We have done a lot of work around 100. Can you name some number sentences using 2 numbers that get us to 100? [*A number line and 100 chart are accessible to the students.*]
STEPHANIE: I know that 50 + 50 = 100.
DAQUAN: Oh, 70 + 30 and 20 + 80 and 60 + 40.
TEACHER: How did you know so many so quickly?
DAQUAN: Because it's like getting to 10.
TEACHER: Can you explain what you mean by that?
DAQUAN: 7 + 3 makes 10 so 70 + 30 makes 100.

TEACHER: Stephanie, can you explain or give another example about what Daquan is talking about?

STEPHANIE: Um, I think so. I think that if 1 + 9 is 10, then 10 + 90 has to be 100. Is that right?

TEACHER: Yes! Now, it seems like we have created a list that uses multiples of 10 to get to 100. I'm wondering if you know any other ways to make 100.

ANDREA: Do you mean like using money? Cuz, I know that 25 cents and 75 cents is equal to $1.00.

TEACHER: Yes, that is what I was thinking about. How do we write that on this chart? What would the number sentence be?

ANDREA: 25 + 75 = 100.

DAQUAN: I'm thinking about something. I think we could add a whole bunch to that list because 99 + 1 is 100 and 98 + 2 is 100. It keeps going.

TEACHER: You all have had some really good ideas for our charts on ways to make 100. We are going to play a game that uses the ideas we have talked about today. When we meet with the rest of the class, I want you to share some of the ideas we have just come up with. These ideas will help you with the game.

Practicing the Game

We play the game more than once to allow students to move from a trial-and-error approach to eventually developing their own efficient strategies. During the first game, I tend to join the groups and just listen in on their conversations. I record the strategies students are sharing with their partners as well as how they are solving their problem. I make note if a student is referring to the strategy charts and whether a student is strategically choosing digits that get close to 100 or whether the digit selection is random. I keep these conference notes to guide the math discourse at the end of class as well as to prepare for the next time we play Close to 100 and for my lessons about addition strategies (see Figure 14–1 on page 120). These conference notes help me guide math conversations and allow me to prepare for my struggling students.

Facilitating Students' Strategies

I carefully choose children to share during our discussion time. When listening in on their conversations, I seek out students who can offer a strategy, a success, or a challenge they faced that may help others when playing the game. This can be an opportune time for a struggling learner to participate, having a specific problem or thought to share.

Stephanie	(worked with before the game)/(partnered with Kavon) cards chosen were pulled from the deck in same order; choosing randomly; combining strategies are good though; partner appears to be getting frustrated when explaining his own strategies
Ana	(working with Sierra) no problem combining numbers but appears to be picking cards randomly; partner is trying to explain her strategies for picking cards but not finding the best words
Shyquell	seems to be relying solely on the 100s chart and counting by 1s
Luis	explains strategy without prompting
Andrea	(worked with before the game) miscalculates the difference from 100, but chooses good cards
Sierra	finds good combinations, but struggles to explain to her partner why she has the best combination (partner was just picking any numbers)

Figure 14–1. Conference Notes Excerpt

Within a few days, the group plays the game again, with a more strategic thought process. Again, referring to my conference notes, I look for students who may need extra support. I decide, for example, whether to put a struggling learner with a partner who can explain the strategy behind choosing particular digits or someone who can guide the selection of cards without giving away the answer. I also look out for the students who can work independently so I can assist those who need more support.

During one particular game, I noticed that Stephanie and Ana (both working with different partners) were successful when adding their two numbers but had difficulty choosing the best digits. It appeared that they both were choosing the cards randomly; the cards were placed near each other, they were taken out of the deck in a particular order, or they saw two digits that got close to 100, such as 8 and 9 and thought that would be a good starting point. So, I decided on day two to have them work together with my guidance. I allowed them to get started before checking in with them.

TEACHER: Hi, girls. How are we doing?

STEPHANIE AND ANA: Good!

TEACHER: I know that when we played this game the other day, you both kept getting really high scores. You know the object of the game is to get as close to 100 as possible. Why do you think you were getting such high scores?

STEPHANIE: I guess I didn't get really good cards.

ANA: Yeah, me either.

TEACHER: Well, sometimes that does happen. You might have all high cards in front of you or even all low cards. Let's look at what you have in front of you now. What can we do? [*cards in the order as they were in front of the students: Stephanie has 7, 5, 4, 2, 9, 3; Ana has 5, 9, 9, 2, 0, 3*]

ANA: I see 92 and that is really close to 100. So I think I can use that.

TEACHER: If you use 92, how much more does it take to get to 100?

ANA: [*counting on the 100 chart*] 8.

TEACHER: What should we do?

ANA: I don't have an 8, maybe I should use 3.

At this point I wondered if Ana saw that she could have added 5, instead of 3, to get even closer, but I was pleased with what she had done. I needed to keep watching because I noticed that she used the cards in the order that they were in front of her. Would she have chosen the 5 if it was in the same place as the 3? It was also important for me to explicitly ask Ana how much more to get to 100. This is a strategy that she can work with when left to play the game with her partner.

TEACHER: OK, Stephanie, it's your turn now. Ana got close to 100. Ana, how many more did you need to get to 100?

ANA: 5 more.

TEACHER: Stephanie, what can you think about?

STEPHANIE: I see the 92 like Ana had and the 3 she used, but I don't have a 0 so I don't think that will work.

TEACHER: I like the way you are looking at all the digits. You can move the cards around if you need to.

STEPHANIE: [*looking over to the strategy chart*] I see 75. That means I need 25 more for 100.

TEACHER: Ana, can you tell me how Stephanie knew she needed 25 more if she started with 75?

ANA: I saw her look at that [*pointing to the strategy chart*]. It says that 75 + 25 = 100.

TEACHER: Ana you did something similar. You chose 92 and then counted 8 more to get to 100.

STEPHANIE: I don't have 25, but I could do 23. No, wait 24. That gets me really close.

TEACHER: Could you use 23?

STEPHANIE: I could but then I'm not that close; 24 gets me closer. It's only 1 away from 25.

TEACHER: Stephanie, does the order of your cards matter when you are looking at them? What I mean is, do you need to make two-digit numbers in the order you are looking at in front of you?

STEPHANIE: No, that's why you said to move them around. At first I didn't see the 24 because the 3 was after, but then I looked more.

TEACHER: So how close to 100 did you get?

ANA: 75 and 24 makes 99, so 1 away. I'm a little closer than Stephanie.

TEACHER: Girls, you did a great job. I want you to think about these strategies when you are choosing the four cards. If you select a number, think about how far away you are from 100 and see if you have something close. You can also look at the Ways to Make 100 chart to help you get started.

Assessing Understanding

I noticed that Stephanie was able to manipulate the numbers into a position other than what was in front of her. At first I wasn't sure because she chose 75 and 23, which came in that order (7, 5, 4, 2, 9, 3). She then selected the 4 to get even closer and didn't need to move the cards in front of her. But, I did explicitly point that out to her that the cards *could* be moved around, and perhaps that made her more aware. Stephanie also looked back to the Ways to Make 100 chart that we had created in the small group before the whole-group lesson. Ana had not been in that group and I made a mental note that she could probably benefit from the additional practice.

Sharing Strategies

After my intervention with the girls, I felt that they would be able to present their ideas to the whole class, so I did ask them to share. I was confident that they would be prepared because of the conversation about strategies we had while they were working together. As they shared, they focused on referring back to the strategy chart to get ideas. I was hoping that by having these two students point this out, others would be more likely to look back at the chart. Ana shared how Stephanie moved the cards around to find her numbers. Stephanie was able to follow up by saying that moving the cards helped her see how close to 100 she could get, looking at the 10s first and then moving over to the 1s. Verbalizing these important strategies represented real progress for these girls. Perhaps the next game, Ana will attempt the strategy of moving the cards around as well as determining how many more she needs to get to 100.

Growth Over Time

Through repeatedly interacting with my reluctant learners in small groups and helping them prepare to share in the whole group, I usually notice growth in these students' abilities to express mathematical ideas. By the end of the year, I only have to ask one or two questions before the students are able to keep the conversation going on their own. When I ask one of my reluctant learners to share his thinking, that student can usually tell the group why a particular strategy was chosen and possibly even offer a second way to solve the problem. I may also ask the rest of the class to explain *in their own words* (a difficult skill to develop) what was shared, and to connect and compare students' strategies.

The following is an excerpt from a conversation that took place at the end of the school year as we reflected on our learning. It's clear that the students are now used to and comfortable with the math conversations we have in our classroom. It takes a long time to get to this point.

June

TEACHER: Throughout this past year, we have done a lot of talking in math. I remember how hard it was for you in the beginning of the year. How do you feel about this now and why do you think we have these conversations?

DAQUAN: I think we talk so that we can talk through our math strategies. Like if we didn't know how to solve 7×8, we could just think about this out loud.

ANDREA: I thought that math in the third grade was hard, but we make a lot of connections to what we did in the second grade. That's what I like about our talking.

ANTHONY: In second grade, I just did the math and I didn't really know why. Now I do math and get to explain my ideas and we talk about it to understand it more. Everything has to do with math, we tell time, we can measure how much we walk.

KAVON: When we talk, it basically helps us learn more. But, basically we are helping others learn too. I might know something someone else doesn't. What I say might help someone. Sometimes I get ideas from other people, too.

TEACHER: What made you comfortable in the class to talk about the math you do?

ANDREA: We do a lot of talking, but I think it's OK, I got used to it. I think that I learned more this year because of it.

STEPHANIE: Yeah and it's OK to make a mistake. Like, I might solve a problem and get the wrong answer, but I don't have to be embarrassed. No one will laugh. I used to be scared though.

DAQUAN: The teacher wouldn't like that.

STEPHANIE: I also know that I can ask for help when I'm stuck.

YASMINE: We talk when we work together, too.

MYREEK: I think we talk a lot because we might help someone else who doesn't get it. I might know how to solve a problem with a picture, but someone else might be able to tell me what kind of math sentence to write.

Stephanie and Myreek are two students who were hesitant to share for the majority of the year. By June, they felt confident enough to say that they weren't sure about something a classmate shared or to share their own thinking even if it was pretty basic when compared to what others were contributing. Myreek was able to ask for help to write an equation to match his picture. Although the majority of the students may not be drawing a picture to show their thinking, Myreek felt secure enough to point out how others could help him. Stephanie's thought about feeling embarrassed is something that many reluctant learners experience. They don't want to share if they know that they don't get the math or if they are afraid of being laughed at. It's important for me to encourage everyone to participate, emphasizing how the class can work together to solve problems. Ideally, a struggling student can contribute something to the discussion that other students can then build on, or the struggling student can reiterate what was said or done to feel she has had an important part in the math discourse.

One student ended this end-of-year conversation by saying "the lightbulb goes off." I asked her what she meant by that and she said, "If we didn't come to the rug, there would be no lightbulbs. We help each other understand the math. We don't tell each other answers, but try to ask questions, like you do. Then the lightbulb happens; we can make our own connections."

Reflections

The process of supporting reluctant learners to participate comfortably in group discussions is complex and multifaceted. Carefully building the mathematics community is the first step. The students need to feel that they are a vital part of the learning environment, helping each other and sharing their knowledge. In the beginning, I use specific questions to establish expectations and to encourage participation. As students become accustomed to our mathematical discourse, they are able to ask for help independently, and I no longer need to pose these questions. I become the facilitator as opposed to having a large part in the conversation.

As a teacher, I know that I need to find ways for all my students to contribute and become valuable participants in any and all mathematical discussions. Foreseeing challenges and finding entry points for all my students to be part of this learning environment is critical to a successful year. I plan ahead by anticipating challenges, finding entry points for all my students, and having accommodations ready when needed. For example, I might meet with struggling students before the whole-group lesson to give them a preview of what we will be discussing, or immediately following the minilesson to do a quick check-in. I review the directions and/or strategies already given, and I can also answer more specific questions they may have. Often, I pair my reluctant learners together so I can work with them, help them identify the strategies they are using, and prepare them to share their ideas in front of the group.

Carefully choosing who shares and keeping track of students' thinking can help get a mathematical conversation going in the right direction. This allows the discussion to stay on target. The strategy charts I post around the classroom for all students to refer to can be particularly helpful as an independent starting place for the reluctant learners. It also gives the entire math community a common language when discussing ideas. The students need to feel safe and be willing to take risks for them to make connections and grow as mathematical learners.

15

Talking About Square Numbers

Small-Group Discussion of Multiples and Factors

Dee Watson

> I'm not here for me, I'm here for you so if there's something you don't understand, I'm here for that.

> I've been a fourth grader myself. I know some of the parts that can get confusing. I want you to tell me when it gets confusing so we can talk about it.

These are some of the things I tell my class to get them comfortable with discussion in my mathematics class. I emphasize discussion in my fourth-grade classroom throughout the year for many reasons: to communicate high expectations for learning and behavior, to offer opportunities for students to take responsibility for their own learning, and to encourage the exchange of mathematical ideas. These open exchanges build a sense of trust in our classroom. I want all of the students, including my students with special needs, to feel safe, take risks, admit confusion, and share ideas and insights. In my experience, all students are able to enter into discussions if I make the rules and routines for the discussions explicit, if I build the community so the students are engaged and feel safe, and if I provide a variety of models and representations to make the mathematical concepts accessible.

Setting the Stage

In the beginning of the year, our discussions set the stage for the mathematical conversations we will have throughout the year, so it is important that behavioral norms are set early. The students and I together determined the following rules for behavior in small groups.

I will look at the speaker.
I will listen to the speaker.
I will participate in discussions.

I will talk about my math work.

I will ask questions when I am confused.

I will focus and concentrate on math.

I will solve the problem on my own or with my partner, then check in with my team.

In addition, I let my students know that I take their ideas seriously and that their ideas and opinions will shape how our classroom community gets developed. For example, when I was disappointed in my students' performance on an assessment, I shared my concerns with them about the scores and solicited their ideas about how to improve. I wanted them to take ownership of the problem. We had an earnest conversation and students came up with good ideas, such as changing their seating to help them work with partners who would facilitate serious work. This discussion and others had a positive impact on students' work habits and reinforced to the students that I have high expectations for their learning and behavior.

Working Through Confusions: What Are Square Numbers?

Although I was pleased in general about the class' attitudes and behavior, I still had concerns about some of the struggling students. One of my strategies with students who struggle with concepts is to bring them together in a small group to uncover their thinking and work through confusions. I want to reinforce the ideas that have come up in our large group, give them time to state their ideas and ask questions, and prepare them to contribute to the subsequent whole-group discussion.

Generally, within the first month of school, I am able to determine which students need extra support. Initially, I use data from assessments to make this determination. For some students, it is a language issue, so inviting them to be a part of the small group not only enables me to review the lesson but also allows them to articulate their concerns in a smaller group without feeling the pressure of a million eyes on them. For other students, some foundational understanding is missing, and in our small group we are able to use various models and visuals that will help these students make connections to understanding certain concepts on a deeper level.

This year, my small intervention group included three girls and two boys. Two were English language learners, one of whom had processing difficulties. The other three students had demonstrated some misunderstandings about the math concepts we had been studying and struggled to keep up with the unit. One of my goals with this group was to get all of their ideas out on the table and pose strategic questions that surfaced what they did understand and allowed them to grapple with examples to build their understanding. I wanted them to know that knowing mathematics entails being able to explain ideas. Another goal was to encourage them to let me know when they are confused.

We had been talking as a class about square numbers. Although the students in the small intervention group were able to name some square numbers, I was not sure that they had an understanding of what a square number means or whether they could use a visual representation to illustrate square numbers and represent how square numbers increase. So I decided to focus on this during one of our small-group sessions.

I began the small-group session with a question from the state assessment about identifying which numbers are square. I wanted the students to practice with these ideas but in a new context, so that they would make better sense of them. I began by eliciting ideas they already had so we could build toward a deeper understanding.

> MALIA: The numbers are 25, 81, and 49.
> TEACHER: Dante, are they all square numbers?
> MALIA: No . . .
> TEACHER: Wait a minute; I want to hear from Dante. Which is a square number, and how do you know? [*Dante looks unsure.*] And remember it's OK to say, "I'm not sure" or "I'm stuck." Dante?
> DANTE: [*softly*] I'm stuck.
> TEACHER: You're stuck. Thank you for telling us that you're stuck. OK, Kendrick what do you think? Are they all square numbers?
> KENDRICK: Yes . . .
> TEACHER: Can you prove it? [*Kendrick mumbles.*] Dante has already told us that he is stuck, so if you're stuck too, you can say so. It's OK.
> KENDRICK: I'm stuck.

I was very pleased the children could express their confusion, especially Kendrick. Kendrick is a very sweet, yet quiet boy who rarely contributes to our group discussions, so to hear him voice something at all was exciting. I had also been working with him in a small group after school where I encouraged him to share some of his thoughts and even confusions, so I was pleased that his courage had stretched to where he could voice something with a different group of students.

> TEACHER: What is it about those numbers that makes you think that they are square numbers?
> KENDRICK: Because all of them are high numbers.

I was encouraged that Kendrick took another risk to express an idea, although it was not correct. I could have told Kendrick that he was wrong, but I decided to see what the other students were thinking so I could listen to what they were all understanding. I chose instead to rephrase what he was saying so that in hearing his idea expressed back to him, he could process for himself whether his idea was reasonable.

TEACHER: Because all of them are high numbers. So, OK, at least you've given me some kind of a reason to work with. So that means to you, any number that is low is not a square number? Is what you're saying? So a square number has to be a high number is what you're saying? [*Kendrick nods.*] OK.

TEACHER: Sharonda, what do you think? Are these square numbers?

SHARONDA: I think one of them is a square number because I think 49 is a square number.

TEACHER: And prove how you know that 49 is a square number.

SHARONDA: I know that because I remember once a lady told me that 7 was a square number and like if you multiply 7, 7 times, you'll get 49 or when you count by 7s to like 1,000, 49 will be one of those numbers. That is how I know that 49 is a square number.

TEACHER: Hmm . . . what do you think, Malia?

MALIA: I think all of them are square numbers because 25 is when you multiply 5 by 5, and when you multiply 9 by 9 you get 81, and when you multiply 7 by 7 you get 49, and so like the number 5 and you multiply it again like 5 × 5 gives you a square number . . .

TEACHER: So what can you tell me about how to *find* a square number?

GIRLS: Ooh [*raising their hands*].

SHARONDA: Yeah. Like when we are looking for factors of a number . . . and like 1 times 12 equals 12, and we're like looking for numbers that are factors of 12, or like sometimes when we are doing 25, and we do, like, 1 times 25 and we do 5, and we ask what can go with 5 and we say 5, and that makes it a square number.

TEACHER: Hmm . . . anyone else want to add to that? Because these are all great ideas, but I want to hear some more. Anyone else have something they want to add?

CHELSEA: I think 25 is a square number like Malia because 5 is a square number.

TEACHER: [*to Sharonda*] You think 5 is a square number too, and you think 7 is a square . . .

SHARONDA: I think all numbers are square numbers.

TEACHER: All numbers are square numbers, is what you're saying?

SHARONDA: Yes, they are.

Sharonda had some kernels of understanding; she seemed to understand that you can square all numbers, but I was not sure she understood that squaring a number is not the same thing as a square number. I was also not sure she was clear about the difference between factors and square numbers. I also noted that the students had mastered some of their multiplication facts, something we could build on.

TEACHER: What do you guys think?

MALIA: I want to say that when you add a number by the same number, you get a square number.

TEACHER: When you add a number by the . . .

MALIA: No! When you multiply a number by the same number, I mean.

TEACHER: OK, when you multiply a number by the same number? [*Malia nods.*] Why?

MALIA: Because, like, if you do an array,[1] you will have the same amount on the top and the same amount on the side.

TEACHER: So, if I have an array, and I have the same amount on the top and the same amount on the side, and you're talking about the dimensions right? If all the dimensions are the same, what shape do I end up with?

MALIA: With a square!

Here, Malia was able to self-correct. When she first said, "When you add a number," she changed to "When you multiply a number by the same number." I was pleased to see her being able to reflect on what she said. I restated her comment using the correct terminology, *dimensions*, because I want students to use precise language during our math discussions. Malia was able to recall the visual representation of an array to help her think about square numbers. I realized that this might be helpful for the other members of the group, so I decided to pursue a discussion of the array representation.

TEACHER: So, why do you think a square number is called a square number?

MALIA: Because when you multiply a number by the same number, you end up with a square?

CHELSEA: Like 12 times 12 is 144 . . . is it going to become a square?

TEACHER: You tell me . . . Does a 12-by-12 array look like a square?

MALIA: It will!

CHELSEA: Yeah . . .

TEACHER: Why? How do you know?

CHELSEA: Because it looks like a square.

---

[1]An array is an area model for multiplication that consists of arrangement of objects, pictures, or numbers in rows and columns.

TEACHER: Oh . . . so if I draw my best square on the board . . . one thing we know about a square is that it has . . .

ALL [*Kendrick loudest*]: Four equal sides.

TEACHER: Very good! You're right Kendrick, 4 equal sides . . . right? If I draw a 1-by-1 array, what do I get?

ALL: It's going to be 1 square . . .

TEACHER: Oh! So then $1 \times 1 = 1$, which makes 1 . . .

ALL: A square number!

The array representation seemed to help further their understanding, so I decided the students were ready to revisit some of their initial confusions. It is important to figure out what representations are meaningful to the students, as opposed to my conducting a "lesson" on arrays.

I was also pleased that by seeing the arrays, Kendrick was able to offer an observation about the attributes of a square. Once he made that connection to arrays, I wanted to return to his original assertion about square numbers being big. Even though he was incorrect, I wanted to validate his willingness to take a risk and to use this discussion to clarify other students' ideas. I said, "So let's talk about Kendrick's idea about all square numbers having to be big numbers . . . what do you think, Kendrick? Do you still think the same? Because 1 is not a big number." I decided to start from a small number and build it, hoping Kendrick would see the number pattern.

TEACHER: So what about a 2-by-2 array . . . will I get a big number?

CHELSEA: That's going to be 4!

TEACHER: So if I write 2×2, that will give me 4, which is . . .

ALL: A square number!

TEACHER: Oh, yeah, because it makes a square! OK . . . since you know this, you can tell me what the next square number will be!

ALL: Three!

ALL: [*except Chelsea*] No! Nine!

CHELSEA: Oh, yeah!

TEACHER: So the next square number is 9?

MALIA: Because it will be a 3-by-3 array . . .

TEACHER: OK. And the next square number will be . . .

MALIA: Sixteen!

TEACHER: And how did you know that?

MALIA: Because 4×4 is 16.

SHARONDA: Yeah, because 4×4 is 16, and if you put the dimensions in and you count the squares in the array you'll get 16, see . . . $4 + 4$ is 8 and then $8 + 8$ is 16!

MALIA: 25!

TEACHER: So, Malia, even though she didn't wait for us, thinks she knows the next square number . . . is 25 . . .

MALIA: [*laughing*] No . . . No . . .

TEACHER: So, she's going to have to prove it! Do you agree?

SHARONDA: No, because after 3 is actually 4 instead of 5.

MALIA: After 4 what goes after it?

SHARONDA: 5 . . .

MALIA: And what is 5 × 5?

SHARONDA: 25! So, if you put . . . oh, sorry! [*laughing*]

TEACHER: Sharonda is having a moment there . . . so 1, 4, 9, 16, 25 . . .

I sensed that they were working on some important ideas. The students thought back to what they knew about squares and how a square figure connects to a square number—that a square number is a number multiplied by itself. They were very excited and engaged. I was pleased that they were thinking beyond just answering the question to being curious about what was actually going on. I constantly encourage my students to think like mathematicians—to be curious about why numbers work the way they do—so to see this happening was quite thrilling for me.

I decided that it was time to review and solidify their understanding, revisiting the array model, but I did not explore what was happening to the array each time the dimensions increase by 1 (e.g., why the pattern goes from 9 to 16 to 25). Although Malia seemed ready for this discussion, I knew that Kendrick and others were not quite ready, and I did not want them to lose focus.

TEACHER: So, is it clear what makes a square number? Think about the shape of a square—equal sides. So 1 by 1, equals 1, which is a square number, and 2 by 2 makes 4, a square number. So, let's look at those numbers again. Is 25 a square number?

ALL: Yes!

TEACHER: What makes 25 a square number?

ALL: 5 times 5!

TEACHER: Which is the same as 5 squared! Remember that, too?

SHARONDA AND MALIA: Oh, yeah!

TEACHER: How about 81?

KENDRICK: That's 9 squared!

TEACHER: Oh, Kendrick, that's very good!

I was pleased with the contribution that Kendrick made during the discussion. Because he is quiet and soft spoken, he sometimes tends to get lost in the crowd during our large-group discussions. And because he also has processing problems, I was especially excited that he was following along with this discussion. Two months ago, I would not have expected him to share as much! It was good that he was able to apply his knowledge of multiplication facts to this context.

SHARONDA: I've got a question . . . How come you put that little 2 on the corner of the 9?

MALIA: Because it means you're multiplying that number by that same number!

TEACHER: So what about 49?

SHARONDA: That's 7 squared!

TEACHER: So are they all square numbers?

SHARONDA: No!

OTHERS: Yes! Yes!

SHARONDA: Oh, Yes!

TEACHER: Are we sure? I am hearing yes and no . . .

SHARONDA: Yes, we just proved it!

Analyzing the Session

The talk we engaged in and the use of the array model helped the students clarify their ideas. After each small-group session, I took mental notes about what each student seemed to understand and where I might go in the next session. From our interactions, I understood what they already knew, so I was able to call on them in the large group when the discussion was at a point when I knew they could contribute successfully. After this session, I knew that I might want to work with Malia about what she noticed about the square numbers increasing (1, 4, 9, 16, 25). I knew I would follow up with Kendrick in a miniconference to review why or why not a number is square. Sharonda did not seem sure of her understanding, so I needed to check in with her, too, to determine what she understood or was still confused about. I was pleased, however, at her use of language when she said, "We just proved it"—it gave me an inkling that she was beginning to understand that mathematical talk involves explaining and justifying your ideas.

I continued to work with this same small group of students, and most appeared to be making progress in understanding what problems are asking and expressing their mathematical thinking. My goal was for them to take what they learned in the small group and feel more and more confident about sharing in the large group.

Contributing to the Whole-Group Discussion

My goal for all of these students was that they fully participate in our math community. It is important to me that children are provided opportunities to articulate their understandings—fragile though they may be—and to be able to have discourse with their peers in a manner that provides further understanding of concepts that may be tenuous. The first step is encouraging them to express themselves in the small group. Once I can get them to say what they are thinking, it gives me a starting place as a teacher to assess what they know, what questions to ask, and what representations and examples to offer. My notes (mental or otherwise) from these small-group conversations allow me to plan how to include these students when we have the large-group discussions. I can refer to ideas they talked about in the small group. For example, I could ask Kendrick, "Do you remember when you talked what you know about 81? Do you remember what you said?"

If we are talking about something that I think is still confusing to them, I can make sure to rephrase the ideas with words and representations that will help clarify the ideas/concepts. Because we have established a community where students feel safe, I can say something like, "Chelsea, did you understand what Kenny was saying?" or "Malia and Dante, make sure you pay attention to what Larnelle is saying. He's talking about how you can decide if a number is a square number. This is something you weren't sure about. Remember?"

I try to facilitate conversation so that students make connections among the strategies that their classmates are sharing. I also know that students will support each other when they get stuck. When we solved multiplication problems, I validated skip counting as one method we can use because I knew that Kendrick and a few others were comfortable solving problems that way. During one class conversation, we were trying to solve the problem 38×21. Kendrick was trying to come up with a shorter way to solve the problem without writing all of the multiples of 38. He understood that the 10th multiple would help him, but thought that he could continue skip counting from there, instead of making the connection that he could do another 10th multiple and have the 20th multiple of 38. Marcus asked Kendrick, "Remember yesterday's before-school work assignment? When we had to find the 10th multiple of 15? Well, if you know the 10th multiple of 38, then you can figure out to solve 38×21. You know the 10th multiple of 38, right? Then you know the 20th multiple because of how 10 is related to 20 . . . right? 10 is half of 20, right?" When Kendrick didn't respond, we paused and used an example of something he already knew—10×10.

> TEACHER: If you know 10×10, how will you find out 10×20?
> KENDRICK: Oh, that's just another 10×10, then you put them together . . . so that's $10 \times 10 = 100$ and another 10×10, which is 100, so all together that's 200.
> TEACHER: Right! So now use that idea to think about what Marcus said about the 20th multiple?

KENDRICK: [*initially looks confused, then light dawns*] Oh, I get it! So, do 38×10 and another 38×10 and that will be 38×20!

All of us were absolutely delighted that Kendrick was able to make this powerful connection. His thinking would not have developed without the conversations that went on in the class and the interest that Marcus took in encouraging the reasoning of his fellow classmate.

Reflections

I know for myself how powerful it is to talk about math with someone. I get clarification, I learn new strategies, and I can build on my understandings. Because discourse is such an empowering tool to understanding mathematics, it is the focal point of all my math sessions. Establishing an atmosphere that makes it safe for students to take risks is key at the beginning of the year. Having regular mathematics discussions allows my students and me to support each other in building mathematical understanding. It allows my students who struggle to practice expressing their ideas, and it helps me understand what they know and what they need to learn.

16 💿

Kindergartners Talk About Counting

The Counting Jar

Introduction

This video shows Lillian Pinet facilitating a discussion with her kindergarten class about an activity called the Counting Jar from the *Investigations in Number, Data, and Space* curriculum (Russell et al. 2008o). During this discussion, Lillian highlights students' counting strategies and involves the whole group in helping a student recognize and correct a counting mistake.

Counting is the main focus of the number work students do in kindergarten and is an important part of the work students do in first and second grade. Students come to kindergarten with a wide range of experiences and understanding of numbers and counting. All students need many opportunities to count, to observe counting, and even to talk about counting to make sense of and learn the action, concepts, and skills of counting.

The Counting Jar is an activity in which students work on multiple aspects of counting. The activity begins with the teacher placing a set of 5 to 20 objects (cubes, golf balls, plastic animals, and so on) inside a clear jar. A few students at a time work on the three different parts of this activity:

1. Students individually count the number of objects in the jar.
2. They make a representation on paper to show how many objects are in the jar.
3. They create a set of other objects with the same number of objects as in the jar. This equivalent set is stored on a paper plate or in a plastic bag or cup.

After everyone in the class has a chance to do a particular counting jar, the students often share their representations and their counting strategies in a whole-group discussion.

In many classrooms, this activity is continued throughout the year with the teacher varying the number and types of objects each time. As students do this activity throughout the year, it supports their growth in understanding counting and developing their counting skills. It gives them an opportunity to independ-

136

ently count within a structure that becomes very familiar. When doing the Counting Jar, students work on a few different aspects of counting: counting a set of objects, representing a count, creating a specific-size set, and connecting the same quantity of two different kinds of objects.

Some students may find this activity challenging. They may have difficulty figuring out a strategy for keeping track of what they have already counted in the jar and what they have not counted. Other students may be able to count the number of objects but not know how to represent the count on paper. Still others might find it difficult to create an equivalent set of objects.

As you watch the video, consider the following questions. You might want to take notes on what you notice.

- How does the teacher use this discussion to help students build an understanding of counting?
- How does she structure this discussion?
- What questions does she ask?
- What statements does she make?

Classroom discussions can be an important part of supporting students who struggle with mathematics. Classroom discussions are an opportunity for students to hear their classmates' ideas or strategies. Students might hear something that helps them with an idea they are struggling with or hear a strategy that might work for them. Discussions are an opportunity for students to practice communicating their ideas and to think through their own ideas, strategies, or even confusions. They are also an opportunity for teachers to focus on specific ideas or strategies they think are important for students to examine or that they think might be difficult for students. However, it can be a challenge for teachers to include a wide range of learners in whole-class discussions in a meaningful way.

In this video, you see Lillian Pinet using this discussion as a learning opportunity for her students and trying to involve all her students in the discussion. She does this through the decisions she makes about which students she asks to share their work, how she asks them to share their work, how she responds to a student's mistake, and the way she involves the whole class in helping this student understand her mistake.

Examining the Video Footage

In the first interview, Lillian says she decided to have Ricardo share his work first because she knew "he would have a clear strategy to share." As Ricardo shares his strategy, Lillian helps him communicate it clearly by asking him to explain out loud and show in detail each of his steps. For example, she asks him to show how he counted, to count out loud, and to explain how he used the number line to help him. By sharing his work, Ricardo has an opportunity to think through and articulate his strategies and practice communicating clearly his ideas to others. As Ricardo shares his strategy, Lillian also repeats out loud what he did in each of his steps, helping the other students get a clear picture of everything he did. The other students benefit from hearing and looking at Ricardo's work because it might give them some new ideas about strategies for counting (for example, when creating an equivalent set, he shows his strategy of taking one shell out of the jar and then putting one object in the cup to match it) or it might affirm some of the strategies they were already using.

Lillian next decides to have Janiris share her work. When Janiris shares her work, it is clear she has made some counting mistakes. Each piece of her work shows a different amount and those amounts do not match the quantity of objects in the jar. When she counts out loud, she skips some numbers. Lillian does not simply tell Janiris she made a mistake nor does she tell her what the mistake is. Instead, she uses Janiris' mistake as a learning opportunity for Janiris and for the rest of the students. As Lillian says in the second interview, "If I helped her realize she made a mistake, it would kind of get into her mind and she would think about it next time she was working in the Counting Jar or anything else. If you just tell them, then I think it becomes just a one-deal thing . . . it doesn't become their own. The ownership part of it . . . by her realizing her mistake . . . it was more of her physically working through it."

Lillian makes this a learning opportunity for all the students through the questions she asks, the ideas she focuses on, and the way she supports Janiris in working through her mistake. In the same way she asked Richardo, she asks Janiris to show how she counted the shells. She does not just tell Janiris that she made a mistake. Instead, Lillian has Janiris compare the amounts she recorded on paper and the amount in her equivalent set to the amount she counted in the jar. Lillian helps Janiris count again and then has all the class count. This gives everyone practice counting and provides Janiris practice with the correct counting sequence. Lillian asks others to share strategies they thought Janiris could use to make sure she got the same amount. This involves other students in the discussion, and it helps Janiris to hear strategies from her peers. Lillian also involves students with a range of understanding of counting in the discussion of Janiris' mistake. She asks the group how many more Janiris would need to have the correct amount (a challenging question for a kindergartner) and asks the student who responds to explain his strategy. Another student simply restates the mistake Janiris made, perhaps trying to process it, and Lillian affirms his statement.

Because of the way Lillian structures the discussion of Janiris' mistake, Janiris and the other students are able to learn more about counting and their counting skills. Janiris is able to identify the mistakes herself, which might help her in her future counting. By listening to her classmates help her count, she could hear the correct counting sequence. The discussion might also help her understand that it is OK to make mistakes and that one can learn from mistakes. Other students might be making similar mistakes and might benefit from watching Janiris work through those mistakes. They might also benefit from counting aloud with the whole group.

Throughout the video, there is evidence that Lillian has worked hard to create a community of math learners in her classroom and that there are clear expectations for how students participate in a discussion. As each child shares her work, the other students watch her closely and seem to be listening carefully. Just as the teacher treats each student's ideas respectfully, the students are expected to treat each other's ideas respectfully, but are also asked to give suggestions to help any student who is having difficulty. Mistakes are not viewed as something to be ashamed of but instead are seen as learning opportunities. Because of the way Lillian has structured discussions and the expectations she has clearly communicated, her young students are able express their ideas to others, listen to each others ideas, and learn from each other.

17 ⊙

What Do We Do with the Remainder?

Fourth Graders Discuss Division

Introduction

This video shows Dee Watson leading a discussion about a division word problem with a class of fourth-grade students in October. The students work through one strategy for solving the problem and, through their discussion of the strategy, figure out what to do about the remainder in the problem.

The students in the video discuss the following problem from the *Investigations in Number, Data, and Space* curriculum: There are 36 people who are taking a trip in some small vans. Each van holds 8 people. How many vans will they need? (Economopoulos et al. 2004). To solve this problem, students are asked to figure what is happening in the problem, decide on a strategy to solve it, and then decide what they need to do with the leftover people. Therefore, although the answer to the problem $36 \div 8$ is 4 with a remainder of 4 or $4\frac{1}{2}$, the answer to this word problem is 5 because an extra bus is needed for the 4 leftover people.

As you watch the video consider the following questions. You might want to take notes on what you notice.

- How does the teacher use this discussion to help students build an understanding of division?
- How does she structure this discussion?
- What questions does she ask?
- What statements does she make?

Classroom discussions can be an important part of supporting students who struggle with mathematics. Classroom discussions are an opportunity for students to hear their classmates' ideas and strategies. Students might hear something that helps them with an idea they are struggling with or hear a strategy that might work for them. Discussions are an opportunity for students to practice communicating their ideas and to think through their own ideas, strategies, or even confusions. They are also an opportunity for teachers to focus on specific ideas or strategies they think are important for students to examine or that they think might be difficult for students. However, it can be a challenge for teachers to include a wide range of learners in whole-class discussions in a meaningful way.

Throughout this video, Dee Watson works hard to help all her students build an understanding of division as they discuss a specific problem. She does so by:

- thoughtfully selecting a strategy to discuss that she thinks is accessible to a wide range of learning and carefully deciding how they talk through and record the strategy
- responding respectfully and with interest to each student's ideas whether they are correct or not
- asking questions about the specifics of the ideas students share

Examining the Video Footage

In this discussion, Dee Watson presents a problem to the students and they work on solving it together. Students share their ideas about what they think is going on in the problem, how they might approach the problem, and what they think the answer is. The way Dee structures and facilitates the discussion helps surface what students are understanding and not yet understanding about division. Dee builds the discussion from the students' ideas. This allows her to hear what they are thinking right away. She treats each student's responses with equal seriousness and consistently asks them clarifying questions about what they said. This seems to communicate to each student that there is something important in what they are saying and to consider whether or not what they are saying makes sense. By asking clarifying questions, Dee is able to dig into what their statements indicate about what they are understanding and what they do not yet understand.

In the first interview, Dee talks about her decision to begin the discussion by pursuing a repeated subtraction strategy suggested by a student. She chose this strategy because she knew that it might be accessible to other students who struggle with division. For students who struggle with the concept of division, using subtraction, a more familiar operation, to solve a division problem may be a good entry point. When doing repeated subtraction, one can actually see each individual group being taken away and that the groups taken away are equal groups. These are important concepts in understanding division, so it is an appropriate strategy to use early in the year. Later in the year, Dee's focus will be on helping her students move toward using more efficient strategies for solving division problems such as using multiple groups of the divisor or breaking the dividend into parts. By the end of the year, she will expect the students to use more efficient strategies like these.

As the students discuss the repeated subtraction strategy, Dee carefully records each step. Recording each step of the strategy may help students keep track of what is being discussed even if they are not participating at that time. Dee's recording is a tangible record of what has been discussed and can be referred to by students to remember what was said and to help them figure out an answer. The recording particularly helps with repeated subtraction because sometimes students find it challenging to figure out where the answer is with repeated subtraction (the number of groups taken away). As Dee records each step, she checks in with the students to see if they are following the strategy by asking "Am I finished?" She also repeatedly asks students what the specific numbers she has recorded represent.

As the discussion continues, Dee uses the students' ideas to try to help them as a group and individually move forward in their ideas about and understanding of division and specifically division with remainders. She does this by asking the students very specific questions about what they are saying to make their ideas clear to the other students and to themselves (whether they are correct or not), by connecting students ideas, and by specifically asking a student about what another student said. For example, when one student says the answer to $36 \div 8$ is thirty-two, Dee responds, "Is thirty-two really the answer? . . . So someone said $36 \div 8$ is how many 8s can we get out of 36. So are you saying we are getting thirty-two 8s out of 36? $8 + 8 + 8$ thirty-two times?" Later she asks this student to listen to another student's idea, which she then rephrases: "This 4 represents the 4 buses, but the 4 also represents the four 8s, which according to Najat is 32, 4×8 is 32, so you are right it does land on 32, but 32 is not the answer."

Participating in Discussions

At this time of year (October), the community in a math class is still developing and students are still figuring out how to be a part of that community. As Dee says in one of the interviews, "In the beginning of the year, it's very difficult to get all the students engaged in the conversation; they are coming from different places. So it is important to do a lot of the modeling, put myself in their shoes, even sometimes talk like them. And make arguments and have discourse back and forth about why this answer doesn't work and so on and so forth." Her strategies—such as using humor, building the discussion from the ideas coming from the students, responding positively to all students' responses and taking their responses seriously, and citing their words in her responses and questions to others—all encourage students' participation. At the end of the discussion, Dee also makes sure to approach those who have not participated and find out what they understood from the discussion. Consistently using these strategies for discussions makes more and more students actively participate in discussions as the year goes on.

There is evidence in the video that the way Dee structures and facilitates discussions already draws the active participation of students with a wide range of understanding of division and numbers in general. For example, one student is comfortable enough to count on his fingers to check the answer to a small subtraction problem, and another student talks about negative numbers in his response. Also, some students show they have some clear ideas about how to deal with remainders, although others share that they think there is no answer to the problem. Through this discussion, Dee tries to help individuals move forward from where they are in their thinking about division as well as helping the whole group move forward in their understanding of division.

Communicating Ideas

In another interview, Dee says that one of her goals is for her students "to be very specific in their answers." Her interaction with one student, Louise, is an example of how she tries to help students clearly communicate their thinking. She repeats what Louise says (that there is no answer to 36 ÷ 8) but turns what she says into a question: "So there's no answer because it went over 32?" This makes Louise think again about her response and whether it is true and whether it is exactly what she wants to say. Dee says a few times, "So there is no answer?" and then expects Louise to explain why she thinks there is no answer. When Louise says something about what is left over that is not quite correct (half of a bus, half people), Dee takes her literally, which forces Louise to rethink how to phrase her idea to exactly reflect what she means. Dee uses humor to illustrate how Louise's answer is not precise, but also to help make the students comfortable.

As Dee helps Louise communicate her ideas, she helps her think through some ideas about division and remainders: Is there an answer to a division problem where the amount in the groups doesn't fit evenly into the total? Can you have leftovers in an answer to a division problem? How do you answer a division problem with remainders? How does the answer in the context of a story problem relate to an answer to a bare numbers problem? What do the numbers represent? Listening to Dee's interaction with Louise may help other students strengthen their understanding of division because they might have similar ideas and confusions and it might be helpful to hear Louise's responses.

By the end of the discussion, there are some things about division that many of the students seem to understand and there are some things they are clearly still trying to figure out. Most of the students seem to understand that in division you are dividing a quantity into equal groups. There is some evidence that students understand there is a relationship between multiplication and division (skip counting by a number to solve a division problem). They are working a lot on the idea of what to do if there is a remainder to a problem: Is there no answer? How can your answer reflect that there are some left over? They are also working on the connections between a division story problem and bare numbers problem and how the answers are related. Finally, they are solidifying which numbers represent the answer in the specific strategy they are using as well as what all the numbers stand for in a division problem and in the answer to a division problem.

Next Steps

In the last interview, Dee talks about how she uses each day's discussion to "craft the kinds of questions I am planning to ask the following day." At the beginning of her discussions, she often reviews what students learned from a prior lesson. After this discussion, she might have the class solve another problem with remainders to check the students' understanding through their oral contributions. Then she might use what came up from this lesson about multiplication, for example skip counting, to ask questions to move to the relationship between multiplication and division, all the while emphasizing that division means splitting quantities into equal groups.

Taking Responsibility for Learning

Introduction

My struggling students just sit there; they don't ask for help.

She has her hand up right away, not even attempting to solve the problem on her own. She is waiting for me to tell her what to do.

He let his partner do all the work and just copied what his partner wrote. When I asked him how the figured out the problem, he had no idea.

We have all heard stories like these about students who are struggling, whether they are students on Individualized Education Programs or others who are having difficulty. Sometimes this "learned helplessness" comes from years of being told what to do, to follow a procedure step-by-step. Other times, after many experiences with failure, these students have internalized that they cannot learn (Mercer 2008).

Seeing oneself as a learner is basic to success in school, no matter what the subject. What can we do about these students who struggle in mathematics class? How can we teach them to be mathematical thinkers? What it means to learn and do mathematics and what that involves is a complicated topic that has been written about by many prominent researchers (Schoenfeld 1992). Although there is no simple answer or list of foolproof techniques, the essays in this section describe strategies that teachers have used to help their struggling students become more confident, independent learners of mathematics. These teachers expect that their students who struggle can learn mathematics with understanding if given support. This approach is supported by research, such as the Cognitively Guided Instruction Project (Carpenter, Fennema, and Franke 1996). This primary-grade mathematics project integrated research findings on how children think about mathematics with findings on how teachers use this knowledge when making instructional decisions. The teachers in the CGI project found that when their students with learning disabilities solved problems with representations and contexts that were familiar to them and with manipulatives and tools that made sense to them, they were able to understand numerical operations conceptually and solve problems (Hankes 1996). Other studies have demonstrated that instead of remediating deficits, encouraging children to develop computation strategies based on their own knowledge increases understanding of operations as well as knowledge of number facts for at-risk students and students with mild disabilities (Thornton, Langrall, and Jones 1997; Karp and Voltz 2000; Behrend 2003).

The teachers who wrote these essays help students establish routines so that they can function independently by taking advantage of resources such as charts and posters in the classroom; developing a series of questions to ask themselves about a problem; and building on each success so that it becomes a reference point in the future. Students learn to ask themselves questions such as, "How did you know that?" and "What did you think about next?" through carefully scaffolded instruction.

The themes in this section tie in closely with other sections of the book, in particular the Linking Assessment and Teaching section. One teacher, for example, had expressed interest in writing about the responsibility theme, only to realize through close assessment that her student was a passive learner because she had major gaps in her understanding of math concepts. As a result, she shifted her focus to the teaching and assessment cycle. You will also recognize aspects of the Making Mathematics Explicit essays here as teachers build their students' abilities to reflect and take responsibility for their learning by highlighting mathematics concepts in activities and making them accessible for their students.

Kristi Dickey teaches first and second grade, looping or keeping the same class for two years. In "Becoming a Self-Reliant Learner," she describes her work with a first-grade student who was a bystander, not engaging in the work of the classroom. Kristi describes how she developed a routine with the student, repeating the problem that the class was solving to make sure the student understood what the problem was asking and checking that she had what she needed to solve the problem. Kristi also asked her questions, such as, "Now, you have two ways. Do you think there is another way?" This structure helped this student engage in the mathematics and progress in her understanding.

In "Getting 'Un-Stuck'," fourth-grade teacher Mary Kay Archer describes how she worked with a new student to help her learn to solve problems independently. She showed the student how to make use of her strengths to enter into the mathematics. As the student drew on her ability to visualize, for example, she was able to see equal groups to make sense of multiplication. Through her work with this student, Mary Kay found that she learned how to ask more precise questions and model strategies that made her a better teacher for all her students.

In "Tasha Becomes a Learner," Candace Chick writes about how she used a Learning Behavior Observation Record, a listing of behaviors that foster habits of good learning, to help her plan for and teach one of her students to see herself as a learner of mathematics. Keeping track of the behaviors on the record helped Candace consider where Tasha fell along various learning dimensions and keep track of Tasha's progress.

These episodes describe teachers who set high but reasonable expectations for their students and plan and teach their students to become learners so that they will be able to make sense of mathematics.

Questions to Think About

What strategies do the teachers use to foster independence and confidence in their students?

What steps do the teachers take to make sure that their students are participating members of the mathematics community?

What evidence do you see that the students in the episodes come to take more responsibility for their learning?

What evidence do you see that the students in the episodes are learning mathematics?

How might the Learning Behavior Observation Record inform your practice?

18

Becoming a Self-Reliant Learner

The Story of Eliza

Kristi Dickey

"Let's play this game, it's fun. Maybe I can get a number to the top this time!"

"Yes! I got a 12!"

"Your strategy is almost just like mine."

Ryan and Jesse are in the art center playing a math game, which requires rolling dice and recording the total. On the floor in the group time area, Olivia and Bekka are playing a math bingo game called Five-in-a-Row (Russell et al. 2008k). Jacob is working on story problems at his own seat, while Curt is writing and solving his own set of more challenging problems. As each one finishes a problem, he shares his strategy with the other.

This is a typical scene during math workshop in my first-grade inclusion class. The math curriculum at my school is investigative in nature; children are encouraged to think, solve problems, and play games together. Children learn that there are multiple avenues to arrive at an answer and that we can learn from each other as we share strategies. Each child is viewed as another "teacher" in the room.

The structure and organization of my math workshop also encourages students to be responsible for their own learning. My students have choices about how they will practice a skill and where in the classroom they will work. They also have some choice about with whom to work. Some days students choose their own partners, and other days I assign them a partner. Once children have learned the routines and expectations, they can work independently, affording me the time to work more closely with individual or small groups of students who need more support.

Teaching responsibility can be challenging in a classroom with a wide range of learners. Often in first grade, children with learning disabilities have not yet been identified, so extra support services are not available to them. Because of their struggles in mathematics, these students often do not contribute to class discussions, ask for help, or work independently during math workshop. In thinking about how to best support these students, I asked myself two questions: Have I thought deeply enough about the connection between taking responsibility for learning and becoming a successful, confident learner? How do I develop this idea of responsibility, particularly among my struggling students? My recent experience with Eliza has given me valuable insight into how I can best help my students take responsibility for their own learning.

Introducing Eliza

Eliza is a seven-year-old first grader who repeated kindergarten. At the start of the year, she appeared to be doing well in mathematics. She could perform some rote mathematical tasks and could count and write numbers to 20. However, as I continued to work with Eliza, I noticed that she sometimes needed help recalling how to write certain numbers when they were out of sequence. She appeared to have one-to-one correspondence at times, but was inconsistent. She sometimes spoke the numbers faster than she could move the objects, making her count inaccurate. I also began to notice that she had trouble comprehending and solving story problems without help. She would sometimes write random answers and turn in her paper without asking for help.

In addition to her struggles with the mathematics content, Eliza also had a passive attitude toward her own learning. She would often sit quietly, appearing to be busy but not really doing any work. She never asked me for help. She tried to blend in while working with other children and frequently attached herself to Katie, a friend from kindergarten. Katie often did Eliza's work for her, thinking she was being helpful. During partner or group games, Eliza wrote down what other children told her to write, with little or no thought of her own about the mathematics in the game. Eliza hardly ever participated during group-time activities. She did not appear to listen to other children as they were sharing, nor did she offer any strategies or ideas of her own.

Along with helping Eliza gain mathematical proficiency, I recognized that I had to help her learn to be an active participant in our classroom community, to see herself as a learner of mathematics, and to be responsible for her own learning. To that end, I developed the following goals for what I wanted to accomplish with Eliza:

- to become less dependent on her peers
- to increase her attention and contributions to the classroom community, in both small- and large-group settings
- to ask for help

As a first step, I wanted Eliza to gain some confidence in her own mathematical abilities. As a more confident learner, she would feel more comfortable asking for help and contributing ideas to the group. Then I would be able to work with her to become less dependent on her peers. I began spending one-on-one time with her as she worked on some math story problems.

Solving Story Problems

One of the first story problems the class solved was: Rosa had 8 books. Max gave her 3 more. How many books does she have now? (Russell et al. 2008f). Eliza's paper had random numbers written on the page (4, 1, 6, 3, 4, 5, 9, 7, 8). During math workshop, I pulled her aside and asked her to tell me about her work. She just stared at me blankly. She didn't have a strategy. I asked her the same questions that I routinely ask all of my students: "Can you tell me the story in your own words?" "Will Rosa have more books or fewer books than when she started?"

I also helped Eliza act out the story with manipulatives. Then I asked her if there was something she could draw that could help tell the story. Eliza drew a line for each book and a number on top of each line (1–11). I continued to work with her closely throughout September and October, repeating this scenario for many other story problems. Figure 18–1 (on page 152) is a sample of Eliza's work from the end of our third unit in November. She was able to do this work independently. Her work met the end-of-unit assessment benchmarks because she was able to interpret the problem and combine the quantities accurately by drawing the books, then counting each one.

I continued to work with Eliza and especially paid close attention when new concepts were introduced. Partner work continued to be a challenge for Eliza. She often depended on peers to do the thinking, particularly when playing games. Games are introduced throughout our curriculum not only to engage children in fun, meaningful mathematics but also to provide repeated practice for specific concepts and skills. Counters in a Cup (Russell et al. 2008k) is a game in which children explore relationships among combinations of numbers of up to 10 and become exposed to the idea of a missing addend. In the game, children work with a certain number of counters. One player hides some of the counters under a cup, leaving the rest to show. The second player looks at the counters in view and figures out how many are in the cup.

Playing Counters in a Cup

I anticipated that this game might pose a challenge for Eliza. As expected, I saw her partner doing most of the thinking for her and telling her what to write. At the first opportunity, I sat down to play the game with Eliza to observe her strategies. We played the game with 8 counters, and I began by hiding 7 counters under the cup and leaving 1 in view.

Name _____ Date _____

Solving Story Problems

Assessment:
How Many Books?

Solve the problem. Show your work.

Our class library has 8 books about frogs.
Mr. B gave us 5 more.
How many books about frogs do we
have now?

M38 Unit 3   Session 3.5

Figure 18–1.

TEACHER: How many counters do you think are in the cup?

ELIZA: I think there is 6. I really don't know.

TEACHER: How many counters did we start with all together?

ELIZA: 8.

TEACHER: Show me 8 fingers.

This was my attempt to show her with her own fingers that 7 and 1 make 8. She couldn't show me 8 fingers, so I physically helped her hold up 8 fingers and together we counted the 8 fingers.

TEACHER: Let's say that this finger [*points to 8th finger*] is the counter that we can see, and the other fingers are like the counters that are in the cup.

ELIZA: [*counts remaining fingers slowly*] 7 in the cup?

TEACHER: How can we find out?

ELIZA: Let's check in the cup. [*Together, we count the counters in the cup.*] There are 7.

TEACHER: Let's try again. [*hides 1 in the cup, 7 counters are showing*]

ELIZA: One in the cup?

TEACHER: How did you know?

ELIZA: It's hard to explain. My daddy taught me there is 1 in the cup.

TEACHER: [*hides 3 in the cup, 5 are showing*]

ELIZA: [*counts the counters that are showing*] 1, 2, 3, 4, 5. [*recounts*] 6? 7? I don't know. [*Together, we count the counters that are showing.*] 1, 2, 3, 4, 5. [*Holding up 1 finger at a time, we continue counting.*] . . . 6, 7, 8.

Teacher: How many fingers are showing?

ELIZA: 3.

TEACHER: How many counters do you think are in the cup?

ELIZA: 3!

I continued working with Eliza, teaching her to count the counters that were showing, then continue on her fingers until she got to 8. After many repetitions, she was successful part of the time on her own.

As Eliza began to have success with these strategies during one-on-one situations with me, I began to scaffold her work with me to her work with a peer. I did this by staying close to her as she worked and shared strategies with a partner, sometimes helping her verbalize her thoughts. I gradually encouraged her to be less dependent upon my support and rely more on her own words. When she was stuck, I asked guiding questions to get her back on track: "How did you know that?" "What did you think about next?" I also made sure to post all of my students' problem-solving strategies as they shared them. This provided students with a place to start working more independently. As they solved new problems, they could refer back to these familiar strategies. I also discussed with the class how to facilitate thinking with a partner so that each partner contributed ideas. We talked about how to help a partner without giving answers and how to come up with good questions we can ask when a partner is stuck.

The next day I observed Eliza successfully playing How Many Am I Hiding? (Russell et al. 2008f), a similar game using the same strategy that had worked well for her when she played Counters in a Cup.

AIDEN: [hides 3 cubes behind his back] How many am I hiding?
ELIZA: [counts cubes in view] 1, 2, 3, 4, 5, 6, 7 [then continues on fingers] . . . 8, 9, 10. Three are hiding!

These initial steps with Eliza seemed to bring her increased understanding of the mathematics and led her to begin to develop some responsibility for her own learning. She began to come to me more frequently for help, and I often observed her in a small-group setting using some strategies that I had made more explicit for her. This seemed to also give her the confidence she needed to share her strategies with the whole class. Her subsequent work on an assessment activity in April provided further proof of the progress she was making.

Assessment Activity: Ten Crayons in All

I have 10 crayons. Some are red. Some are blue. How many of each could I have? How many red? How many blue? Find as many combinations as you can. (Russell et al. 2008i)

Eliza listened to the instructions and then went to the manipulative shelf and got 10 red cubes and 10 blue cubes. She then came to me and asked for help. I read the problem aloud and Eliza connected together the 10 red cubes.

TEACHER: I'll read the problem again, and let's check to see if we have all the parts of the problem. "I have 10 crayons." Do we have 10 crayons?
ELIZA: [counts 10 cubes]
TEACHER: "Some are red, some are blue." Do we have red and blue crayons?
ELIZA: [takes off 2 red cubes and replaces them with 2 blue]
TEACHER: How can you show on paper what you have here?
ELIZA: [writes: 8 red + 2 blue]
TEACHER: Is there another way?
ELIZA: [takes 1 blue cube off and replaces it with 1 red, records 9 red + 1 blue]
TEACHER: You have two ways now. Do you think there is another way?
ELIZA: I can switch them around! [builds with cubes and records 2 red + 8 blue and 1 red + 9 blue].

TEACHER: Good! What other ways can you find?

ELIZA: [*finds the rest of the combinations*] I think I'm done.

I felt so encouraged that Eliza kept trying until she felt she had all the combinations (see Figure 18–2 on page 156).

During group time, when the class was sharing combinations of 10 red and blue crayons, Eliza raised her hand.

ELIZA: 8 red and 2 blue.

TEACHER: How do you know?

ELIZA: I said 1, 2 [*holds up fingers as she counts*] 3, 4, 5, 6, 7, 8, 9, 10.

Several things happened during this assessment that showed me how far Eliza had come in taking responsibility for her own learning.

1. Eliza listened to the instructions.
2. She knew the materials she needed to be successful with the activity.
3. She determined that she needed help and came to find me.
4. She persisted until she found all of the combinations.
5. She volunteered to share her work with the class.

Next Steps

Although I know my work with Eliza isn't finished, I feel as if we have made good first steps. I will continue to explicitly model strategies that work for her, keeping in mind that I need to take my cues from the strategies that are already her own. Trying to impose strategies might impede connections that she is making herself. I will continue to work one-on-one with her, then scaffold her to partner work. Past observations tell me that I need to vary her partners so that she learns to work with a range of people and not become dependent on any one person. I am confident that eventually Eliza will be able to choose an appropriate partner herself.

I will work to make sure the activities are not too hard for Eliza, but push her just beyond what she can do independently (her "zone of proximal development" [Vygotsky 1978]). When playing games or learning a new concept, I will back up to numbers that she is comfortable with and move from there. I've wondered, for instance, what would have happened if I had started her off playing Counters in a Cup with only 5 counters instead of 8. Would she have been able to develop her own strategies with the smaller number of counters and then been able to move on after developing a solid foundation? I am pleased that she has progressed to be able to play the game with 10 counters, but I will think carefully about starting with smaller numbers when the next challenge arises.

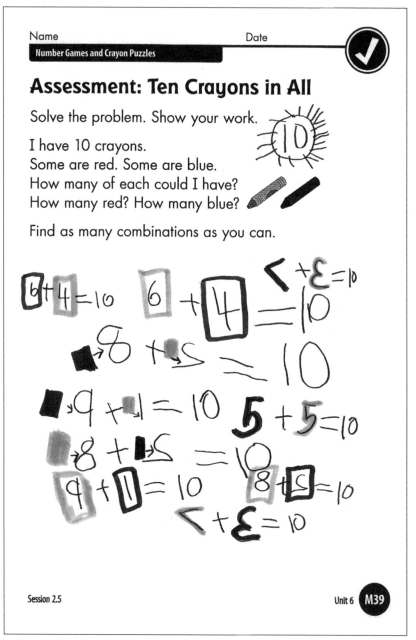

Name _____   Date _____

Number Games and Crayon Puzzles

Assessment: Ten Crayons in All

Solve the problem. Show your work.

I have 10 crayons.
Some are red. Some are blue.
How many of each could I have?
How many red? How many blue?

Find as many combinations as you can.

$6+4=10$ $6+4=10$ $7+3=10$

$8+2=10$

$9+1=10$ $5+5=10$

$8+2=10$

$9+0=10$ $8+2=10$

$7+3=10$

Session 2.5   Unit 6 M39

Figure 18–2.

Eliza and I also need to spend some more time working on her metacognition—thinking about her own thinking. I will continue to help her find words to explain strategies as she is solving problems. We will continue to have discussions about her own strategies and relate her strategies to those of other children that are shared and posted in the classroom.

I will also continue to help Eliza plan ahead what she can share at group time, and she and I will communicate regularly about my expectations of her participation in whole-group settings. Knowing my expectations and practicing with her what she might share seem to make her feel more confident. Finally, I will work toward the goal of asking Eliza to identify her own strengths and weaknesses and helping her set goals for herself. Periodically, we will revisit the goals and the progress she is making to reach them. During regular individual conferences, we will meet together to look at work samples from her math portfolio. We will discuss the specific areas in which she thinks she is getting better and those that might still be difficult. These conferences will help her become more aware of the progress she has made and encourage her to continue to be responsible for her learning.

Reflections

As I reflect on my work with Eliza and think of all other struggling learners I have taught and will teach, I return to the questions I posed for myself at the beginning of the year. Have I thought deeply enough about the connection between taking responsibility for learning and becoming a successful, confident learner? How do I develop this idea of responsibility, particularly among my struggling students? I am more convinced than ever that the idea of responsibility for learning plays an important role in helping these students on their journey to becoming mathematically proficient. Often these students lack confidence in their abilities because they have not experienced success, which in turn causes them to exhibit avoidance behaviors like Eliza's. By letting other people do the work for her, not asking questions, and not sharing at group time, Eliza could hide. She could get by without anyone noticing her difficulties. By helping her develop strategies and find words to explain them, become comfortable asking for help, and share her ideas with the whole group, Eliza has taken the first steps toward developing responsibility.

Although I have always tried to encourage students to be responsible for their own learning, my work with Eliza has helped me become more explicit about teaching responsibility. Not only did I learn to be more explicit with Eliza, I also became more explicit with the whole class in my expectations for learning, for example, how to work well together with partners. The strategies I used to encourage Eliza to be a confident independent learner will benefit all of my students.

19
Getting "Un-Stuck"

Becoming an Independent Learner

Mary Kay Archer

Many of my students are capable of verbalizing what a particular mathematics problem is asking them to solve and what strategies they might use. Other students may struggle a bit more but are able to recognize when they are struggling and are willing to ask me for guidance. However, there are a few students in my fourth-grade classroom who are often unable to find an entry point into a problem and do not ask for help. They tend to be quiet and appear as if they are on task and working hard. However, when I ask them to explain a problem or share their strategies, they often say they don't know or attempt to explain but quickly become confused. Some of these students quietly await my direction before they even attempt to solve a problem, others jump into a problem without thinking through details, and many are not able to use strategies that worked for them before. In this essay, I reflect on my work with one of my students, Heather, to articulate the thinking I do to make mathematics more accessible for my struggling students so that they can become more confident, independent math learners.

Introducing Heather

Heather was new to our school in September. From the beginning of the year, she received special education services out of the classroom with a certified special education teacher for reading, writing, and a review of math games and activities. When Heather said she was tired, had a stomachache, needed to use the restroom, or go to the office, I assumed she was adjusting to our school and that she needed time to build trust with her fellow students and me. But, as the weeks went by, Heather continued to find reasons to escape math class. She is an excellent helper in the classroom, sometimes offering to sharpen pencils or straighten books. In retrospect, she was probably thinking of activities to do instead of completing her math assignments.

I wanted Heather to feel safe taking risks. I was hoping that she could become an active and engaged participant in our math community. However, I was troubled that Heather might not have had enough prior experiences to solve problems independently. She had not yet developed habits that would allow her to take responsibility for her own learning and thinking: she did not yet contribute to large-group discussions; she depended entirely on her partner during paired work; or she came up with excuses to avoid the work entirely. She also used familiar coping skills to make herself look like she was studious and usually appeared as if she wasn't having difficulties at all. She parroted what others said or copied what her partner wrote. When asked how she was thinking about a problem or why she wrote what she did in her math journal, she would shrug her shoulders and say she forgot. I knew I had to plan some targeted interventions to help Heather and a few of my other students who were passive learners. First, I had to assess what she had learned and what confused her.

Assessing Multiplication: Understanding Heather's Learning Profile

Because it was early in the year, I still did not have a full picture of Heather's mathematical understanding. I knew this was important information so I could plan appropriate accommodations to help her become an active, engaged learner. The first formal assessment of the year presented an opportunity for me to understand her thinking and reasoning. The assessment asked students to represent 8×6 through the use of arrays, pictures or models of groups, and story contexts (Russell et al. 2008c). During the assessment, Heather rested her head on her arm and drew small figures on the paper. I asked what she could tell me about the numbers. She told me that the only thing she knew how to do with numbers was to count the dots on each number so she would know "how many the number was." To explain what she meant, she drew the number 6, placed 6 dots along the lines of the 6, touched each dot, and counted by 1s to 6. She said, "I only know about those dots, I'm not good in math, and nothing is nice for me in math." Clearly, I needed to find an entry point for Heather, so I began an unplanned interview.

TEACHER: What else do you know about 6?
HEATHER: There are 6 legs on a ladybug.
TEACHER: Great! If there are 6 legs on a ladybug and I had 2 ladybugs in my hand how many legs would I see?
HEATHER: [draws the ladybugs, counts by 1s] 12.

I wondered if she might be able to work with 8×6 if I coached her to use repeated addition, so I asked "What would happen to the number of legs if we had 8 ladybugs?"

After drawing 8 ladybugs, Heather had to recount the number of ladybugs at least 3 times and recount the number of legs many more times. As she counted the legs, she often lost track of her count. She was unable to skip count and was even having difficulty keeping track of numbers as she counted by 1s. I wondered how she would ever be able to reason through the process of double-digit multiplication problems in the future.

This interview and my other observations were the beginning of my own understanding of why Heather wasn't able to function as an independent learner in my fourth-grade class. I recognized that to be a more independent learner, she needed many more experiences making sense of numbers as she explored key mathematical concepts.

Playing Factor Pairs

An early opportunity to help Heather arose during a math workshop one day in October when I observed students playing a game called Factor Pairs (Russell et al. 2008c). In this game, students use array cards to find products of any multiplication combination up to 12 × 12. Factor Pairs is engaging for students and provides opportunities for students to work on multiplication combinations. The goal is for students to focus on using easier combinations they already know to determine products of more difficult combinations with which they are not yet fluent. To play the game, students take turns picking up an array card with the factor side faceup (see Figure 19–1). They have to name the product either by "just knowing it" or figuring out an efficient way to count the squares. If their answer is correct, they keep the card. Students play with a partner and keep track of combinations they know by dividing a recording sheet into two columns: "Combinations I Know" and "Combinations I'm Working On."

A small group of students, including Heather, were having a great time playing the game and seemed to be working cooperatively, but I suspected they were playing the game without thinking about the mathematics. I stopped to listen to their conversation and observe their actions to determine what strategies they were using. It quickly became clear that they were simply going through the motions of playing the game. They would turn over an array card, say they knew the product, and put the card into the pile of combinations they knew. When I asked if the factor pair belonged in the pile of combinations they were working on or was a combination they already knew, they would frequently say they knew it even when it was clear that they did not. These students were simply guessing, not reasoning about multiplication.

On the other hand, those students who were playing the game using mathematical reasoning would look at the array, talk with each other about how to break the factors into workable numbers, use the arrays as visual models, ask each

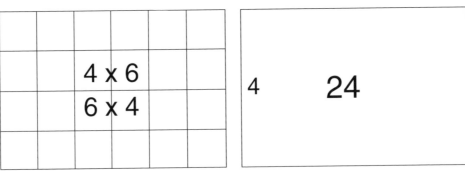

Figure 19–1. Array card with factor pairs on the front and product and one dimension or factor on the back.

other questions, correct each other, and give each other clues. They knew which combinations they still needed to work on and discussed ways to learn more difficult combinations by using combinations they already knew. I wanted Heather's group to acquire these skills and play the game with a clear purpose and strategy.

Gaining Entry into the Mathematics

Based on what I heard and saw in Heather's group, it was clear that I needed to revisit the reasons for playing the game and the mathematical concepts they were supposed to be learning. The following day, I gathered Heather's group together as the other students played the game in pairs. I began by asking the group if they remembered what they did yesterday with the Factor Pair game. As they demonstrated how to play the game, I asked what they were learning. I was not surprised when they couldn't answer. At this point, I reviewed what it feels like to be stuck in a problem and what we might need to do to become "un-stuck." In other content areas, the class had worked on reflecting on their learning using the following prompts based on the Thinking Dispositions from the Artful Thinking Program (Richhart, Turner, and Hadar 2008):

REASONING
What do you think is going on? What are your reasons? What makes you say that?

QUESTIONING AND INVESTIGATING
What would you like to find out? What do you think you know? What questions or puzzles do you have? What might you need to explore?

OBSERVING AND DESCRIBING
What do you notice?

COMPARING AND CONNECTING
How does it connect to other things you know about?

I used prompts such as these to discuss what to do in math when we are struggling to learn new concepts. During this particular discussion I wanted these students to become more aware of when they were not able to move forward in solving problems. The Comparing and Connecting prompt was particularly applicable. I asked if they remembered being stuck with anything before. They gave examples, including a story of actually being stuck in the mud. Using this story, I explained that the way they were playing the game was like being stuck in the mud without a direction or a reason for getting out.

I told them we would be playing the game again, but this time I wanted them to tell their own stories of what they were learning from playing the game. We slowed the game down, not in the sense of repeating directions or asking students to slow down, but by methodically reviewing the game to investigate connections to prior knowledge and taking the time to focus on the important mathematical concepts.

I became an active member of the group, modeling my thinking as I played the game along with the students. If the array was 4×8, I would say "Maybe 4×8 is a combination I need to work on, so I am thinking of an easier combination I already know, such as 4×4." I would point to a smaller part of the array to show the 4×4 area, write the equation on my whiteboard, and ask students if I was finished finding the product of 4×8 (see Figure 19–2). Sometimes students recognized that I was not finished, but they were unable to explain what I needed to do next. I would then think aloud and say, "I have solved part of the area of the whole array, now I need to figure out the dimensions of the other part of the array that I did not use to find the product of 4×8. So, what do I need to do next?" My goal was to encourage students to think of the next steps. I also explicitly used mathematical words and wrote number sentences to illustrate the distributive property $(4 \times 8 = [4 \times 4] + [4 \times 4])$, and the commutative property (8×4 or 4×8).

I set the small group off to play the game in pairs and immediately checked in with Heather and her partner. I began by asking them to explain the purpose of the game. They answered, "Multiplication and using what we know." They were simply reading back the words I had written on the board earlier to explain what was going to happen in math that day. I asked, "What makes you say the game is about multiplication and using what we know?" They said, "Because that is what is written on the board." I then asked, "How does using what you know help you with combinations you are working on?" and they replied, "We count the squares" (in the array). They counted the squares by 1s. I was not convinced that they understood that they could use easier combinations to solve for more difficult combinations. So, I drew two small arrays that fit into one bigger array to demonstrate visually how the different combinations might help them figure out the bigger array combination (see Figure 19–3).

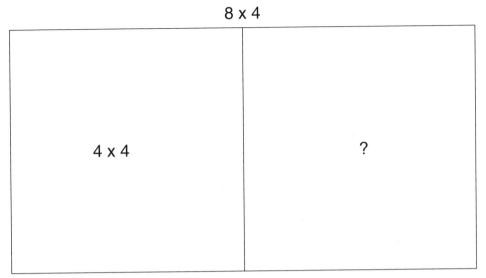

Figure 19–2.

Implementing Structures and Routines

I wanted Heather and a few other students to be able to use what they know and the resources available in the classroom to help them solve problems. I became more explicit about the structures and routines I had put in place to help foster independence among all my students. I wanted them to apply the routines that we had used in other content areas to mathematics. I encouraged students to make use of the dispositions of thinking routines (Richhart, Turner, and Hadar 2008) and

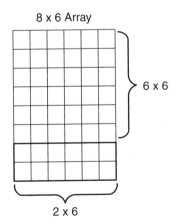

Figure 19–3.

question posters we had posted for reference, such as a poster that asks: What's going on? What do you see that makes you say that? I also suggested that they refer to the messages on the board explaining the math focus of the day and the list of thinking words designed to help students express their mathematical ideas and reasoning. To ensure that the class used these resources, I began to explicitly point out when a student referred to the posters, written messages on board, or thinking words. We noted which questions seemed to help students move their thinking ahead in specific situations. With all students beginning to use these resources more frequently, Heather became more aware of the opportunities for support and when to use them.

I also began to plan specific accommodations for Heather depending on what the activity required. For example, there might be a need to reread a problem, discuss vocabulary words, provide a variety of manipulatives, or use smaller numbers. I asked Heather specific questions about the assigned problems before she began work.

- What is the important information in the problem?
- What is the problem asking?
- What does the problem remind you of that you have worked on before?

These types of questions were also posted in our room to scaffold students' problem-solving work. I would also tell stories or draw situations to help Heather visualize what a particular problem was asking.

Additional Math Practice

At the end of January, our school's principal, along with all of the second-, third-, and fourth-grade classroom teachers, decided to add thirty minutes of math instruction for those students who were struggling in each grade level. We called this math club. By reworking my schedule, I was able to carve out time before lunch each day to work with Heather and eleven other fourth graders. Because the math club was held before the math lesson each day, I pretaught the math concepts to the twelve students and gave them opportunities to explore and rehearse strategies we would use in class later that day. I was explicit about the purpose of the group: we were going to learn how to develop strategies for solving problems, become aware of what helped us learn and what we needed to learn, and build our mathematical understanding. By openly stating our goals, it gave students permission to use the small group as a place to ask questions about what they didn't understand. Because the group was small, I came to understand how each student approached problems, and I conferenced with students more frequently to help them clarify their thinking. This small group with Heather among them, became a community of learners who worked out mistakes together and revised their work when an answer didn't make sense.

The following is an example of how I structured experiences for my math club students to prepare them for the work we would be doing in class. In class, we were preparing to be able to read and locate numbers on a large class 10,000 chart that we made together (Russell et al. 2008h). I knew the students in the math club would need practice with adding and subtracting multiples of 10 and 100 before they could understand the place value of numbers on the 10,000 chart. First, I gave them extra practice with their 1,000 books, which they had created themselves, earlier in the unit. The 1,000 books consisted of 10 partially filled 100 charts. The students fill in enough landmark numbers on each chart so that they can locate any other given number (see Figure 19–4).

Next, we used the 1,000 books to play a game called Changing Places (Russell et al. 2008h). In this game, students start at any given number and move to a new position in the book by adding and subtracting multiples of 10 and 100. For example, they might start at 275 and then move +20, –30, +300 to land on 565. They then fill in this new number in their 1,000 book. After we reviewed the directions for the Changing Places game, the students played for five minutes. We then discussed what was happening to the starting numbers as they added or subtracted multiples of 10 and 100. Students noted, for example, that if they added a 20, the 10s place changed and sometimes the 100s place changed, but the digit in the 1s place did not. After a few more examples and sharing of thoughts, I asked the question, "What would be different or the same about finding numbers

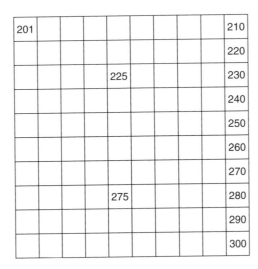

Figure 19–4.

on a chart that has 10,000 squares instead of your 1,000 book that has 1,000 squares?" The first response was, "There would be way more squares, like . . . maybe at least more than 1,000 more squares." Another student said, "We can figure out how many more squares if we know how many thousands." Another student mentioned that there would be 10 thousands because "that is what it means when we say 10,000 out loud." I gave examples of adding and subtracting multiples of 10, 100, and 1,000 on the 10,000 chart to see if they would use what they learned from the 1,000 chart. For example, if they knew how the value changed with 386 + 100, could they similarly figure out how the value changed with 3,860 + 1,000 or 3,860 + 100? After a series of examples, we discussed what digits changed as the students added or subtracted multiples of 10, 100, and 1,000.

That day in class we made the 10,000 chart. Heather and the students in the math club were able to complete the task independently. Their experience working with the 1,000 books helped them visualize the structure of 10,000. A few days later, the class worked on the Changing Places activity again, this time on the 10,000 chart. The students from the math club had the opportunity to share their strategies with the class, extending their strategies from locating new numbers in the 1,000 book to the 10,000 chart. They were able to identify what digits changed and explain why. The students in the math club had become comfortable and confident with these larger numbers as a result of:

- creating and reviewing the 1,000 book
- practicing adding and subtracting multiples of 10 and 100 through the Changing Places game
- discussing what they needed to pay attention to when playing the game
- constructing the 10,000 chart
- locating numbers by adding and subtracting multiples of 10, 100, and 1,000

I was especially pleased that Heather could successfully participate in this activity.

Learning About Learning

As the year went on, I continued to see evidence of Heather's progress. Heather volunteered to share more frequently, realizing that she not only had an approach for solving a problem but was also able to explain it. For example, during a math club discussion about Quick Images, Heather was very explicit in her description of how she determined the number of dots shown in Figure 19–5 (Russell, Economopoulos, Wittenberg, et al. 2008). Heather circled groups of 3 in the first arrangement of 9 dots, and she was able to explain that she knew there were 9 because she counted by 3s. She then explained that she knew how many were in the other

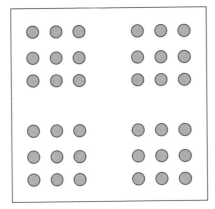

Figure 19–5.

3 groups (9) and then wrote 9 + 9 + 9 + 9 on the board. Next, she wrote 9 + 9 = 18 twice and then 18 + 18 = 36. One day, she explained to other students that multiplication was about how many groups and how many were in each group. Instead of counting the squares by 1s as she did during the Factor Pairs game, Heather was now able to chunk the groups of dots, add the groups together, and not lose track of the total she was counting. Although she was not yet using the multiplication expressions that other students were using, such as 9 × 4, she was building her understanding of equal groups. Some of the students told her that she helped them see the groups differently. I was thrilled to see her developing her math understanding and her sense of confidence.

Heather continued to apply her strengths, such as visualization, to solve a variety of problems. During our study of fractions, when some students were struggling to visualize $\frac{3}{4}$ and $\frac{5}{6}$, Heather spoke up and said, "What helps me is when I picture it in my head and when I can draw it in my notebook. Like if we had two sheets of brownies and cut one sheet into 6 pieces and the other into 4 pieces, I think of which piece is bigger." Other students said they had not thought of the problem like that before and that using Heather's example helped them figure out if $\frac{3}{4}$ was equal to, less than, or greater than $\frac{5}{6}$. After this conversation, I added Heather's example to our classroom poster about fraction strategies, and it became a point of reference for the class.

Becoming Confident Learners

Heather and the other members of the math club began to understand that they could think mathematically, and they developed multiple ways to enter into the mathematics of a lesson. They had begun to expect that they would be questioned about their thinking and were able to offer explanations and listen to the strategies of their classmates. Their progress was brought home to me during another math club session when the group described a lesson taught by a guest teacher. During the course of a lesson on rate of change, the guest teacher had written the following: $3 + 5 + 5 + 5 + 5 + 5$. My students wondered why she wrote all of those 5s and explained to her that it would be more efficient to write $3 + (5 \times 5)$. I realized the guest teacher had written exactly what was in the teacher's edition, not realizing that these students could see $3 + (5 \times 5)$. The students told me that she didn't ask questions about what they were thinking, Heather added, "It is just that when you or other kids ask questions, the questions help me think about what I'm supposed to do. Sometimes I get started but can't figure out what to do next. You don't tell us what to do but you ask us a question to help us think about the problem." Heather was describing how she becomes un-stuck.

Reflections

This was an enormous change from the small group of reluctant learners I had worked with at the beginning of math club to the group who ended the school year with more confidence and ability to use reasoning to solve problems. The math club had a clear purpose that the students and I all shared: to help them understand how they think, know what to use to help them when they are stuck, build on their strengths while understanding their gaps, and use what they have learned to determine entry points for the daily math work.

Before each session I was explicit about our mathematical goals. To accomplish these goals, I always reviewed the prior lessons, and together we worked through examples that would provide connections to the current work. With each example, we talked about not only what their solution was, but how they arrived at it and what they needed to pay attention to.

Not only did Heather demonstrate growth in understanding number concepts, she also helped me clarify and further develop the strategies I use to assess learning, build understanding, and foster independence and confidence with all my students. As my students said near the end of the year, "If we say we don't know, you don't give up on us." I hope never to give up on any student and believe all have the ability to be mathematical thinkers.

20

Tasha Becomes a Learner

Helping Students Develop Confidence and Independence

Candace Chick

When we think about students who struggle to learn mathematics, we often focus on the skills and concepts they haven't mastered. Although it is important to assess what mathematical knowledge students need to learn, it is also critical to assess students' learning behaviors—their attitudes and actions that indicate how they approach learning. Development of these behaviors is key to students' ability to take in new information and access what they already know. Students who manifest these behaviors take an active role in their learning; they approach their work independently and confidently. My role with students who are struggling is to document how they approach learning and introduce strategies that will help them develop positive learning behaviors.

The Learning Behavior Observation Record

I have found that unless my struggling students begin to see themselves as confident, independent thinkers, their progress in learning mathematics will be limited. One tool I have used to guide my work with these students is the Learning Behavior Observation Record (see Figure 20–1). This tool was developed by teachers and researchers in the NSF-funded Accessible Mathematics project and represents a list of the behaviors they found to be significant indicators of student success in mathematics. The tool gave me a way to think about these specific behaviors instead of generalities such as "learned helplessness" that don't provide a starting point to help students.

The marks along each line are meant to help keep track of a student's progress over time. Because the record presents the development of these behaviors as a continuum, it is an extremely helpful tool for documenting students' current status, tracking their progress, and identifying specific goals for improvement. I find that it is sometimes useful to share this tool with the students themselves and with

Sees oneself as a learner

Is willing to take risks

Perseveres

Knows when to ask for help

Able to work independently when expected

Actively participates in mathematical discussions

Listens to ideas of others

Tries to understand what problem is asking

Makes connections to prior knowledge

Applies new knowledge to a variety of contexts

Evaluates own work and compares to others' solutions

Checks reasonableness of answers

Uses organization to facilitate thinking and solve problems

Figure 20–1. The record has blank lines on the bottom because the list may be expanded, according to the needs of each child.

parents, as it illustrates what I am talking about, and it can provide a jumping-off point to talk about where students have improved and where they still need to demonstrate progress.

In addition to thinking about whether a student is exhibiting these behaviors and how often, noting the context in which a student exhibits the behaviors can also provide valuable insight. For example, there are many factors that might affect a student's willingness to take risks. When I notice that a student is occasionally willing to take risks, I make note of the learning context in which this happens. Was it during a whole-group discussion or during small-group or independent work? What was the mathematical focus of the problem (i.e., number, geometry, data)? Was it a problem-solving situation or a computation problem? Similarly, if a student is making connections to prior knowledge, I consider the context of the lesson. How was the lesson introduced? Were explicit connections to prior knowledge made? What is the mathematical content of the lesson? Might the context be particularly applicable to that student? These kinds of questions are extremely helpful in understanding more about how a particular student learns.

The following vignette describes how I used the Learning Behavior Observation Record to guide my interventions with Tasha, a student who was initially charted at the low end of the continuum on many of the learning behavior dimensions. Tasha entered an inclusion class in fourth grade, after spending her first three years in a special education class for children with behavior problems. Figure 20–2 is Tasha's Observation Record representing where she was on the continuum in October of her fourth-grade year and in the spring of her fifth-grade year. (I was able to document the progress over two years, because I "looped" or stayed with these students in both fourth and fifth grades.) To give an idea of how Tasha presented herself initially, the strategies I used, and the progress we achieved, I have selected a few of the learning behavior categories to discuss.

Sees Oneself as a Learner

At the beginning of her fourth-grade year, Tasha's self-esteem was very low, as evidenced by her comments such as, "I can't do this" and "I'm bad at math." She was very nervous in class and unwilling to take risks or participate much. So, my first priority was to help Tasha focus on seeing herself as a learner. Many students with learning difficulties have experienced so much failure in school that they assume that they cannot learn. When encountering new content, they make only halfhearted attempts to learn, assuming that they will fail. It is extremely important to help them see that they are able to learn. This will facilitate their ability to use all of what they already know and take the risks necessary to build new skills and knowledge.

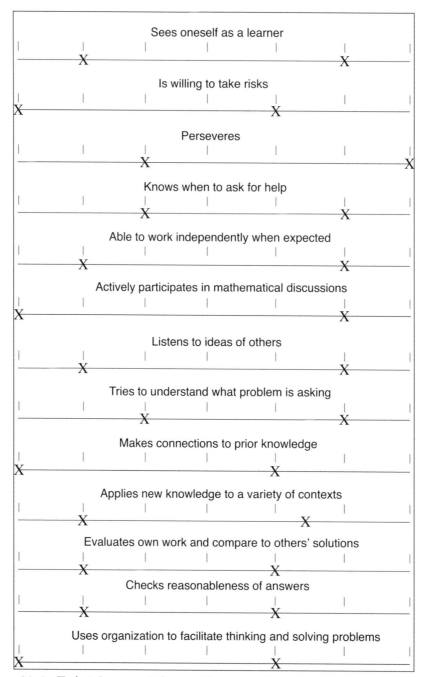

Figure 20–2. Tasha's Learning Behavior Observation Record representing where she was on the continuum in October of her fourth-grade year (X's on left side of the lines) and in the spring of her fifth-grade year (X's on right side of the lines).

One strategy I use to help students see themselves as learners is to set clear expectations for acceptable academic and social behaviors and to hold my students accountable for their participation in class. To that end, I ask my students to evaluate their own work by giving themselves a score based on the following questions.

Did I actively participate in learning?
Did I try my hardest?
Did I use *everything* I know to help myself with the problem?
Did I get distracted, off task?

Points are determined at the end of each academic period or task. The number of points is determined by the degree of difficulty of the task or the length of the period. For example, 8 points might be given for science, which is a ninety-minute block, 6 points for reading workshop, which lasts sixty minutes, and 4 points for swimming, which is forty-five minutes long. Students tell me what they think they have earned, and I record the points on a sheet for each day. The points are then totaled for the week. Student can use the points to buy free time once a week if they have earned 75 percent of the total possible points that could be earned for the week. If students don't give themselves full points, they need to explain why (i.e., "I gave myself 4 points out of 6, because I was talking at the beginning of reading workshop and wasted time"). This helps students to acknowledge their actions, or inaction. Students come to accept responsibility for their learning.

Like many students, Tasha was initially overly critical of herself. If she had a difficult time with part of a lesson or got off task even for a minute, she gave herself a 0. With practice, Tasha was able to be more objective about her behavior. The questions I asked encouraged her to consider all aspects of her learning. Without the questions, Tasha tended to get trapped by thinking that she was terrible at math or that she was bad because she got off task for a minute or two. The questions acknowledged partial success and prompted her to try using anything and everything that she knew about how numbers worked to help her solve problems.

At the beginning of fifth grade, I grouped Tasha with some other girls who were also struggling to build their self-esteem. Tasha realized that she wasn't the only one who didn't understand some of the mathematics and that it was OK to not be perfect and to ask for help. Tasha was performing the best in that group, which gave her a sense of self-assurance. Once she gained confidence, I sometimes grouped her with a stronger student so she could learn from someone with more advanced strategies. I wanted to give Tasha the message that she was capable of learning more complex strategies from her peers. For example, when I wanted Tasha to move to working with larger multiples (e.g., 250 instead of 25), I paired her with another student who would also be patient in showing Tasha the relationships between the multiples.

Her partner explicitly pointed out the relationship between 25 and 250, so that Tasha was eventually able to use 250 in solving problems.

Checks Reasonableness of Answers

Prior to joining my class, Tasha had not had much exposure to mathematical thinking. She had been taught only rote procedures and didn't view math as something that was supposed to make sense. As a result, she had no way of judging whether her answers were reasonable. I modeled ways to help her make sense of mathematics. In one instance, a problem asked which multiple of 100 was nearest to a series of numbers. Tasha wrote that the multiple of 100 nearest to 130 is 200. When I asked her why, she said because it is already over 100. I asked, "Is 130 closer to 100 or 200?" She quickly replied, "100." I recorded the multiples of 10 between 100 and 200 and asked which are closer to 200 and which are closer to 100. She drew a line at 150, to indicate that everything greater than 150 was closer to 200. Seeing the multiples written out provided her with a way to structure her thinking.

Eventually, with all of the modeling I did and the strategies we shared in class, she applied what she knew and could assess whether or not her answer was reasonable. For example, this is her work for 32×9.

$$32 \times 9 = \quad \begin{array}{r} 1 \\ 30 \times 9 = 270 \\ 2 \times 9 = 18 \\ \hline 32 \times 9 = 358 \end{array}$$

But, I know that $32 \times 10 = 320$, so 358 can't be the right answer for 32×9. It's wrong. I need to go back and check my work. There's a mistake.

$$32 \times 9 = \quad \begin{array}{r} 30 \times 9 = 270 \\ 2 \times 9 = 18 \\ \hline 32 \times 9 = 288 \end{array}$$

I see what I did wrong. I added up wrong. I did the 8 twice and it was lined up all wrong.

By working on ways to break up larger problems into smaller, meaningful chunks using the multiplication facts she was fluent with, Tasha was able to recognize that if $30 \times 9 = 270$, then 32×9 could not possibly equal 358 because 2×9 only equals 18. Even though Tasha made a computation error, the important point here is that she was using mathematical reasoning to critique her own solution.

Actively Participates in Mathematical Discussions

I used a variety of specific strategies to encourage Tasha's participation in discussions and help build her confidence. I asked her questions in the large group that I knew she could answer (e.g., what is another fraction for $\frac{1}{2}$?). I also did some "preteaching"—going over directions and activities in advance so she would be

My number is odd.

My number is a multiple of 9.

My number is a square number.

My number has two digits.

Figure 20–3.

My number is smaller than 50.

It is a square number.

It is a multiple of 5.

Figure 20–4.

able to participate in the group. This was particularly effective with Guess My Number Puzzles (Tierney et al. 2004; see Figure 20–3). Students who struggle with mathematics often have problems developing a strategy to figure out these puzzles. They tend to guess at numbers that work for only one or two of the clues. For example, when I presented the puzzle in Figure 20–3, Tasha started out by calling out square numbers randomly. I knew I needed to help Tasha approach this problem more systematically, so I started out by posing simpler puzzles with a smaller range of numbers or fewer clues (see Figure 20–4). Having a smaller range helped her focus on the possibilities.

Additional strategies I used to help Tasha solve the number puzzles included:

- making clear that the number must fit all the clues
- explicitly showing what "process of elimination" means
- offering 300 charts, scrap paper, and calculators for skip counting
- helping her find ways to keep track of the numbers to help her develop a method for eliminating the ones that don't fit the clue
- showing her how to use the 300 chart to circle all the multiples of 9 between 50 and 100

- discussing possible order of clues that narrow the search quickly (for example, after recognizing the range, is it more efficient to list all the odd numbers or list the multiples of 9 or the square numbers?)
- reviewing definitions of words such as *multiple, factor, prime, even, square numbers*
- providing supplemental work with multiples, factors, and squares

Gradually, Tasha began to participate in discussions and was often able to supply reasonable answers using some of the strategies listed here. As she experienced more success, she gained confidence and began attempting to explain her mathematical work, which in turn built her understanding of mathematics.

Makes Connections to Prior Knowledge

It was also important for me to learn about Tasha's strengths and find ways to help her apply those when encountering a new problem. For example, Tasha often used money as a tool to solve problems. When I wanted to introduce her to doubling and halving as a strategy, I started with a context involving money. I knew that Tasha and her sister often went shopping together, so I presented the following problem: If I gave you $2.50, how would you share this equally with your sister? At first Tasha used actual coins, but eventually she was able to solve more problems like this mentally. Tasha was then able to make connections to the doubling and halving strategy in other problem contexts.

Another strength of Tasha's seemed to be visual representation. The array model appeared to make sense to her. Reminding her of this strategy helped her get started on and solve multiplication problems (see Figure 20–5). When Tasha was unsure about how to start a problem, I prompted her to remember concepts from previous lessons that could provide an entry point, for example, "Do you remember how you made a list of factors of 100? How could those factors help you find the factors of 300?" I often reminded Tasha and her group, "What have we done before that was like this?" Another strategy I used to stress the importance of making connections to prior knowledge included posting strategy charts around the room. These charts highlighted problem-solving strategies that students came up with. I even developed a miniature version of a strategy chart that students could use at their desks. Eventually, Tasha used these resources to help her with her work. For example, Figure 20–6 represents Tasha's solution to the following division problem: How many groups of 4 pencils can you make with 720 pencils? Not only were the methods she used from the strategy chart, but she was able to show her work and explain her thinking. (She used an algorithm that my students called the "Forgiving Method" and a second method using clusters to check her work.)

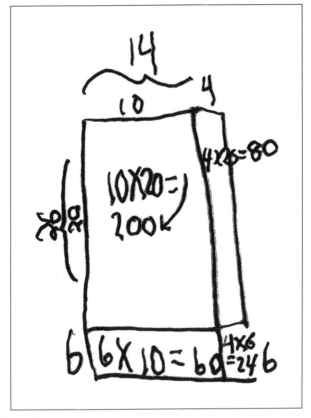

Figure 20–5. 24×14

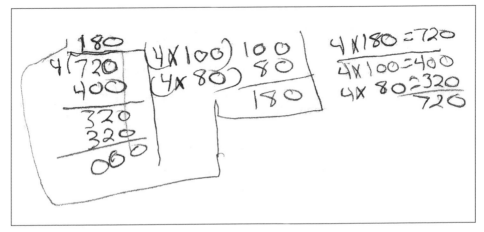

Figure 20–6. $720 \div 4$

Uses Organization to Facilitate Thinking and Solve Problems

Tasha had organizational problems, both in keeping track of her classwork and homework and in organizing her written work. This lack of organization was compounded by her fine motor limitations (difficulty with cutting and handwriting). Tasha's organization improved with the help of specific interventions. I clearly labeled areas of the room—places to put finished work, where the supplies are, and so on—and also gave Tasha checklists to help keep her organized (see Figure 20–7).

My Morning Checklist

- I got my homework, notebooks, and everything I need out of my backpack.
- I put my coat and backpack away.
- I checked in all of my homework, and my reading log, and put them in the basket.
- I checked in my weekly rubric and put it in the binder.
- I'm ready to begin ten-minute math and word study.

My Afternoon Checklist

- I wrote my homework in my agenda.
- I had all the materials that I needed to do my homework: reading log, reading response, social studies notebook, math sheets, writer's notebooks, etc.
- I understood how to do my homework.
- I asked my teachers all the questions I had about confusing things.
- I put away all the books, supplies, and materials that I used today.

Figure 20–7.

I adapted worksheets to give Tasha more space on a page to accommodate her large and inconsistent handwriting and provided lined or graph paper to assist her in vertically aligning the numbers. I also showed Tasha how she could "box things off" to divide the page into meaningful chunks. By fifth grade, Tasha was able to use this strategy to organize all of the equations that formed her solution to a problem.

I also developed an organizational structure designed to provide Tasha with an entry point into more open-ended problems (see Figure 20–8). I gave her an example of a completed template as well as a blank one. This helped Tasha organize her thinking so that she could work more systematically. When Tasha was presented with an open-ended task such as "What do you know about 125?" it was difficult for her to know how to begin, and once she began, it was difficult for her to organize her writing and know what to include. By giving her an organizational framework for the task, including some prompts for the type of information I was looking for, Tasha was able to give a higher-level response and use her knowledge of multiplication and division instead of just listing simple addition and subtraction sentences that equal 125 (e.g., $124 + 1 = 125$, $126 - 1 = 125$), the way she did in the beginning of the year.

What do you know about 125?	
Multiples 125, 250, 375, 500, 625, 750, 875, 1000, 1125	**Factor Pairs** 1, 125 5, 25
Multiplication Problems $1 \times 125 = 125$ $25 \times 5 = 125$ $125 \times 1 = 125$ $5 \times 25 = 125$	**Division Problems** $125 \div 1 = 125$ $125 \div 5 = 25$ $125 \div 125 = 1$ $125 \div 25 = 5$
Other Number Facts I Know	
125 is an odd number. 125 is not a prime number or a square number. It is a composite number. Double 125 is 250. 125 is hard to split in half because it's odd. But half is 62½.	

Figure 20–8.

Reflections

Students arrive in my classroom with a variety of prior experiences that influence how they see themselves as learners of mathematics. The Learning Behavior Observation Record provided a framework for me to think about the characteristics of my students as mathematics learners and how these behaviors evolved over time along the different dimensions. It was particularly helpful in working with a student like Tasha, whose needs seemed overwhelming at first. By thinking about each of the dimensions on the chart, I was able to focus on specific characteristics and keep track of how she was doing over time and in different contexts. At first, I filled out Tasha's chart before and after each curriculum unit. In fifth grade, when I knew her better and had a built-in sense of how things were going, I tended to fill it out at the end of each term, as I tried to do for my other students. I worked hard on helping Tasha see herself as a learner, building her confidence, and helping her use what she knew. I thought carefully about the strategies with which Tasha was fluent, and I used those as a starting place to develop more efficient strategies. Toward the end of fifth grade, when I saw her volunteering to present her work and sharing strategies that she understood, I realized she had come a long way, and I felt optimistic about her future as a learner of mathematics.

Working Collaboratively

Introduction

Although ongoing collaboration between classroom teachers and special education teachers is widely acknowledged (Nolet and McLaughlin 2005; Mutch-Jones 2004; Friend 2007) to be essential to improve the learning of students with special needs in inclusive classrooms, it is unfortunately not a common occurrence. There are a number of possible reasons for this lack of collaboration. Special education teachers are often responsible for fulfilling the time-consuming requirements of the Individuals with Disabilities Education Act, for example, administering batteries of tests, attending meetings, and writing Individualized Educational Programs. In addition, the primary subject of instruction in special education is literacy. During their preservice program, special education teachers take many more courses in literacy than in mathematics. Their inservice professional development opportunities tend to focus either on the legal aspects of their role or on literacy-related topics.

Classroom teachers also have pressures and requirements that may interfere with time for collaboration, such as the testing and meetings associated with the No Child Left Behind Act, and administrative and nonteaching responsibilities (e.g., bus duty, committee meetings).

Despite these barriers, many teachers, including those whose essays follow, are able to make collaboration work. They make the effort because they view the relationship as a form of professional development and because they understand that their collaboration increases the opportunities for students with special needs to access the mathematical ideas and concepts put forth by the National Council of Teachers of Mathematics Standards-based curricula.

The development of structures that promote joint planning and reflection is central to a successful collaborative relationship (Friend and Cook 2006). In their planning meetings, the special education and regular education teachers in these essays familiarize themselves with the mathematics content and pedagogical strategies for upcoming lessons and anticipate difficulties that students might experience. They also discuss what student strengths and prior knowledge might help with the next series of activities and concepts.

Studies of collaboration have found that students learn more when special education and classroom teachers are flexible, adjusting their plans to meet students' needs, and when they share compatible pedagogical strategies, such as maximizing students' engagement and providing a consistent structure. The special education teacher is an active partner, not an assistant, who actively instructs her students, providing additional practice and opportunities for the students to encounter important mathematical concepts (Mastropieri, Scruggs et al. 2005; Kloo and Zigmond 2008).

Because the special education teacher is more likely to work with students either one-on-one or in small groups, her observations often become the focus of the debriefing meetings. These meetings involve reviewing student work and assessments with the classroom teacher, as both try to make sense of what the students understood and what areas of confusion remained. The teachers note what strategies seemed to work well in addition to those that did not seem to help the students gain understanding. The classroom teacher provides the crucial perspective of how the students are performing in the context of the whole-class mathematics community. In the essays that follow, the teachers detail aspects of their collaborative relationships. What does it look like when teachers collaborate? What do they talk about? How can we get beyond the generalization that collaboration is good and figure out how it actually can work?

In "Collaborative Planning," Michael Flynn writes about his collaboration with a paraprofessional in his second-grade classroom. He meets with the paraprofessional regularly to go over the mathematical focus of the upcoming lesson and to plan how she might support the students to make sense of the concepts that he is teaching to the whole class. He also describes how he and the paraprofessional built trust and were able to have honest and open exchanges about working with these students to best serve their needs.

In "A Double Dose of Math," Marta Johnson describes how her relationship with a special education teacher evolved over time, from a pullout model to a coteaching situation. The two teachers worked together to provide instruction that was philosophically consistent with the school mathematics curriculum and to provide appropriate experiences and practice for the students. The episode focuses on their work to help one of Marta's fourth graders who was struggling to understand fractions.

In "Planning Guided Math Groups," John McDougall recounts the joint efforts of two fifth-grade classroom teachers and a Title I teacher to use literacy strategies to improve students' mathematics comprehension with multistep word problems. The episode describes their planning and debriefing meetings in detail, particularly how they familiarized the Title I teacher with the mathematics content and how the Title I teacher brought her expertise in literacy to the mathematics classroom.

All these teachers engage in practices that contribute to their students' mathematics learning. They have worked hard to develop mutual respect and trust and a sense of shared responsibility. Their writing makes it apparent that fostering collaboration requires a great deal of time and effort. The teachers find the relationships worthwhile, appreciating what they learn from each other in terms of mathematical content, teaching strategies, and shared insights into the students' thinking. Although the roles and contexts are different, in all of the essays, you will see that the focus of the collaboration is on providing consistent support to help their students with special needs make sense of mathematics.

Questions to Think About

What roles do the classroom teachers and special education teachers play during these episodes?

What structures promote sustained communication in these episodes?

What knowledge does each teacher contribute?

What evidence is there that students benefited from collaboration?

What challenges do the teachers face as they work together?

21

Collaborative Planning

It's More Than One-on-One

Michael Flynn

As a teacher in an inclusive second-grade classroom, I have often supervised paraprofessionals in their work with my students who have disabilities. My goal is to establish a collaborative relationship in which we can learn from each other and provide a wider range of instructional supports for our students. Fortunately, most of the support staff who have been in my room have followed their students since kindergarten or first grade and know the children really well. I rely on their knowledge of the students as I plan and coordinate lessons, and they rely on me to help them understand both content and pedagogy.

This is particularly true when it comes to math instruction. Our mathematics program encourages instruction that helps students make sense of mathematics. It looks very different from the way we were taught, and most of our paraprofessionals do not have an education background or experience with supporting students to build number sense and become confident mathematics learners. I have found that often their first tendency is to simply tell students what to do rather than help them make connections and develop their own understanding.

For this collaboration to work, it is up to me as the teacher to establish the working relationship. I have learned that the best way to ensure success is to devote specific times during the week for joint planning, as I did with Pam, a paraprofessional assigned to work with Robert and Steven, two of my students with severe special needs. Fortunately, Pam had worked with these two boys in first grade and had developed some understanding of their learning styles. The following vignette is an example of how our collaboration progressed over the course of the year.

Planning Together

In the early spring, I taught a unit on patterns and functions. As part of our planning process, Pam and I sat down to go over some of the math activities together. I find these conversations constructive, because not only do they help help us anticipate difficulties the students might have but they also help the paraprofessionals understand the mathematics in the lesson. If they understand the math, then they can offer appropriate support in the lesson.

The lessons we discussed required students to construct buildings using cubes. In this series of activities called Cube Buildings, each cube represents a room and each row of cubes represents a floor in the building (Russell et al. 2008e). A building might start off as a row of 3 cubes. This would be a 1-story building with 3 rooms. Each time a new floor is added, the total number of rooms increases by 3. Therefore, this same building with 5 floors will have a total of 15 rooms.

In the lesson I describe here, I took the process a step further by introducing tables. After the students constructed each floor of their buildings, they tallied the total number of rooms they had to that point and entered this data in their two-column tables (the first column listed the "Total Number of Floors" and the second column was labeled "Total Number of Rooms"). They continued these steps, working floor by floor, until they constructed the building 5 floors high. At that point the table jumped to 10 floors (see Figure 21–1).

As Pam and I were going over the activity during our planning process, the following exchange took place.

PAM: So they just have to double the fifth floor to get the tenth.
MICHAEL: Well that's what we'd like to see, but most kids won't be ready to make that jump right away. They'll have to build to the tenth floor a few times so they can get a sense of what a 10-story building looks like.
PAM: But wouldn't doubling be quicker?

Total Number of Floors	Total Number of Rooms
1	
2	
3	
4	
5	
10	

Figure 21–1.

MICHAEL: Absolutely! And I hope all the students begin using that strategy, but most will have to construct the whole building before they're ready to think about a shortcut.

This exchange illustrates a typical interaction between us. Together we have discussed the benefits and drawbacks of just telling our students what we can see so clearly ourselves. I strongly believe that students need to make sense of mathematics ideas—often incrementally, as they would when working floor by floor to the top of a building even if these ways seem less "efficient."

Pam's conception of appropriate support has changed in many important ways during the year. When she first began assisting her two students, she often did most of the work for them. When they were working on story problems, she picked the manipulatives they would use, counted out the appropriate number of cubes, determined the operation for them, and then talked them through how to count and find the total. Their papers had all the correct answers, but they were not developing their own understanding of addition situations or strategies to solve these types of problems. I decided to model the kind of support I thought she could offer. This turned out to be exactly what she needed. She was able to see that her students could do much of the work and that her role was to support their learning through questions such as: "What's happening in the problem? Will your answer be more than 20 or less than 20? How do you know? What could you use to help you solve it?" By asking questions, she helped the students become learners.

Although she had developed many effective strategies to help her students, she would sometimes revert back to a more traditional method so her students would solve problems quickly. We continued to have conversations about how to best support her students' understanding.

PAM: I know Steven will be able to double, but Robert will have to build it.
MICHAEL: Steven should build it too, though. Otherwise he won't really understand why he's doubling. In fact, I'm probably going to require that each student build to 10 floors a few times so they get a sense of what's happening to the building.

Steven was one of her students who had been diagnosed with developmental delays and needed a great deal of support with work that emphasizes reasoning and problem solving. However, his computation skills were fairly strong. I had no doubt that he would be able to use the doubling strategy if someone pointed it out to him, but he wouldn't understand why it worked. To me, making sense of what was happening as each floor was added and figuring out a strategy from that experience was the most significant aspect of the activity.

At this point, I felt that Pam understood the main mathematical focus of the lesson, and I wanted to get a sense of how she felt her other student, Robert, might fare. Robert was diagnosed with a developmental delay also. However, his computation and number sense were much weaker than Steven's. Ordinarily, we would make many accommodations to the activities to provide an entry point for Robert, but this lesson did not require it. I wanted Robert to practice counting groups of objects and this activity was perfect for him. I was more concerned about the level of abstraction with the materials (cube = rooms, rows = floors, and so on). This is where Pam became invaluable and I could rely on her expertise. She knew what types of directions or activities were confusing for Robert and could anticipate the types of support he might need.

MICHAEL: Do you think Robert will be able to follow all of the steps?

PAM: I'll probably have to walk him through most of it, but he should see the pattern with the numbers.

MICHAEL: The first few are predictable patterns like 2s or 5s, but they will get trickier.

PAM: What should I do if he gets stuck?

MICHAEL: I don't think he'll get stuck because even if he loses the counting pattern, he can still count the cubes in the building. Just take notes on how he does and find me if he hits a snag.

PAM: Should the boys sit for your introduction?

Michael: I don't know. What do you think? It would help for them to see how the ideas are developed with the other students.

PAM: They might have a hard time paying attention.

MICHAEL: It may engage them; at least in the beginning when we are constructing the building. Why don't we have them come to the floor for that part and then play it by ear? If they check out, then you can introduce the rest of the activity to them separately.

Because of the ongoing communication Pam and I had established, we were able to engage in brief conversations like this that allowed us to have strategies in place for her students, with backup plans if our first course of action didn't work.

Providing Support for Students

The next morning when it was time for math, I introduced the activity to the group while Pam sat by her two students. They did engage in the introduction and both helped build a floor of the building. Pam and I made the decision, in the moment, to keep them with the whole group because they were participating. Pam could then support them as they worked on the assignment.

As Pam went off with the students, I circulated around the room to check in on the rest of the class. Early in the year, Pam and I established a system where she would take notes on what her students were doing in an activity based on the mathematical emphases in the lesson. To help her with a focus and a structure, I would identify what I wanted her to pay attention to on an observation sheet, which listed the names of all students. She could then make comments beside each name as she observed them. This also helped her focus on the important mathematical goals of the lessons.

Once a lesson was over, we would use part of our preparation period to debrief what happened. Pam's input was a big help because I couldn't always observe the boys each day. She would also observe other students if her students were not in the room. Having this second set of eyes helped me with my ongoing assessment and planning for the next lesson. Her interactions with the other students not only increased her knowledge of the range of strategies that students develop but also strengthened our collaboration.

When I was making the rounds in the classroom, I went over to see how the boys were doing. Robert was diligently constructing the first building and systematically recording the information on the table with Pam's assistance. Every time he finished a row, he would count all of the cubes starting from the first floor and then write the total on the table. This is exactly how I expected him to approach this task, and I was glad to see him make the connection between the physical object and abstract table.

It was also great to see how well Pam worked with him. As he finished a step, she would simply ask, "Now what do you have to do?" or "What should you do next?" This gave Robert ownership of the activity while still providing support.

Steven's first table was completed perfectly and he began working on the second building (5 rooms per floor). As I watched him work, I saw him build the first floor of 5 rooms. Once he saw how many cubes were on the first floor (5), he began writing the counting-by-5s pattern down the second column on the table. I expected this much of him because he knew many counting patterns and would have no trouble continuing one. However, he was not constructing a building and this worried me. I wondered how much he was getting out of the lesson.

After he got to the fifth floor, he began to write a 3. This wasn't surprising because he wasn't paying attention to the numbers in the first column. He also had no building to refer to. For him, it was an exercise in counting patterns. So I expected him to write 30 because it would be the next number in the pattern. However, he quickly erased the 3 and wrote 50.

MICHAEL: Now why did you write 50?

STEVEN: Mrs. Reil said to double the last number.

I was disappointed because he clearly had no idea why he was doubling. Pam sensed my disappointment and began to explain.

PAM: He really picked up on the pattern so I think he has it. He just needed help to not continue the pattern for 6 floors. Once I showed him the 10, he got it.

I wasn't going to disagree with her in front of Steven, so I just let it go. I knew we would debrief and I could talk to her about it then. I finished making my rounds and then called the class to the floor to wrap up for the period. When the students left for art class, Pam and I sat down to talk about the lesson.

Debriefing the Lesson

This could have been an awkward situation, but Pam and I had established a sense of openness early in the year. Having worked with other paraprofessionals in the past, I realized the importance of open communication. Before the start of the year, we agreed that we should both feel comfortable being open and honest in our communication. She knew that I might question how she did something, and she also knew that she could question me. Neither of us had all the answers, and it was important that we could respectfully disagree and ask questions. Establishing these norms early on helped both of us improve as teachers.

Of course, it did take time for this type of relationship to develop. It is one thing to say you are going to be open in your communication; it is another thing to do it. We both took tentative steps during the first few months of school. When I wanted to suggest she try a different approach with a student, I would go out of my way to praise everything she was doing already and eventually get to my suggestion. She in turn would do the same when making suggestions to me. Eventually, as with any relationship, we developed a comfort with each other and began speaking more frankly.

As we sat down to debrief, she already knew what I was going to say.

PAM: I know, I know, I showed him how to double, but he really had it. He was just flying. He finished the other 2 buildings before you called the class to the floor.
MICHAEL: See, I think that's the problem though. He was flying through the activity, but I don't think he really understands what he's doing.
PAM: I think he does. He didn't even need to build the buildings. He saw the pattern right away.
MICHAEL: Right, but remember this activity is about more than counting. We want the students to connect what they're building to the table. He can't do that if he's not making the building.

PAM: So what should I do with him then?

MICHAEL: I would do exactly what you were doing with Robert. That was perfect. We're doing a similar activity tomorrow.

PAM: But Steven is too quick to work with Robert.

MICHAEL: Steven needs to slow down. That's half his problem. He just goes on autopilot and does things without understanding. Do exactly what you were doing with Robert and help Steven make those connections.

PAM: Should he build it to 10 floors?

MICHAEL: If he has to, then let him.

PAM: I don't think he will. He really does know when to double.

Pam was still missing the big mathematical point in the lesson. She really wanted her students, particularly Steven, to work at the same pace as the rest of the class. It was easy for her to worry that the boys were falling behind and natural for her to want them to "catch up." However, I strongly believe that if we rush students at the expense of their understanding, then we make it harder for them to develop sound mathematical ideas. This math activity was about much more than simply having the correct numbers in the table, and the next day's lesson would prove that.

MICHAEL: Well tomorrow's activity is pretty much the same as today's, but the tables will go to 6 rows before jumping to 10. We'll see if he really gets it. I'm betting he'll double the sixth floor to solve for the tenth. What do you think?

PAM: OK, you made your point. He was just moving so fast with the patterns. I thought he would get it.

MICHAEL: In terms of computation, he does get it, but working with the tables is pretty abstract stuff. He's going to need a lot of support to make sense of it.

Implementing Accommodations

The following day, Steven did exactly what I predicted. Pam laughed and I jokingly gave her an "I told you so." For the rest of the period, she worked with Steven much the same way she worked with Robert. She spent her time helping him connect what was happening in his building to what was happening on the table.

This process was much slower, but Pam was beginning to realize that although he was getting the correct answer very quickly, he didn't understand what he was doing. Students really have to understand what happens as the buildings grow to understand why doubling the fifth floor would work. The students in my class who noticed that doubling would work were able to justify in a few different ways during our discussion at the end of the period.

CHRIS: You can double the 25 and get 50 because you're just adding 5 more floors. There are 25 rooms when it's 5 floors so 25 more is 50.
SAVANNAH: [*breaking the 10-floor building in half*] See, these are the same. They each have 5 floors, so it's double.

The students also had ideas about why you couldn't double the rooms in a 6-story building to figure out the total in a 10-story building. Jessica said, "If you double the sixth floor then that would tell you how many rooms are on the twelfth floor. That would be 60."

Another student demonstrated this with cubes much like Savannah did earlier. Still another student further elaborated on the idea by saying you could double the total on the second floor to find the total on the fourth floor, and you could double the total on the fourth floor to find the total on the eighth.

These student explanations helped Pam understand that the math in the activity went beyond counting patterns and doubling. I think it helped her to see the level of knowledge needed for students to justify the doubling strategy. When the students left for music class, we debriefed.

PAM: I can see why using the buildings helps.
MICHAEL: Absolutely. That's why I make everyone build them even if they notice that they can double to solve for the tenth floor. Do you feel like Steven was making the connection?
PAM: Not at first. I had to introduce the whole process all over again. He forgot about the rooms and floors. He really didn't know what he was doing. But it was good because I had Robert work with him and sort of teach him how to make the buildings.
MICHAEL: That was good idea. How was the pacing with both of them?
PAM: It was actually fairly balanced. Steven needed a lot of support constructing the building and Robert needed help with the table so they were able to help each other.

I understood why Pam wanted to push Steven's strengths to help him with the activity. If all the activities were like the first ones, he would have aced all of them. However, once she understood the bigger picture, she knew he needed much more.

Reflections

As Pam became more proficient at observing and analyzing students while they worked, she began thinking like a teacher. For example, she made better decisions about what level of support a student might need. She was able to focus her support on building understanding of the mathematical ideas of the lesson instead of rushing her students to keep the same pace as the rest of the class. Over time, I found that she needed less direction from me during the lessons. Unfortunately, she will be moving on with her students as they go to third grade, and I'll have to start the cycle all over again next year with a new paraprofessional. I will build on what I learned from my collaboration with Pam, about how to accommodate students' learning styles, and about how to make the big mathematical ideas explicit in supervision.

22

A Double Dose of Math

Collaborating to Support Student Learning

Marta Garcia Johnson

Each year, my fourth-grade class* includes a few students who need additional assistance from a special educator to access mathematical ideas and build confidence for sharing their ideas. Often collaboration between special education teachers and classroom teachers can be challenging because special education teachers usually focus on literacy instruction and are not afforded the opportunity to learn the school mathematics program. However, for six years, I have been fortunate to collaborate with Diane, a special education teacher who is both knowledgeable about mathematics and enthusiastic in supporting the math learning of our students. Diane benefited from attending our district's professional development workshops that incorporated the content and pedagogy that were aligned with our school mathematics program. She valued the program's emphasis on problem solving, reasoning, and student thinking and was able to implement many of the strategies she learned. Over time, we have developed a productive working partnership that supports the math learning of my students with special needs.

Diane came into my classroom once a week to work with my special needs students. She also provided additional assistance for these students in a pullout group that met for thirty minutes each week. We had many conversations about how to connect the work that was happening in the classroom with the support teaching she was doing both in the classroom and during the pullout time. We worked hard to provide our struggling students with extra practice that was consistent with the problem-solving approaches that we use in our school mathematics program. We regularly scheduled joint planning and debriefing meetings to discuss students' progress and plan for instruction.

---

*Chapter 8 is another essay about this class.

During one particular year, Diane and I worked closely together to support the progress of Jhali, a student with multiple learning challenges. Our work during this time allowed us to both strengthen our collaboration strategies and support the growth of this student's mathematical understanding.

Planning for Our Work with Jhali

In addition to being an English language learner, Jhali had specific learning disabilities in the areas of reading, written expression, and mathematics. As we began work on our fractions unit, it was clear that this content would be particularly challenging for Jhali. I knew it would be important to work closely with Diane to map out and execute a course of instruction that would help us meet the following state benchmarks:

- interpreting the meaning of *numerator* and *denominator*
- understanding that fractions refer to equal parts
- visualizing fractions
- identifying relationships between unit fractions
- ordering fractions with like denominators and justifying their order through reasoning

In preparation, I spent some time assessing Jhali's current understandings about fractions and discovered she was struggling in several areas:

- She had difficulty creating a mental image of a fraction.
- She was unable to make up a story that described a fractional relationship.
- She would use either the numerator or denominator—whichever was larger—when comparing two fractions.
- She was using an additive approach to look at the relationship between the numerator and the denominator. For example, in describing $\frac{2}{5}$, she remarked that "5 is 3 more than 2."

I also gathered information about how Jhali incorporated the work she was doing in Diane's pullout group during the regular mathematics education block. For example, when Jhali's small group in my class began to make a deck of fraction cards (Russell et al. 2008d), Diane volunteered to make additional cards for the unit fractions and wholes with unit fractions to give Jhali extra practice in the pullout group (e.g., $1\frac{1}{2}$) (see Figure 22–1). We used these cards to order fractions and to match the fractional notations with pictures of area models of the fractions. Because of the extra practice with these card games she was getting in her pullout group, Jhali was confident in her ability to support her small group's work in the regular math block by making the deck of fraction cards.

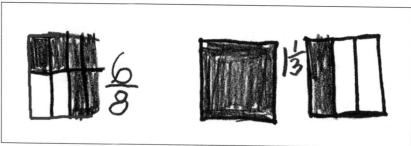

Figure 22–1.

While I was assessing Jhali's work in my classroom, Diane was assessing how Jhali was articulating her ideas in the pullout group. To be sure that we had the same learning goals in mind, I asked Diane to focus her assessments on:

- whether Jhali's limited use and understanding of the vocabulary associated with fraction concepts was hindering her understanding and her ability to express the ideas she did understand
- how consistent Jhali was with her explanations of how she was comparing fractions
- whether or not Jhali was using vocabulary such as *numerator*, *denominator*, *whole*, *greater than*, and *less than* in ways that were consistent with her strategies for comparing fractions

I knew that the words *numerator* and *denominator* were not making sense to Jhali in the abstract and that we needed to talk about fractions in the context of representations. Based on our assessments, Diane and I developed a plan for working with Jhali, both in the small pullout group and in the regular classroom, that incorporated some of the same representations we were using in class. The following is an excerpt from our initial planning conversation.

MARTA: I've noticed that Jhali is using the terms *denominator* and *numerator* correctly, but I am not certain that she understands how those parts of a fraction are related. When I ask her to describe a fraction such as $\frac{3}{5}$, she says things like "the denominator is bigger 'cause it is 5, but then the 3 is going to be smaller but the numerator is going to make it bigger."

DIANE: We've worked a lot on vocabulary. Here, I brought her folder with the cards and pictures we have made, but I think we have a lot more work to do on what a fraction is. Maybe she can work on drawing more models.

MARTA: Yes, I think it's helpful that you've worked with Jhali on these terms so that she can follow our class discussions when those terms are used.

But it's clear that although she can use the words, she's not yet able to compare fractions with like numerators.

DIANE: Today we were looking at two fractions in a word problem and she tried to say something about the bigger the number, the smaller the pieces. But she got confused and started talking about the numerator.

MARTA: That's what I have noticed as well. She starts off very confident and seems to begin connecting what she has worked on previously, and then she moves on to use a completely different and inefficient method for comparing the two fractions.

DIANE: I think part of this is her inability to stay focused. Even in our small group every day, she jumps from one idea to another without finishing what she had started to say. I think we should have her work with the same three fractions for a few days, comparing those same ones each day and see if she is consistent in how she explains her strategy.

MARTA: Would you be able to work on using different representations with her for several days? Let's stick with $\frac{1}{2}$, $\frac{1}{3}$, and $\frac{1}{4}$. And then I can reinforce her practice as the class moves on to other fraction comparisons. Let's check back later next week.

Implementing the Plans and Assessing Progress

Because I had planned the learning trajectory that our class would follow during our work with fractions, I suggested the sequence of activities and assessments that Diane would use to support Jhali in accessing the ideas that our whole class would be studying. Diane was able to use individual interviews and formative assessments with Jhali more frequently then I was. We agreed that these assessments would focus specifically on the individual goals we had set for Jhali, in particular, visualizing fractions and identifying relationships between unit fractions. I would continue to offer suggestions for subsequent activities and assessments that would meet Jhali's needs. Through repeated practice, we wanted her to connect representations to symbolic notations of fractions, to verbalize her ideas before applying them as a consistent strategy, and to connect the formal language of mathematics with her own ideas.

For the next two weeks, Diane had Jhali manipulate fraction bars and circles and explain the images on the fraction cards we made in class. She also provided Jhali time to practice explaining her reasoning when comparing the three fractions. Because Diane had more time with Jhali than I did, she was able to listen carefully to how Jhali was using the vocabulary and how she was developing an understanding of the meaning of the words *numerator* and *denominator*. We especially wanted to assess if Jhali was moving away from viewing the numerator and denominator as two separate whole numbers.

Although Jhali needed this additional time with Diane, it was also important that she continue to be exposed to the mathematical ideas that we were working with in class and to participate in that larger classroom community. I use flexible grouping in my classroom so that my struggling students have opportunities to collaborate with their peers who are working with grade-level ideas successfully. So, while Diane narrowed her work with Jhali to a specific focus (the meaning of *numerator* and *denominator*), I assessed Jhali's understanding of the concepts being investigated by the rest of the class. These students were creating representations for a variety of fractions including fourths, sixths, eighths, tenths, and fractions representing more than a whole. They then made all kinds of fraction comparisons, including fractions with like and unlike numerators and denominators.

I needed to find out how Jhali was making sense of this mathematics. Was she able to use the strategies she learned with Diane and apply them to these new fractions? I checked in with her, asking her to explain the models she had drawn and how the numerator and denominator represented the fraction. Jhali stated: "The denominator is how many pieces [sometimes she would say lines] and the numerator is how many I colored." Although she used this description consistently, I wasn't sure if she would be able to draw upon these images when she had to compare fractions without a visual model. A few days later, I spent some time assessing the development of Jhali's understanding.

TEACHER: Which of these is the larger fraction: $\frac{1}{5}$ or $\frac{1}{3}$?

JHALI: $\frac{1}{3}$ because if I cut the rectangle I have only 3 pieces instead of 5.

TEACHER: So you said you have 3 pieces. Why do you think $\frac{1}{3}$ is more than $\frac{1}{5}$?

JHALI: See, I mean the pieces would be bigger because you only have 3. So you take 1 piece and I take 1 piece but my pieces will be fat and bigger than yours.

This was progress! Jhali based her second comment on her first idea. Next, I wanted to see if she would stay with her strategy:

TEACHER: What about $\frac{1}{5}$ and $\frac{1}{4}$?

JHALI: Maybe $\frac{1}{5}$ is bigger.

TEACHER: What is different about these two fractions from the others you just compared? Let's look at these.

JHALI: Oh, the $\frac{1}{4}$ because the pieces are fatter than the $\frac{1}{5}$ pieces. See.

Jhali then drew two circles (one divided into fourths and one into fifths) and pointed out how the fourth pieces were bigger. (Although her pieces were not of equal size, she had attempted to make the fourths larger than the fifths.) I went on to see if she could compare two fractions when the numerators were not equal to 1.

TEACHER: Which of these two do you think is the biggest, $\frac{2}{4}$ or $\frac{2}{5}$? Before you answer, think about what you just said about $\frac{1}{4}$ and $\frac{1}{5}$.

JHALI: I don't get it because they are the same because they have the same number.

TEACHER: What number is the same?

JHALI: The numerator, the top number. So they are equal.

TEACHER: Look at the $\frac{1}{4}$ and $\frac{1}{5}$. They have the same numerator but you told me that the $\frac{1}{4}$ was larger. Why did you say it was larger?

JHALI: Because the pieces are bigger. But now the pieces are the same.

I could tell she was getting frustrated and I was not sure where to go next. I wondered what mental image she was creating for $\frac{2}{4}$ and $\frac{2}{5}$.

TEACHER: Can you explain to me what picture you see in your mind for $\frac{2}{4}$?

JHALI: 2 colored pieces and 2 not colored and for the other, 2 colored and 3 not colored.

TEACHER: Which has the bigger pieces?

JHALI: Oh, the $\frac{2}{5}$ is smaller because I had to cut the pieces skinnier to make 5 of them.

I was very pleased that Jhali was able to visualize and explain that the bigger denominator signified "skinnier pieces."

Planning Next Steps

Diane and I discussed my interview with Jhali and used that information to plan the next set of activities: comparing fractions with like denominators and unlike numerators ($\frac{1}{4}$, $\frac{2}{4}$, $\frac{3}{4}$). My knowledge of where the class was headed with our work in fractions and my observations of how other students in the class accessed the ideas were critical to this planning decision. At the same time, I depended on Diane's expertise about how learning challenges can be supported with accommodations and her understanding of how Jhali's language difficulties affected her understanding. Because we knew that Jhali had comprehension problems and was still building a listening vocabulary in English, it was important to make sure our explanations made sense to her. We needed to listen carefully to how she described her ideas to see if they indicated mathematical confusion or a limited repertoire of vocabulary.

For the next two weeks, we made sure that Jhali was getting a "double dose" of the same sequence of tasks. Our class continued comparing fractions with like denominators, such as $\frac{1}{4}$, $\frac{2}{4}$, $\frac{3}{4}$, but we had also moved on to comparing fractions with unlike denominators. Diane continued to review the fractions with like denominators with Jhali and her small group. Diane and I both noted that Jhali was applying comparison strategies consistently. One day, Diane shared that Jhali had volunteered several times to explain to the group how she had "stories" that she could tell that would explain how she knew which fraction was greater. We were pleased that she connected the work I was doing with her to the sequence of tasks that she worked with in Diane's room. The consistent practice helped Jhali begin to make sense of fractional relationships. *Numerator* and *denominator* were no longer just *words*. Jhali was able to represent and tell stories to describe relationships. Diane shared one of Jhali's stories about comparing $\frac{1}{4}$ and $\frac{1}{6}$:

> You see, there is this rich man that has a big car. When 4 people get in, they have lots of space but when 6 people get in, they are all squished because the space gets split up into 6 parts. So more people is less space so you only get a little piece, it is only a 1 little piece of 6 spaces. That's why $\frac{1}{4}$ is bigger, those people have 4 spaces in the car and they get 1 of the 4 spaces.

Although Jhali's story did not take into account whether or not the people were of equal size, she was able to describe the relationship that more people would mean less space for each, that each would only have a smaller fraction of space available.

Reflections

An important aspect of working with Jhali was working through this assessment-teaching cycle in close collaboration with Diane. This collaboration ensured that Jhali's mathematical experiences were consistent and provided her with multiple opportunities to practice the same concepts over time in a variety of contexts. Because Diane had participated in mathematical professional development with the classroom teachers, she and I shared a common language and approach. Diane did not simply offer Jhali a set of manipulatives, but she varied the representations and focused on Jhali's expression of the fractional relationships. Because of Diane's support, Jhali could continue to participate in the work that the rest of her class was doing while still receiving the support she needed to build her skills. I am convinced that Jhali benefited both from listening to our classroom discourse and from having the additional practice with Diane. Providing these consistent experiences for Jhali took a great deal of planning by Diane and me.

It was essential that Diane and I made the time to meet together. She was eager to hear about the information I gathered about Jhali from seeing her in class every day and about the mathematical goals I had identified for the unit of study. I found her reporting of Jhali's mathematics in the pullout group to be very valuable in my planning for Jhali during the regular mathematics block. For example, when Diane shared with me the story that Jhali told about the car, it gave me an entry point for the type of story that Jhali might be able to relate to in the whole group. Our collaboration allowed us to make frequent assessments of Jhali's progress, and these observations enabled us to focus our combined efforts in the areas that would best meet Jhali's needs. Both Diane and I found our collaboration to be worthwhile, especially in terms of the progress Jhali made, but also in contributing to our professional growth.

23

Planning Guided Math Groups

A Collaboration Between Classroom Teachers and Title 1 Staff

John MacDougall, with Marta Garcia Johnson and Karen Joslin

For the last year and a half, Karen and her Title I assistants have been working with students in my class and Marta's on small-group literacy instruction focused on comprehension strategies. The three of us began to talk about the potential for extending our collaboration to mathematics. Karen felt strongly that mathematics and reading should not be considered such separate subjects and that she could bring her expertise in reading to help students understand mathematical problems. Because Marta and I teach both literacy and math with our fifth-grade classes, we too saw the connections between the two disciplines. At the same time, we realized that some of our students were not doing well in math because of their struggles with reading and comprehending word problems. Many students, across the grades, were proficient computational thinkers but struggled to understand complex situations represented in word problem form. Marta and I are on the school math committee, and we brought up the possibility of working with the Title I teachers on math literacy. With the math committee's backing, Marta took the next step of approaching the school improvement team, consisting of Marta, a teacher-representative from each grade level, the principal, and the librarian. The school improvement team gave us the approval to form math literacy groups with grade 3–5 students that would meet once a week for approximately thirty minutes.

Implementing the Small-Group Math Instruction

As classroom teachers, we understand the importance of collaborating with our special education colleagues to improve the learning of our students who are struggling. Working together in mathematics can be particularly challenging because we often find that the special needs teachers we work with have a stronger background in literacy than in math.

Karen has a unique perspective and set of experiences that allows her to engage with the children in a way that a classroom teacher in a whole-class setting would be hard pressed to match. Because we knew that she was doing very good work with the students in literacy and that she was well aware of their strengths and gaps, we began this relationship with a high level of mutual trust and respect. Karen had worked extensively with our struggling students throughout the year using KWL (What I Know, What I Want to Know, What I Learned) charts to understand reading passages as well as using visualization, inferring, making connections, determining importance, and questioning in small-group reading lessons. Karen is a master at guiding children through these thinking processes while reading and has a relatively strong mathematics background. It was a very natural transition for her to adapt those strategies for mathematical situations. In our meetings, Karen was able to share her experience merging her literacy comprehension strategies with math problem-solving strategies. We knew she would be able to make connections to math work with the students in our classes because we worked with her closely during reading and writing instruction. We were fortunate that she was eager to take on this additional responsibility and add to her knowledge of teaching mathematics.

It was clear that a productive collaboration between the classroom teachers and the Title I reading staff (led by Karen) would be key to the success of these groups. We knew we needed to work together to determine when and how to use reading comprehension strategies to help students make sense of the mathematical problems they were trying to solve. Given our focus on comprehension, we all determined several goals for the math literacy groups:

1. Students will carefully read and unpack each math problem, taking it apart and figuring out what each piece of the problem means and what it is asking. All of our students have been working extensively with KWL charts to aid in reading comprehension, so for our mathematics work, we will use a variation of the KWL chart—a KWC (What I Know; What I Want to Know; What are the Constraints or Conditions of the Problem) chart.

2. Students will use a variety of reading comprehension strategies to help them understand and solve the problem, including visualizing, inferring, making connections, determining importance, and questioning.

The school's math committee developed and led a monthly, school-based professional development series, involving the entire school-certified staff, based on the book *Comprehending Math: Adapting Reading Strategies to Teach Mathematics, K–6* in which particular strategies to develop comprehension in math are outlined (Hyde 2006). This book's approach is only one tool to foster math comprehension, but as our entire staff was trained in this strategy, we believed it would be effective. At our meetings, we collected, shared, and analyzed student work based on the comprehension strategies we were using from the book.

The Planning

Karen began coming into our rooms for the small-group math instruction a few months into the year. At the time, all of the classroom teachers were using the same, nonroutine word problems, which students worked in homogenous groups to solve. The students we focused on were in a group with the literacy specialist (Karen, in our cases) while the classroom teacher rotated among the other few small groups in the room. (This kind of grouping is how Title I reading groups are organized, so we decided to stay with this familiar structure.)

We realized that it was crucial for the three of us to meet to plan the word problems we would be focusing on, to work on the mathematics in the problems together, and to discuss what comprehension strategies would support students' understanding of those particular problems. We decided that Karen would start out working with a group from Marta's classroom, then we would debrief, and she would use what she learned to adjust her teaching for the group in my classroom.

We wanted to choose a problem that involved the application of the ideas surrounding the number work we had done with students with the operations of multiplication and division, as well as fractions. We also wanted to choose a problem that would require the students to navigate a significant amount of language to understand the problem. The problem we chose was:

> One day, the Lugnut Car Factory produced 315 cars. The cars were silver, black, or white. One-ninth of all the cars were silver. For every 3 black cars made, 2 were white. How many of each color did they produce? (Wheatley 2002)

During our discussion, we talked about what Karen should focus on during the lesson.

- strategies for unpacking the problem to figure out what it is asking
- possible representations to support students' visualization of the problem
- possible strategies for computing the solution
- places where students might be confused

Unpacking the Problem

It was important that we took the time to unpack the problem and solve it ourselves. This allowed us to "think like the students" and gave Karen the opportunity to learn about the different kinds of math thinking our students were doing and where their comprehension might break down.

We began with a discussion of how to use a KWC chart to help our students slow down and think carefully about the information in the problem, one sentence at a time. After the first sentence of the problem, we agreed that we wanted students to realize that there are 3 groups of cars within the 315. Then we determined that the students would need to realize that the $\frac{1}{9}$ is an important piece of information.

KAREN: Well, I'd say, "What's important in that sentence?" Hopefully they'd say $\frac{1}{9}$ of the cars are silver.

JOHN: At this point, they might infer what fraction is not silver. Or actually how many cars are not silver.

MARTA: Yes, you may want to stop at that point and say, "If $\frac{1}{9}$ of the cars are silver, how many ninths, are not silver? The black and the white together make how many ninths? That's $\frac{8}{9}$, that is almost 1 whole, so, you hardly have any silver cars at all."

KAREN: That's where the visualization comes in, to compare the silver cars with the nonsilver cars.

MARTA: You don't have a number but you can already visualize this little tiny group and then these two other groups. Now it is time to go to the next sentence.

JOHN: There were more cars made, they were black and white. We need to know how many of each.

Introducing Representations

At this point, we discussed why it might be important to suggest that students use a physical model to represent the problem. In this case, we decided that different-colored cubes would be an appropriate model.

MARTA: They might use groups of 5 cubes, 3 black and 2 white, to represent the relationship between the number of black and white cars. You might ask, "If you have 6 black cubes, how many whites would you have?" That's one way to model or represent the black and white cars.

JOHN: I wonder if at that point when it is time to solve it, the students will try to build a chart with a row for each set of 5 cars [*see Figure 23–1*] or if they'll be able to work directly with the number of nonsilver cars. Are they going to try to go each step? You know, go: 3 black, 2 white; 6 black, 4 white; 9 black, 6 white?

MARTA: I hope not. With the blocks and the chart, I am hoping that they will see the ratio as a constant. Every time you get 3 more black cars, you'll get 2 more white ones and vice versa. And you will always be able to see groups of 2 and groups of 3 no matter how large your numbers get.

JOHN: For every 3 black cars, 2 are white. That means $\frac{3}{5}$ of the remaining nonsilver cars are black.

Black Cars	3	6	9	12	15	18
White Cars	2	4	6	8	10	12

Figure 23–1.

What Is the Question?

Once we had worked on the visualization and representations, we returned to the "unpacking part."

> KAREN: So, now we are down to where we are actually computing numbers to answer the question. We actually need to know how many of each color they produced. We talked about the constraints, that there have to be 2 white for every 3 black, and there has to be $\frac{1}{9}$ silver.
>
> JOHN: Instead of saying $\frac{1}{9}$ of the cars are silver, another way you could think about it is 1 out of 9 is silver. Then they have to figure out how many groups of 9 are in 315.
>
> MARTA: You might even want to model that with cubes. 9 cubes, 1 of which is silver. So, you could ask, "If you have 18, how many silver would you have? If you had 27, how many silver would you have?"
>
> JOHN: So continuing the pattern, they will need to figure out, how many groups of 9 are in 315.

Working Through the Computation

At this point, we discussed how to best support students' computational strategies. This discussion would also support Karen, who was not as cognizant of the strategies that the students had at their disposal. When Karen worked with students in math class before, she often found herself asking the students to explain how they were approaching a computation simply because she didn't understand their strategy. Although the articulation of their strategies reinforced students' understanding of their own thinking, Karen knew that it was useful for her to be aware of how to support students as they applied their computation strategies to a particular problem, so we discussed possible strategies in some detail.

> KAREN: Are they going to want to divide 315 by 9?
>
> MARTA: A lot of them might chunk it, something like this: 10 9s = 90; 10 9s = 90, 10 9s = 90. That's 30 9s = 270. Five more 9s = 45. 270 + 45 = 315.

	20	20	10	6
5	100	100	50	30

Figure 23–2.

So there are $10 + 10 + 10 + 5 = 35$ silver cars. Then there is another part. They are going to need to subtract to find out how many cars are not silver. There are 280 cars left.

JOHN: So now we are back to visualizing 3 black cars for every 2 white cars. We want to continue that representation using an array model. The array model of division would work well in determining how many groups of 5 are in 280 (the number of nonsilver cars) [*see Figure 23–2*].

MARTA: So the students have to visualize these groups of 5, with 2 white and 3 black like we did before until they get to 280 cars.

JOHN: And hopefully instead of counting each car, they will look at them in groups of 5. So, you might ask, "If we had 10 groups of 5, how many of each color would you have?"

MARTA: And they should be able to say, well, there are 20 groups of 5 in 100. Twenty in another 100, which would be 40. Another 10 would be 50, and then you would need 6 more. That would be 56 groups of 5 in 280.

KAREN: So, what we are trying to do is get them to see 280 in groups of 5.

MARTA: Right, once they get that there are 56 groups, they should think that in each of those 56 groups of 5, there are 3 black cars and 2 white cars.

JOHN: So, they are going to have to multiply the number of groups by the number of cars of each color in each group.

KAREN: So, 56×3 black cars and 56×2 white cars.

MARTA: And 56×2 would be 112 white cars and 56×3 would be 168 black cars.

JOHN: Which would you give you the 280.

Preparing for Points of Confusion

Throughout our discussion, we all noted places that might be difficult for the children, and we developed strategies to help them work through those challenges. We knew that keeping track of what the problem was asking—figuring out how many cars were silver and then splitting up the remaining cars proportionately to figure out the totals—would all be areas of challenge for these students. We saw the KWC chart as a tool to help them organize the information and understand what the question was asking. Establishing the representations, such as cubes and arrays, to help them visualize and solve the problem was also particularly important. Using precise language such as "in each of the 56 groups of 5, there are 3 black cars and 2 white cars" would help the students keep track of the numbers and remind them of what they were trying to solve.

When the meeting was concluded, we had all worked through the problem and thought deeply about the ways the students could see success. We asked Karen how she felt about the task and how well prepared she felt, and she showed a high level of confidence and enthusiasm.

The Small Guided Group Meeting

On this particular Friday, Karen joined Marta's fifth-grade classroom. She brought a group of seven students together. Some of the students have identified learning challenges in reading comprehension and mathematical problem solving, some are English language learners, and some have special needs in math. A whiteboard, markers, and cubes were close at hand. Karen reminded the students that they would be working on one problem for the entire time and that they would spend the first part of the session "unpacking" the problem using the KWC charts.

The problem that day was the same one we had worked on together: One day, the Lugnut Car Factory produced 315 cars. The cars were silver, black, or white. One-ninth of all the cars were silver. For every 3 black cars made, 2 white ones were produced. How many of each color did they produce?

Karen began by asking the students to not read the whole problem at once because they would be discussing each sentence in the problem, one at a time, and using the KWC chart to understand the problem. She asked a student to read the first sentence: "One day, the Lugnut Car Factory produced 315 cars."

KAREN: OK, stop there.
JAY: That's a lot of cars.
JULIO: We can write that in the Know column.

Karen asked Glenda to read the next sentence: "The cars were silver, black, or white." The group wrote the new information in the Know column on their KWC charts: "There were silver, black, white cars." Karen reminded the group that they were now noting that the cars were going to be split into 3 groups. Sally read the next sentence: "One-ninth of all the cars were silver."

JAY: We could do $\frac{1}{9}$ of 315, and that will automatically give us the silver. We could break up 315 into 9s. You could do 10×9 and then 15×9 and see how close you get.

KAREN: Are you saying that we need to multiply?

GLORIA: Shouldn't we divide? If we did multiply we would get too many.

This was an opportunity to talk about what the students already knew: as Gloria said, there are 315 cars in all and if we multiplied 315 by 9, we would increase the total number of cars. Jay was approaching the problem differently, though, using multiplication combinations that he knew to figure out how many 9s were in 315. In retrospect, Karen realized that she could have pursued a discussion of the differences between these two approaches.

At this point, several of the children wanted to start dividing. Karen asked them to wait until they had read the entire problem. This was a common behavior for this group of students: They often began computing with the numbers in the problem before they had a complete understanding of what was required to find a solution to the problem.

Jay read the next sentence: "For every 3 black cars made, 2 were white."

JAY: We can write BBBWW, BBBWW.

KAREN: Let's write that on the chart.

JULIO: We have $\frac{2}{3}$ black cars.

KAREN: Let's get this sentence [*"For every 3 black cars made, 2 were white"*] on the chart and think about it for a bit.

After the new information was noted on the KWC, Karen pulled out some black and white cubes. She asked, "What do you notice about this group of cubes that might help us with this problem?"

NINA: There are 5 cubes in the group.

KAREN: Nina, tell us more about that.

NINA: [*putting together a row of 3 black cubes and 2 white cubes*] Well, there are $\frac{3}{5}$ black and $\frac{2}{5}$ white.

KAREN: We are going to be looking at $\frac{3}{5}$ and $\frac{2}{5}$ of what number?

TASHIA: We have to figure it out of the silver.

KAREN: Let's read the last sentence to figure out what we want to know. [*The group reads the question—"How many of each color did they produce?" — and adds it to the KWC chart under W.*]

SETH: We want to know how many of each color car there is.

KAREN: Are there any constraints?

NINA: Yes! Every time we have 2 white cars, we have to have 3 black ones.

TASHIA: And the silver are $\frac{1}{9}$. [*We then added these constraints on the KWC charts.*]

JAY: Can we divide now?

KAREN: OK, now let's figure out the silver cars.

Karen was glad that we had discussed possible computation strategies prior to the lesson. She was able to support the students as they computed 315 divided by 9, using their strategy of breaking up 315 into groups of 9 with "friendly numbers," such as 10×9 and 15×9. From her schooling, Karen was only familiar with the long division algorithm, but she was beginning to see that methods such as "chunking" foster a deeper conceptual understanding.

KAREN: It looks like all of you got 35. So we know we have 35 silver cars. What do you think we need to do next?

NINA: We need to figure out the black and white. The $\frac{2}{5}$ and $\frac{3}{5}$.

KAREN: Do we know what number we are going to take $\frac{2}{5}$ and $\frac{3}{5}$ from?

SALLY: Not yet.

TASHIA: We have to find how many are left after we take out the silver. So we can find out about the black and the white.

KAREN: OK, so let's find that out.

The students worked to find out the difference between 315 and 35. This group of students was fairly proficient with basic operations, so Karen didn't need to give them much support to be successful with this step.

SETH: We have 280 cars left.

TASHIA: And some of those are black.

SALLY: And the rest are white.

JULIO: Let's make a chart. [*Other students add rows to Nina's row of 3 black and 2 white cubes.*]

KAREN: OK, let's look at the groups of 5 cubes we have started. How could they help us make a chart or to solve the problem? To make the problem easier? [*see Figure 23–3*].

JAY: We can go 5, 5, 5, 5 times a number.

KAREN: It might take a long time to count by 5s.

JULIO: We could divide 280 by 5.

JAY: It might have a remainder.

NINA: I don't think so.

The students worked to find the number of groups of 5 in 280. Karen was really impressed with the way the students split apart the 280 into 100, 100, and 80 and found how many groups of 5 there were in the total by adding 20, 20, and 16.

KAREN: So now we know there are 56 groups of 5.

JAY: We could take $\frac{1}{2}$ of 56.

KAREN: OK. So let's look at the cubes. There are 56 groups like this.

JULIO: We will divide them.

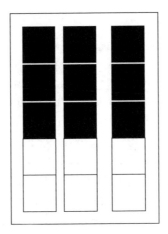

Figure 23–3.

JAY: Divide them in half.

NINA: But they aren't half white and black.

KAREN: Why are we dividing?

Julio thought that they needed to separate each of the 56 groups of 5 cars into black cars and white cars.

GLORIA: We need to multiply.

KAREN: Why do you think that?

GLORIA: If you divided them, the number would be small and we have to have 280 cars.

KAREN: So if I take my white cubes, then I have 56 groups of the white cubes.

NINA: And we have 2 in each group so we multiply 56 × 2. [*The students quickly compute the answer to 56 × 2.*]

KAREN: So how will I find the black cubes?

TASHIA: Take the black cubes, you take the 3.

NINA: The 3 times the 56.

KAREN: How are we going to know that we have all the cars?

TASHIA: We add them all up!

SALLY: We add up the silver the black and the white and we get 315.

Karen realized that she could have connected Julio's idea about dividing the groups of five white cars and black cars to Nina's computation of 56 × 2 and 56 × 3.

The Debriefing Meeting

The following Monday, we met to discuss how the small-group discussion unfolded. This was an opportunity for Karen to point out her successes and challenges while providing us with another perspective and set of insights about the children's thinking. We then took what we learned and planned adjustments for Karen's next meeting with my students.

KAREN: So, basically, it went really well. I was really impressed with their thinking. We started out doing a sentence at a time, as we had talked about in our meeting. Then we did the KWC, and I was pleased that they made use of this strategy to help them organize the information. I was surprised at the way they worked straight through the $\frac{1}{9}$; they didn't need to discuss it at all. They were just like "Oh, we're going to have to divide and that will tell you how many cars are silver." I didn't even bother to stop at that point to draw a representation because they seemed to see it already in their heads. The other thing they also knew immediately was that we had to take the 35 silver cars away from the total of 315 cars. The second part with the ratio of 3 to 2 was a little trickier, so we got out the cubes. And again it didn't take as long as I thought it would for them to notice that it was groups of 5.

MARTA: So they did notice it was groups of 5?

KAREN: Right. I think I had to prompt them and say, "So how many are in the groups?" One student noticed it right away and helped the others see that it was groups of 5 and that they needed to see how many of these groups of 5 would go into 280. It was nice to see Nina becoming more involved and speaking out, because she is usually so quiet. Then that was where it got interesting. Once they figured out there were 56 groups of 5, the 3-to-2 ratio confused them.

MARTA: Did anyone actually articulate that it was 56 groups of 5 that were composed of black and white cars? Did anyone actually say it like that, that you recall?

KAREN: They knew that they were the black and white, and they were very clear that the silver was out of the way and taken care of. It became an issue of what to do with the 56 groups. It took some doing.

MARTA: Do you remember what questions you asked to guide them when they got to that 56, or were they just talking among themselves?

KAREN: They were really just talking among themselves at this point. It has gotten to the point where four of them are pretty verbal and play off of each other. But, as some of them were moving forward, one student kind of threw his hands into the air and said, "This is over my head," and another really tried to stay with us, but when we got to the ratio piece, her thinking started to break down.

JOHN: So that was when you used the cubes to represent that situation?

KAREN: Yeah. I made the cubes into a physical model, matching the black and white cubes with the black and white cars in the situation. I modeled the groups of 5 several times, and had the students visualize that the groups would continue until there were 280 cars. I think we had 4 groups of 5 out at that point. One student wanted to keep separating the groups, emphasizing that you can *divide* them. Once again, it was Gloria who noticed that that just wouldn't work. She brought up that the total had to be 280 black and white cars.

MARTA: Ahh . . . that's really important.

JOHN: So she remembered to maintain that quantity.

KAREN: Yeah, she said if you divide the 56, you're not going to end up with 280 cars. Then I led the conversation so that we started talking like we did in our conversation, like we've got this group of 5, and there are 2 white and 3 black. And we started putting the groups together like that, using the cubes to make rows of 3 black cars and 2 white cars. Then they realized that we have to multiply.

MARTA: So, I heard you mention our earlier conversation. Did our conversation about having the 3 and the 2 help you sort of scaffold for the kids?

KAREN: Yes, because I knew where we needed to go when the thinking was getting off track. When they got stuck, I had a plan to pull them back by using the cubes to model the problem.

JOHN: Nice. So, when you do this problem again, with my class or with one of your tutors that goes into other classes, what can we do to help it go more smoothly? What would you do differently?

KAREN: I felt ready! They pulled out what they knew, and that went very well. They are comfortable with the KWC, whether they want to do it or not. But, this was a problem with so much information that even the reluctant ones were like, "OK, I need to do the chart."

MARTA: This was a great problem for showing them the necessity of the KWC chart.

KAREN: The biggest problem was that a couple students just wanted to read the whole problem at once without figuring out what the problem was asking. But you can't just do something to 315 and come up with an answer. This problem has a lot of steps. I'm not sure what other strategies to use to help those students understand what they are trying to solve.

MARTA: We had sort of anticipated that they would hit a wall when they had to split up the black and white.

KAREN: And we were right! Talking through the problem beforehand made a major difference for me. Knowing what the kids have been exposed to and the possibilities of the strategies that they might do, they might go to fractions, they might do percents, or whatever. I felt like I was prepared, because there were several different ways that it could go, and I had an idea of how to deal with that.

JOHN: Were their computation strategies ones that you were used to seeing? I know we went over some of those in our earlier meeting.

KAREN: Well, I have gotten pretty used to them now. When they explain it to me, it just reinforces that they understand what they are thinking. Even if it's not how I would solve it, the explaining just solidifies it for them. I think it went really well.

We proceeded to look over the student work, noticing the elements of each child's KWC chart. Karen was really pleased at one student's reaction when he said, "It looks really hard, but if you do a KWC it makes it easy!" I noted that one child began to make a chart to represent the 2-to-3 ratio, but that after about the twentieth step, it became too cumbersome. Karen noted that this was when that child decided to use multiplication to work more efficiently.

Then we worked on creating a similar problem, but with a candy bar context, rather than cars. The problem was a little more complicated, but we felt that the students would be able to make connections from the previous work that would help them tackle the similar problem.

Reflecting on Our Collaboration

The collaborative work for the lesson that we engaged in was invaluable for helping us guide the students' learning. We were able to share perspectives on the children's thinking while thoroughly exploring the many avenues on which the students' thoughts might travel. It was crucial that we met both before and after each lesson and that the meeting beforehand included doing the problem together. Marta and I were able to help Karen anticipate some of the challenges that students might face during the problem and suggest some questions and representations that might be helpful.

After the lesson, Karen was able to reflect on what went well, how each student approached the problem, and what parts of the lesson were challenging for her. We then used what we learned from the lesson to plan future activities for the students. Karen took what she learned from this collaboration to her training of Title I assistants who collaborate with teachers in other classrooms. All three of us hope that this positive experience of working together can be a first step toward increased collaboration among classroom teachers and special education staff. It is our hope that as we continue to work in collaborative groups, both teachers and students will cease to view these as isolated, subject-specific strategies and more as general thinking and problem-solving skills to be used across the curriculum and in everyday life.

We are confident that giving our struggling students extra practice with comprehension and using similar approaches in literacy and math will help students develop effective and efficient strategies to solve mathematics problems.

References

Asera, Rose. 2006. "Pipeline or Pipedream: Another Way to Think About Basic Skills." *Carnegie Perspectives*. Stanford, CA: Carnegie Foundation for the Advancement of Teaching. Accessed at www.carnegiefoundation.org 12/22/08.

Behrend, Jean. 2003. "Learning-Disabled Students Make Sense of Mathematics." *Teaching Children Mathematics* 9 (5): 269–73.

Bell, Max, Jean Bell, John Bretzlauf, Mary Ellen Dairyko, Amy Dillard, Robert Hartfield, Andy Isaacs, James McBride, Kathleen Pitvorec, and Peter Saecker. 2007. Place Value, Number Stories, and Basic Facts. A first-grade unit of *Everyday Mathematics*, 3rd ed. Chicago: Wright Group/McGraw-Hill.

Boaler, Jo. 2008. *What's Math Got to Do with It?* London: Viking Penguin.

Carpenter, Thomas, Elizabeth Fennema, and Megan Loef Franke. 1996. "Cognitively Guided Instruction: A Knowledge Base for Reform in Primary Mathematics Instruction." *The Elementary School Journal* 97 (1): 3–20.

Clarke, Doug. 2001. *Early Numeracy Research Interview Booklet*. Melbourne, Australia: Department of Education, Employment and Training, Victoria. http://www.education.vic.gov.au/studentlearning/teachingresources/maths/assessment.htm#1

Clements, Douglas, and Julie Sarama. 2008. "Focal Points—Pre-K to Kindergarten." *Teaching Children Mathematics* 14 (6): 361–65.

Dr. Seuss [pseud.] 1963. *Hop on Pop*. New York: Random House.

Duckworth, Eleanor. 2006. *The Having of Wonderful Ideas: And Other Essays on Teaching and Learning*. New York: Teachers College Press.

Economopoulos, Karen, Cornelia Tierney, Ricardo Nemirovsky, and Susan Jo Russell. 2004. Arrays and Shares. A fourth-grade unit of *Investigations in Number, Data, and Space®*. Glenview, IL: Pearson Scott Foresman.

Friend, Marilyn. 2007. "The Coteaching Partnership." *Educational Leadership* 64 (5): 48–52.

Friend, Marilyn, and Lynne Cook. 2006. *Interactions: Collaboration Skills for School Professionals*. Boston: Allyn & Bacon.

Hankes, Judith. 1996. "An Alternative to Basic-Skills Remediation." *Teaching Children Mathematics* 2 (8): 452–58.

Hiebert, James, et al. 1997. *Making Sense: Teaching and Learning Mathematics with Understanding*. Portsmouth, NH: Heinemann.

Hong, Lily Toy. 1995. *Two of Everything: A Chinese Folktale*. New York: Harcourt Brace Publishers.

Hyde, Arthur. 2006. *Comprehending Math: Adapting Reading Strategies to Teach Mathematics, K–6*. Portsmouth, NH: Heinemann.

Kamii, Constance. 2000. *Young Children Reinvent Arithmetic: Implications of Piaget's Theory*. New York: Teachers College Press.

Karp, Karen, and Deborah Voltz. 2000. "Weaving Mathematical Instructional Strategies into Inclusive Settings." *Intervention in School and Clinic* 35 (4): 206–15.

Kliman, Marlene, Cornelia Tierney, Susan Jo Russell, Megan Murray, and Joan Akers. 2004. Mathematical Thinking at Grade 5. A fifth-grade unit of *Investigations in Number, Data, and Space*®, 1st ed. Glenview, IL: Pearson Scott Foresman.

Kloo, Amanda, and Naomi Zigmond. 2008. "Co-Teaching Revisited: Redrawing the Blueprint." *Preventing School Failure* 52 (2): 12–20.

Lampert, Magdalene, and Paul Cobb. 2003. "Communications and Language." In *A Research Companion to NCTM's Standards*, edited by J. Kilpatrick, W.G. Martin, and D. Schifter. Reston, VA: National Council of Teachers of Mathematics.

Livingston, Andrea, and John Wirt. 2005. *The Condition of Education in Brief* (NCES 2005-095). U.S. Department of Education, National Center for Education Statistics. Washington, DC: U.S. Government Printing Office.

Mastropieri, Margo, Thomas Scruggs, et al. 2005. "Case-Studies in Co-Teaching in the Content Areas: Successes, Failures, and Challenges." *Intervention in School and Clinic* 40 (5): 260–71.

Mercer, Cecil. 2008. *Students with Learning Disabilities*. Upper Saddle River, NJ: Prentice Hall.

Mutch-Jones, Karen. 2004. Collaborative Insights: The Work of General and Special Educator Pairs in Inclusive Mathematics Classrooms. Cambridge, MA: Harvard Graduate School of Education (unpublished dissertation).

National Center of Education Statistics. 2007. *The Condition of Education*. Washington, DC: Institute of Education Sciences.

National Council of Teachers of Mathematics. 2000. *Principles and Standards for School Mathematics*. Reston, VA: Author.

National Joint Committee on Learning Disabilities. 2005. "Responsiveness to Intervention and Learning Disabilities." *Learning Disabilities Quarterly*. 28 (4): 249–61.

Neuschwander, Cindy. 1998. *Amanda Bean's Amazing Dream*. New York: Scholastic.

Nolet, Victor, and Margaret McLaughlin. 2005. *Assessing the General Curriculum: Including Students with Disabilities in Standards-Based Reform*. Thousand Oaks, CA: Corwin Press.

Richhart, Ron, Terri Turner, and Linar Hadar. 2008. Uncovering Students' Thinking About Thinking Using Concept Maps. Paper presented at the annual meeting of the American Educational Research Association Conference, New York. March 26, 2008. Available at http://pzweb.harvard.edu/Research/UncoveringStudentsThinking.pdf.

Russell, Susan Jo, Karen Economopoulos, Lucy Wittenberg, et al. 2008. Multiple Towers and Division Stories. A fourth-grade unit of *Investigations in Number, Data, and Space*®, 2d ed. Glenview, IL: Pearson Scott Foresman.

Russell, Susan Jo, Karen Economopoulos, Lucy Wittenberg, et al. 2008a. Counting and Comparing. A kindergarten unit of *Investigations in Number, Data, and Space*®, 2d ed. Glenview, IL: Pearson Scott Foresman.

———. 2008b. Counting, Coins and Combinations. A second-grade unit of *Investigations in Number, Data, and Space*®, 2d ed. Glenview, IL: Pearson Scott Foresman.

———. 2008c. Factors, Multiples, and Arrays. A fourth-grade unit of *Investigations in Number, Data, and Space*®, 2d ed. Glenview, IL: Pearson Scott Foresman.

———. 2008d. Fraction Cards and Decimal Squares. A fourth-grade unit of *Investigations in Number, Data, and Space*®, 2d ed. Glenview, IL: Pearson Scott Foresman.

———. 2008e. How Many Floors? How Many Rooms? A second-grade unit of *Investigations in Number, Data, and Space*®, 2d ed. Glenview, IL: Pearson Scott Foresman.

———. 2008f. How Many of Each? A first-grade unit of *Investigations in Number, Data, and Space*®, 2d ed. Glenview, IL: Pearson Scott Foresman.

———. 2008g. How Many Tens? How Many Ones? A second-grade unit of *Investigations in Number, Data, and Space*®, 2d ed. Glenview, IL: Pearson Scott Foresman.

———. 2008h. Landmarks and Large Numbers. A fourth-grade unit of *Investigations in Number, Data, and Space*®, 2d ed. Glenview, IL: Pearson Scott Foresman.

———. 2008i. Number Games and Crayon Puzzles. A first-grade unit of *Investigations in Number, Data, and Space*®, 2d ed. Glenview, IL: Pearson Scott Foresman.

———. 2008j. Pockets, Teeth and Favorite Things. A second-grade unit of *Investigations in Number, Data, and Space*®, 2d ed. Glenview, IL: Pearson Scott Foresman.

———. 2008k. Solving Story Problems. A first-grade unit of *Investigations in Number, Data, and Space*®, 2d ed. Glenview, IL: Pearson Scott Foresman.

———. 2008l. Stickers, Number Strings and Story Problems. A second-grade unit of *Investigations in Number, Data, and Space*®, 2d ed. Glenview, IL: Pearson Scott Foresman.

———. 2008m. Trading Stickers, Combining Coins. A third-grade unit of *Investigations in Number, Data, and Space*®, 2d ed. Glenview, IL: Pearson Scott Foresman.

———. 2008n. What Comes Next? A kindergarten unit of *Investigations in Number, Data, and Space*®, 2d ed. Glenview, IL: Pearson Scott Foresman.

———. 2008o. Who Is in School Today? A kindergarten unit of *Investigations in Number, Data, and Space*®, 2d ed. Glenview, IL: Pearson Scott Foresman.

Saland, Spencer, and Elaine Hofstetter. 1996. "Adapting a Problem-Solving Approach to Teaching Mathematics to Students with Mild Disabilities." *Intervention in School and Clinic* 31 (4): 209–17.

Schifter, Deborah, Virginia Bastable, and Susan Jo Russell. 1999. *Developing Mathematical Ideas: Building a System of Tens* and *Making Meaning of Operations*. Parsippany, NJ: Dale Seymour Publications.

Schoenfeld, Alan. 1992. "Learning to Think Mathematically: Problem Solving, Metacognition, and Sense-Making in Mathematics." In *Handbook for Research on Mathematics Teaching and Learning*, edited by D. Grouws, 334–70. New York: Macmillan.

Scruggs, Thomas, Margo Mastropieri, and Kimberly McDuffle. 2007. "Co-Teaching in Inclusive Classrooms: A Metasynthesis of Qualitative Research." *Exceptional Children* 73 (4): 352–417.

Sullivan, Peter, Judy Mousley, and Robyn Zevenbergen. 2006. *Developing Guidelines for Teachers Helping Students Experiencing Difficulty in Learning Mathematics*. Mathematics Education Research Group of Australiasia (MERGA) Conference Proceedings.

Thornton, Carol, Cynthia Langrall, and G. Jones. 1997. "Mathematics, Instruction for Elementary Students with Learning Disabilities." *Journal of Learning Disabilities* 30 (2): 142–50.

Thurlow, Martha. 2001. "Students with Dyslexia and High-Stakes Testing." *Perspectives* 27 (4): 4–5.

Tierney, Cornelia, Susan Jo Russell, Megan Murray, and Joan Akers. 2004. Mathematical Thinking at Grade 5. A fifth-grade unit of *Investigations in Number, Data, and Space*®, 1st ed. Glenview, IL: Pearson Scott Foresman.

Tomlinson, Carol. 2003. "Deciding to Teach Them All." *Educational Leadership* 61 (2), 6–11.

United States Department of Education. 2002. *Twenty-Fourth Annual Report to Congress on the Implementation of the Individuals with Disabilities Education Act*. Washington, DC: Office of Special Education and Rehabilitative Services.

Vygotsky, Lev. 1978. *Mind and Society: The Development of Higher Psychological Processes*. Cambridge, MA: Harvard University Press.

Wheatley, Grayson. 2002. *Developing Mathematical Fluency*. Bethany Beach, DE: Mathematics Learning.

Contributors

Mary Kay Archer is a fourth-grade teacher in a rural community in Michigan. Teaching mathematics and paying attention to student thinking have long been special interests of hers. She has provided professional development in her district and is a workshop leader for the *Investigations in Number, Data, and Space* curriculum.

Candace Chick teaches an inclusion class in the Boston Public Schools. She teaches fourth and fifth grade, looping or keeping the same class for two years. She also serves as the school's Intermediate Grade (3–5) Literacy Coordinator. Candace has long been passionate about helping students with special needs see themselves as learners and experience success in school.

Kristi Dickey is a teacher in Oklahoma. She teaches first and second grade, looping or keeping the same class for two years. She loves looping because it provides a consistent learning community. Kristi is also a district math leader, a mentor, and a workshop leader for the *Investigations in Number, Data, and Space* curriculum.

Nikki Faria-Mitchell is a third-grade teacher in the Boston Public Schools. She has been a leader in several National Science Foundation-funded professional development projects, including Foundations of Algebra and Developing Mathematical Ideas. Nikki is particularly interested in facilitating mathematical conversations that include all learners.

Michael Flynn is a second-grade teacher in western Massachusetts who teaches in an inclusive classroom. Michael is the recepient of the 2009 Horace Mann Award of Teaching Excellence, a national award given to only five teachers in the country each year. He was also honored as the Massachusetts Teacher of the Year in 2007–2008. In addition to his math teaching, Michael focuses on science and integrating technology across the curriculum.

Arusha Hollister is a research and development specialist at TERC. She was one of the writers for the revision of the *Investigations in Number, Data, and*

Space curriculum and now works on revising and creating professional development for the second edition. Before working at TERC, Arusha was an elementary school teacher for ten years and a math coach. Arusha is particularly interested in the mathematical learning and thinking of children in the younger grades.

Marta Garcia Johnson is a fifth-grade teacher in a small city in North Carolina. She has taught in classrooms with diverse learners for more than twenty years and also works with teachers as a staff developer. In 2005, Marta won a Presidential Award for Excellence in Mathematics and Science Teaching. She particularly enjoys thinking with her colleagues about what students understand and what they need to learn and how she can apply that to her teaching.

Karen Joslin is an experienced Title I lead teacher in a small city in North Carolina. She is also National Board Certified in Literacy K–8. Karen is passionate about seeing the connections among subject areas to meet children's needs. She was instrumental in developing her school's initiative to incorporate math comprehension as part of Title I.

John MacDougall is a fifth-grade inclusion teacher in a small city in North Carolina. He is a third-year teacher who has taken on leadership roles in mathematics programs such as, Foundations in Algebra, and the Investigations in Number, Data, and Space workshops, and he serves on the school-based math literacy team, which has had a special focus on improving math instruction for struggling students and on closing the achievement gap.

Laura Marlowe is a kindergarten teacher and workshop leader in Michigan. She has always found it rewarding to work with students who struggle in mathematics—by listening and trying to understand students' thinking and using what they already know to make new concepts explicit for them.

Maureen McCarty is a first-year teacher in a town outside Boston. Before becoming a classroom teacher, Maureen worked with children and adults as an art museum educator where she used questions to foster their understanding of art. In the classroom, she has been especially interested in applying the questioning strategies she used in art museums and the formative assessment work she did in graduate school to help figure out what her students already know and what they need to learn.

Christina Myren is a consultant teacher for the Beginning Teacher Support and Assessment program in Thousand Oaks, California. She works with new teachers in a formative assessment program that is mandated for all new teachers in the state. Sarah Bruno, the teacher featured in Christina's chapter, is a second-year teacher in this program. Christina is a former winner of the Presidential Award for Excellence in Mathematics and Science Teaching.

Anne Marie O'Reilly is a second-grade teacher in western Massachusetts and a workshop leader for the *Investigations in Number, Data, and Space* curriculum. Starting in the 2008–2009 school year, she is assuming a new role in her school, half-time math coach and half-time teacher. Anne Marie finds it especially rewarding to work with a range of learners.

Michelle Perch was a third-grade teacher who worked in the Clark County School District in Nevada for over eighteen years and was a professional developer for more than fourteen years. She was particularly interested in differentiating her instruction by working with guided math groups.

Lillian Pinet is a kindergarten teacher in the Boston Public Schools System. She has taught in both bilingual and sheltered English instruction settings. Lillian is passionate about educating all of her young learners. Her motto is, "Many children, many walks of life, but only one love . . . a passionate desire to teach the multitude."

Lisa Seyferth is a kindergarten teacher in a suburb of Boston. She has also been a leader in several professional development projects related to elementary school math. She enjoys teaching kindergarten because the children are so curious, energetic, and full of surprises. Lisa is always seeking ways to be more precise and effective as a teacher.

Heather Straughter taught in an inclusion class in the Boston Public Schools. She looped with her students, which means that she worked with the same students in fourth and fifth grades. Heather is currently raising a family, and she continues to be passionate about the education of students with special needs.

Ana Vaisenstein is a math teacher and coach in a public elementary school in Boston, working with classroom teachers to support students who struggle with mathematics. She is currently participating in the National Science Foundation-funded Foundations of Algebra Project. Her interest is in exploring the use of early algebraic ideas to strengthen understanding of the operations among students with math difficulties.

Dee Watson is a fourth-grade teacher in the Boston Public Schools. She is also a facilitator for the Developing Mathematical Ideas workshops. Dee is passionate about focusing on talk in her teaching of mathematics because as a child she was taught mathematics in a rote way, was not allowed to ask questions, and found it very confusing.